THE ASSA

Edward Burm
read Philosophy at the U
Leeds. He lived in Tehran for five years,
travelling extensively in Iran and
neighbouring countries. He now lives and
works in Italy and is the author of
The Inquisition: The Hammer of Heresy
(1984) and *The Templars:*
Knights of God (1986).

THE ASSASSINS

EDWARD BURMAN

First published 1987
© Edward Burman 1987

British Library
Cataloguing in Publication Data

Burman, Edward
The Assassins.
1. Assassins (Ismailites) — History
I. Title
297'.83   BP195.A8
ISBN 1-85274-027-2

Crucible is an imprint of
The Aquarian Press,
part of the Thorsons Publishing Group

Printed and bound in Great Britain

1   3   5   7   9   10   8   6   4   2

CONTENTS

PREFACE

THE Assassins have had a bad press. Since the thirteenth century their name has been associated with an act which appears to us today abominable, but which was not then considered so in its specific, almost strategic, use for political motives. Far bloodier stories and societies exist in the chronicles of western history, while even in the Moslem world there has never been a dearth of assassinations for avowedly political reasons. Yet the modern term 'assassin' derives its origin from this sect.

The reason is that the reputation of the Assassins stems from hostile sources which provided biased and sinister accounts, crusaders who viewed their suicidal courage with awe and Moslems who considered them as heretics. The innate secretiveness of the Isma'ilis of whom the Assassins, or Nizari Isma'ilis, were a branch, has made it almost impossible to gain reliable information about them until very recently. It is only with the twentieth century that scholars have begun to piece together a reliable history of the Isma'ilis.

Hasan-i Sabbah, founder of the Assassins in Persia, is usually portrayed as a ruthless, tyrannic leader of a band of murderers who lived in the impregnable valleys of the mountains of Persia. While such an account may be based on fact, it must not be forgotten that Hasan was a theologian and philosopher of extreme subtlety. The revolutionary Islam which underpinned his political activities derived from careful philosophical reasoning, and his thought and powers of argument were recognized and admired even by Hasan's enemies in Persia. Perhaps it was from this that the initial fear stemmed?

Throughout the history of both Christianity and Islam there have been heretical sects, but few survive longer than their leaders and immediate disciples, and most are eventually worn down by the omnivorous longevity of the central 'Churches'. Isma'ilism first appeared during the ninth century AD, became widely known through the Isma'ili Fatimid dynasty of Cairo (909–1171), and achieved notoriety with the Assassins. But it survived the downfall of Cairo and that of Alamut, and resurfaced in the public eye in the mid-nineteenth century in India, although pockets had survived in both Persia and Syria.

Today, the sect is represented by that extraordinary religious leader, the Aga Khan, whose immediate ancestors were quite as unusual in their own way as Hasan-i Sabbah — from whose successor as Grand Master he claims direct descent. A sect of such long and curious history deserves to be known for more than acts of assassination, and it is in terms of their longevity as a sect and their importance as part of the 'history of ideas' within Islam that this study has been written. Although a hundred or so sources have been consulted and mentioned in the text, I should like to make a general acknowledgement to the scholarly work of Marshall Hodgson and Bernard Lewis, who have contributed much to the study of the Assassins and without whose publications this general survey would have been impossible. Specific reference are given in the notes.

INTRODUCTION

EVEN today access to the castle of Alamut, the fortress retreat of Hasan-i Sabbah, which became almost legendary after the supposed 1273 visit of Marco Polo and his description of the 'Old Man of the Mountains' and the 'Ashishin', is difficult.

Alamut, the 'Eagle's Nest', stands in the Alborz Mountains north-west of Tehran and north-east of the city of Qazvin. Today, the use of good dirt tracks and motorized vehicles has rendered the journey relatively fast: until the beginning of this century the trip from Qazvin to Alamut — by far the easiest route to the fortress — took at least three days. From the turn about two kilometres before the roundabout at the eastern end of Qazvin on the modern Tehran–Tabriz road, to the point at which even today cars must be exchanged for mules, is ninety-six kilometres of rough, rock-strewn track which the presence of brigands still renders dangerous, and which requires about three hours driving.

It is important to realize that local villagers do not know the castle, or its ruins, by the name Alamut, which is used of the whole valley rather than of any particular place. In his paper written after a study of the Alamut area in 1929, Ivanow states that the district then comprised sixty-six villages. It seems likely that in Hasan's time, too, the word 'Alamut' was used to refer to the whole area dominated by the Assassins, and it will be used in this way throughout the present study. This area includes the valley of the Alamut River, and the larger and more important valley of the Shahrud River into which it drains. The Shahrud runs parallel to the main Tehran-Tabriz road, and from its valley begin all the mountain passes which allow communications between the Central Iranian Plateau to the south, and the Caspian Sea to the north. The Shahrud itself flows west into the Sefirud, which then flows northwards into the Caspian.

Turning right just before Qazvin the dirt road stretches almost straight across the plain for eighteen kilometres. It then climbs through spectacular serpentines into the Alborz Mountains, through a barren landscape only occasionally broken by rice fields and orchards. Higher up the main crops are millet and wheat, on fields which appear almost miraculously in otherwise rocky valleys and gullies.

Roads through villages are often much worse than those between them, with drainage channels and heavy use destroying the mud streets and creating dangerous slippages, ruts and holes. In the last twenty kilometres, from the village of Moallem Kelayeh, the road deteriorates rapidly with hairpin bends over unprotected precipices rendered perilous by a thick covering of very fine dust on the road surface. After three or four hours of twisting roads, precarious-looking iron-girder bridges and suspicious guards and villagers, vehicles except those with four-wheel drive and stove-pipe exhausts reach the end of their journey at a village called Shotorkhan. And even these specialized vehicles might not be able to continue at all times of the year. May and early autumn are the best periods: in winter the passes are often blocked by snow for months on end, while in spring the apparently innocuous streams turn into violent torrents capable of rolling huge boulders along their course and sweeping away roads and bridges. The river which runs past Shotorkhan to the east, and over which the path leads, comes straight down from the rock of Alamut.

From Shotorkhan there is a final trek up to the village of Ghuzur Khan at the foot of the rock. Within an hour's walk Alamut itself becomes visible in the distance as the sloping plateau leading upwards to the fortress begins. It appears at turns in the path, or at the end of a small gully. The rock, a hump-shaped, gloomy and awe-inspiring outcrop, appears strangely pale against the darker mountains which rise dramatically behind it to four-thousand metres. The high plateau surrounding the rock is relatively sheltered, and larger fields of millet and wheat explain how the Assassins were able to maintain a large garrison in the area.

From that point the village of Ghuzur Khan is a further three hours or so of fairly stiff climbing. Beyond the steep slope on which the village stands is the rock, with the strange but perhaps appropriate tin-roofed school building built on the most obvious camp-site on a small area of good grass beside a crystal clear mountain stream. But the site is not ideal: heavy rain makes camping impossible for much of the year, while even in summer — when it is too hot to make the journey comfortably on foot — the temperature drops towards freezing during the night. But these minor hardships are preferable to the mosquitoes of Shotorkhan.

The final ascent to Alamut, which stands within a high mountain valley like an overturned ship's hull, requires a perilous walk along the side of the looming main rock. The flat ground on which the school stands is connected to the rock by a narrow neck like a causeway. Where this neck ends, an almost vertical bow-shaped wall renders direct assault impossible. In fact the only gully which might be climbed by chimneying up is closed off by an ancient-looking brick wall. To the right, the ground falls sharply away towards Ghuzur Khan; but to the left a tiny loose-shingled track runs along the northern edge of the rock, which is inclined at about forty-five degrees. Scree constantly slips past during the two-hundred metre walk to a point at which a saddle mid-way along the rock announces the main entrance: at that point the path turns upwards at a sharper angle that would clearly have been impossible for an armed fighting force to climb under attack from above.

Inside, almost any track across the shard-strewn ground seems to end in a vertical drop, and the atmosphere is often rendered mysterious and menacing by passing clouds which temporarily envelop the whole rock. The ruins of the fortress or fortified village stand at about two-thousand metres above sea level, and although the rock itself rises only two-hundred metres above the surrounding valley it seems much higher as the result of near-vertical fall-off in every direction.

A short time within the strangely evocative fortress area is in itself sufficient to explain much of the fantasy associated with the legend of Hasan-i Sabbah. Massive walls constituting the remaining shell suddenly come to an end where the mountainside has slipped away. The area inside is more a fortified village than a castle, with the remains of living quarters, mosques, work-rooms, underground rooms and water cisterns and irrigation channels cut through solid rock. The very inaccessibility of the site renders plausible the fact that the original castle was probably built about AD 860–1 by religious refugees from the Abbasid caliphs.

From this extraordinary fortress, Hasan-i Sabbah ruled the castles of the Assassins for thirty-four years. With unique intensity and rigour he developed his Order into a body of men whose operations at some time struck fear into the hearts of men from Karakorum in Mongolia to Marseilles in France. In the whole period of residence at Alamut, Hasan is said to have left his house twice, both times onto the roof. It was at Alamut that the idea of using the Isma'ili faithful for political assassinations seems to have originated, and Alamut always remained the point of reference in the two-hundred years in which the Assassins appear in history.

PART I: THE PERSIAN ASSASSINS

THE ORIGINS
OF THE ASSASSINS

THE history of Islam is in many ways a history of schisms, dissension
and disputes concerning the problem of succession – often violent
and involving murder. The sect known as the Assassins, or more
accurately as the Nizari Isma'ilis, was one of the last of a long series
of dissident sects which Islam spawned. In order to have a firm
understanding of the origins of the political and religious views of
the Assassins we shall make a brief review of the most important
schisms and disputes.

Since religion dominated all aspects of life in Islamic society, any
social, economic or political discontent tended to be expressed in
religious terms. Sectarianism was necessarily the only refuge of the
oppressed or underprivileged in societies where the official creed was
identified with civil and military rulers. The history of Islam began
with a schism which still represents the characteristic division and
underlies the geographical distribution of that religion today, namely
that between *Sunni* and *Shi'a*.

The initial cause of these schisms, which ultimately led to the Nizari
Isma'ili movement, may be traced to the Prophet Muhammad, who
died in AD 632 without having designated a successor to lead the
community he had founded. That community had been based upon
two groups, the *Muhajirun*, or 'Emigrants' and the *Ansar*, or
'Supporters': the former had accompanied Muhammad when he left
Mecca for Medina to form the earliest Moslem community, while
the latter were the people of Medina who had provided both spiritual
and material support for Muhammad in his new city. On his death,
the first dispute concerning the succession developed between these
groups.

It might have seemed that the most legitimate candidate for the succession was Ali, cousin of Muhammad, and one of the first two or three believers. His claim would have been strengthened by the fact that he was also the Prophet's son-in-law, having married his only surviving daughter, Fatima. But decisive action by a triumvirate of the elders in the community resulted in Abu Bakr, Muhammad's father-in-law, being designated as caliph (*khalifa*), or deputy. Thus began the institution of the caliphate, with the caliph, or 'Prince of the Faithful', functioning as both religious and temporal head of the small community. There was, however, already a group of people who believed that Ali should have been appointed caliph. They were known as the *shi'atu 'Ali*, or party of Ali, but at this stage they succeeded in hiding any resentment or disagreement concerning the succession.

Abu Bakr was occupied for most of his short caliphate (632–4) with the so-called wars of secession. These wars consisted of a series of attempts to bring back into the nascent Moslem fold tribes and leaders who on the death of Muhammad had removed their homage and allegiance, and also sought to convert new Moslems by force.[1]

The great general Khalid ibn-al-Walid first brought Arabia and Syria completely under the control of the caliph in Medina. Then during the caliphate of 'Umar ibn-al-Khattab (634–44) he brought Iraq and Persia into the fold, so that 'at the end of a single generation after the Prophet the Moslem empire had extended from the Oxus to Syrtis Minor in northern Africa'.[2] On 'Umar's death in 644, seniority again caused Ali to be by-passed in the succession: Uthman (644–56), who represented the Umayyad aristocracy of Medina, was elected. The new caliph was responsible for the definitive form of the words of Allah in the Koran, and was an extremely pious old man. But he failed to control his greedy relatives, and excessive nepotism created resentment against his rule to such an extent that he was murdered in Medina whilst reading the Koran on 17 June 656.

Then Ali's turn came: he was proclaimed the fourth caliph, last of those known as the orthodox caliphs. But his rule was to be brief, bloody and difficult. In the words of Edward G. Browne, 'The death of Uthman destroyed once and for all the outward semblance of unity which had hitherto existed in Islam, and led directly to wars wherein for the first time the sword was turned by Muslims against their fellow-believers'.[3] Once Ali had solved the problem of rivals at home, his attention was turned to Mu'awiya, Governor of Syria and kinsman of the murdered caliph. Mu'awiya had refused to acknowledge Ali, and challenged him by exhibiting Uthman's blood-stained shirt in the mosque at Damascus and presenting Ali with the dilemma: 'Produce the assassins of the duly appointed successor of the Prophet or accept the position of an accomplice who is thereby disqualified from the caliphate'.[4] Beguiled by the eloquence of the wily Mu'awiya, Ali accepted his request to negotiate a way out of the armed deadlock in which their forces found themselves. But, betrayed, he was assassinated on 24 January 661 on his way to the mosque at his capital, al-Kufah.

This murder appeared to Ali's followers as a martyrdom. Ironically, as Hitti observes, 'Ali dead proved more effective than Ali living'.[5] In death he appeared almost as a romantic hero, perceived by many as the ideal Arab; he was courageous, wise, eloquent, loyal to friends, magnanimous to his enemies, and the paragon of Moslem chivalry. The epithet accorded to his sword, 'the Cleaver of Vertebrae', speaks for itself. Moreover, he is attributed a swarthy complexion, large black eyes, and a long white beard, which complete this romantic picture. Today his influence is second only to that of Mohammad himself, and for believers in the *Shi'a* his tomb at al-Najaf is an object of pilgrimage equal to Mecca. His revenge for the initial slight in not being given the first caliphate was slow to materialize, but when it did come it created a permanent divide in Islam.

The Shi'a and the Umayyad caliphate (661-750)

With the proclamation of Mu'awiyah as caliph in Jerusalem in 660, the caliphate was shifted to Damascus and took on a completely different character. The Umayyad dynasty that Mu'awiyah founded eventually extended from Spain to Kashgar in China. But members of the *Shi'a* denied legitimacy to this caliphate, since for them Ali was the only rightful successor to the Prophet. Furthermore, this right descended to his sons and ancestors. Grievances against the ruling dynasty began to be expressed through Shiism, although at the beginning the *Shi'a* continued to maintain a low profile.

Shi'a revolts occurred throughout the Umayyad caliphate, and any possibility of the influence of the party of Ali diminishing was destroyed by the emotional response to the murder of Ali's son Hosein at Karbala in the reign of the second Umayyad caliph Yazid (680–3). Ali's elder son Hasan had been proclaimed successor to Ali in Iraq, although he was more interested in the harem than political life and power. However, since he was the son of Ali he was made a martyr by the *Shi'a*, even though it seems that he was in fact poisoned as the result of an intrigue developed in the harem and might not therefore appear worthy of such an honour. [6] His younger brother Hosein was then elevated as leader, but he too was killed — though in battle — together with about two-hundred supporters at Karbala in 680, on the tenth of the month of Muharram. This event is still commemorated in *Shi'a* Moslem countries, with passion plays of the death of Hosein. The gory representations of the event are quite dramatic, and include self-flagellation — which had become so bad that it was banned in Pakistan in recent years. It is also worth noting that the Ayatollah Khomeini resided in Karbala for many years, and that it was from there that he began his successful overthrow of the Shah of Persia.

Karbala is one of the most holy cities of *Shi'a* Islam, where Shiism as a separate faith and dogma began. In Hitti's words, 'The blood of al-Husayn, even more than that of his father, proved to be the seed of the Shiite "church"'. [7] Shiism became powerful as Arab hegemony faltered with the introduction of people of non-Arabian race or culture into the Moslem world. Shiism was never limited to a race or a tribe, and quickly became the vehicle of dissent, stimulated and strengthened by the martyrdom of Hosein.

A second key event in forming the *Shi'a* doctrine was the revolt led in the name of Muhammad ibn al-Hanafiyya — a son of Ali, though not by Fatima — by Mukhtar of Kufa in 685. Although Mukhtar himself was defeated and killed in 687, this movement in favour of Ali's son flourished. When Muhammad ibn al-Hanafiyya died around 700 many people believed that he had actually gone into hiding in the mountains near Mecca. They claimed that he would return to bring justice to the world and triumph over his enemies. [8] This new concept of the *mahdi*, or Messiah, was an example of the incorporation of ideas which were not part of the original Islamic faith which the various sects of the *Shi'a* willingly embraced — in this case a concept of Judeo–Christian origin.

Many, especially among the poor and underprivileged, found comfort in the belief in a charismatic leader, a member of the House of the Prophet, who was endowed with more than human qualities and was, therefore, destined to satisfy their hopes for a better life in this world and be their guide to the blessedness of the world to come.[9]

This idea became essential to the Isma'ilis, and the appeal of the *Mahdi* must have been one of its most appealing characteristics to the oppressed people who accepted the doctrines of Isma'ili missionaries.

The Shi'a *and the Abbasid caliphate (750-1258)*

As the Umayyad caliphate declined from its zenith, the Shiites became more active against the caliphate, and were joined by the Abbasid claimants to the throne. The Abbasids, descendants of an uncle of Mohammad called al-Abbas, were clever enough to bring the Shiites over to their cause. Shiites who had established themselves in the north-eastern Persian province of Khorassan joined these two groups to form a winning coalition that overthrew the Umayyad dynasty. After three years of revolt beginning in Khorassan and moving west, abu-al-Abbas was made the first Abbasid caliph at al-Kufah in 750. But although the Shiites, both of Iraq and of Khorassan, had been instrumental in enabling the new caliphate to come into being, they were soon forced into opposition again.[10]

Abu-al-Abbas (750–4), who referred to himself as al-Saffah, the 'bloodmaker', and was ruthless in eliminating the Umayyads, was the first caliph. But it was his brother al-Mansur (754–75) who effectively began the dynasty, since the next thirty-five caliphs descended in direct male line from him. As these brothers gradually established the new dynasty, the *Shi'a* grew 'both as an undercurrent of discontent and a movement of open revolt'.[11] The first open revolt took place in Mansur's reign: two Shiite brothers, Mugammad the Pure Soul and Ibrahim (who both claimed to be descendants of Ali) rebelled in Medina and Basra, respectively. Neither revolt was successful. Muhammad was defeated in battle and gibbeted; Ibrahim, after some success in Basra and Ahwaz, was captured near Kufa, decapitated, and his head sent to al-Mansur.[12]

What is perhaps most interesting from the point of view of a history of the Assassins, is that a third brother of these rebels, Yahya, continued their rebellion in the reign of Harun al-Rashid (786–809), greatest of Abbasid caliphs and contemporary of Charlemagne. Yahya eventually

fled to the kingdom of Daylam, where Shiism had already taken root
and was welcomed by the population there. Daylam was in western
Persia south of the Caspian Sea, and was the area where the Assassins
later established themselves under Hasan-i Sabbah. The story of Yahya
illustrates that this remote and mountainous area was already potentially
the root of dissent and rebellion two centuries earlier.

In the reign of al-Ma'mun (813–33), al-Rashid's son who became
caliph on his elder brother's death, another intriguing revolt occurred
in Kufa. It was led by a certain Abu 'l-Saraya in the name of an Alid
named Ibn Tabataba:

Ma'mun, recognizing the strength of the Shi'a and holding views similar
to theirs with regard to 'Alid claims, proclaimed in 201 A.H. (AD 816),
as his heir to the caliphate, 'Ali Rida b. Musa Ja'far al-Sadiq, and ordered
that the black colour, emblem of the Abbasids, be replaced by the Alid green.
The Abbasids in Iraq denounced Ma'mun's decision, and swore allegiance
to his uncle, Ibrahim b. al-Mahdi. On learning of this, Ma'mun hurried
back from Khurasan to Baghdad. During the journey, 'Ali Rida, who
accompanied him, died suddenly in Tus, probably poisoned.[13]

In this period another refuge was open to rebel Shiites beyond that
in the Kingdom of Daylam. In 864, Hasan b. Zayd founded an Alid
state in Tabaristan after defeating the Abbasids. This state was the
refuge of members of the house of Ali until its demise in 928.

Thus throughout the Abbasid dynasty the Shi'a represented a focal
point for protest. The second half of the eighth century was a period
in which endless local dynasties sprung up as central Abbasid power
visibly weakened:

The foundations of confidence and assent in the Islamic universal policy
were crumbling, and men began to look elsewhere for comfort and
reassurance. In these uncertain times, the message of the Shi'a — that the
Islamic community had taken the wrong path, and must be brought back
to the right one — was heard with new attention. Both branches of the
Shi'a, the Twelvers and the Isma'ilis, profited from these opportunities, and
at first it seemed as if the Twelvers were about to triumph.[14]

This was the time when most of the dissident, heretical or alternative
sects of Islam came into being. The essential characteristic of the greater
part of these sects, distinguishing them collectively from the orthodox
twelver Shi'a, was that they proclaimed allegiance to the seventh imam.

Twelver and Sevener Shiites

After the division into Sunni and Shi'a, the next important schism in Islam was that between the so-called twelver Shiites and what might be called the Sevener Shiites. The undisputed succession of imams from Ali is as follows:

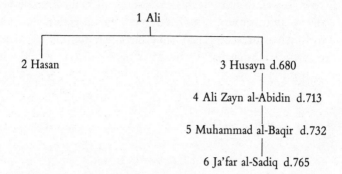

```
                            1 Ali
        ┌───────────────────────────────────────────┐
    2 Hasan                                   3 Husayn  d.680
                                                   │
                                    4 Ali Zayn al-Abidin  d.713
                                                   │
                                    5 Muhammad al-Baqir  d.732
                                                   │
                                    6 Ja'far al-Sadiq  d.765
```

Ja'far al-Sadiq had designated his son Isma'il as his successor, but Isma'il was disinherited — or, according to the Isma'ili version, died before his father — and the greater part of the *Shi'a* recognized his brother Musa al-Kazim as the seventh imam. Thus the line continued with the following important division:

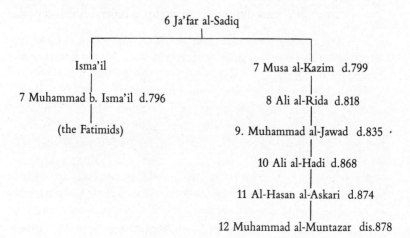

```
                        6 Ja'far al-Sadiq
             ┌────────────────────────────────────┐
         Isma'il                           7 Musa al-Kazim  d.799
             │                                     │
 7 Muhammad b. Isma'il  d.796              8 Ali al-Rida  d.818
             │                                     │
     (the Fatimids)                        9. Muhammad al-Jawad  d.835  ·
                                                   │
                                           10 Ali al-Hadi  d.868
                                                   │
                                           11 Al-Hasan al-Askari  d.874
                                                   │
                                           12 Muhammad al-Muntazar  dis.878
```

For the twelver Shiites, the last imam disappeared in 878. Thus Muhammad al-Muntazar, son of Hasan al-Askari, is still awaited as the *Mahdi* of the majority of Shiites, especially in Persia where twelver Shiism has been the official religion since the sixteenth century.

The sect which later became known in its various manifestations as the Isma'ilis, on the other hand, held that Isma'il had appointed his own son Muhammad as his successor. This Muhammad left Medina and went underground for what is known as the period of occultation, during which accounts become necessarily vague and confused. The very name of the current imam was considered a secret and withheld even from the majority of his own followers. It was during this period that there emerged the various sects which characterized 'sevener' Shiism and provided the political and theological background for the last in the series, the Nizari Isma'ilis, or Assassins.

Sects: Batinites or Isma'ilis

From their secret refuges, the hidden imams sent out a series of missionaries, or *da'is* to preach their doctrine. They were generally known as *batinis* rather than Isma'ilis as a result of the doctrinal distinction between *batin* and *zahir*, which will be examined in detail later. While the *batin* was the hidden or esoteric meaning of the Koran, which was available exclusively to initiates and could only be discovered by means of allegorical intepretation, the *zahir* was the outer form or 'veil' intended to keep the inner, esoteric truth from the eyes of the uninitiated.

This system was perfected by a certain Abdullah, son of an obscure oculist who had worked in Ahwaz and Jerusalem. He first set up headquarters at Basra in south-eastern Iraq, which with the Brethren of Purity had become a focal point for breakaway sects, and later established himself in Salamyah in northern Syria. Abdullah and his successors sent secret missionaries throughout the Moslem world. His method appears to antedate that used by Assassin *da'is* later, as we shall see in Chapter 4. They would begin by discussing religious matters in such a way as to arouse scepticism in their would-be followers, and then direct the audience's attention to the great *Mahdi* or Messiah who was about to appear.

At a time of great enmity between Persian and Arab Moslems,

Abdullah easily gained a strong following amongst those discontented
with Abbasid rule. His ultimate project, which might have served
as a model for Hasan-i Sabbah's remarkably similar initiative, was based
on the idea of establishing a society of initiated free-thinkers who
would use the power base provided by religion to overthrow the
caliphate.[15] Although for the moment the caliphate was not to be
overthrown, this system devised by Abdullah was to have far-reaching
consequences.

Sects: Qarmatians

After nearly a century of complete occultation, Isma'ilism emerged
in southern Iraq towards the end of the ninth century. This new
phenomenon was led by Hamdan b. al-Ash-ath, an Iraqi peasant who
had been influenced by the ideas of Abdullah. Hamdan, whose
nickname of Qarmat caused the new sect to be known colloquially
as the Qarmatians, readily found converts amongst the heavily exploited
peasants and uprooted tribesmen of the area.

The Qarmatians were fundamentally a secret society in which
initiates enjoyed something which has often been described as close
to the modern idea of communism. It seems that they shared all
property between members of the sect, and willingly paid financial
contributions imposed by their leaders. In each village a single person
in whom the whole community trusted was put in charge of all
property, and distributed their wealth in such a way that no one was
ever in need and individual poverty was abolished. The consequence
of this was that each peasant was induced to work harder, so that
the village or community obviously prospered. No one was exempt
from this idea of common property: even young boys who made a
little extra by scaring birds away from the crops, and women who
worked part-time spinning, contributed these casual earnings to the
pool.[16]

Another unusual characteristic of these Qarmatian communities,
which again formed part of the Assassin ethos, was their willingness
to controvert a fundamental Islamic law in taking the blood of co-
religionists. They soon managed to establish an independent state on
the shore of the Persian Gulf, while other groups were established
early in Syria. From these bases, they conducted raids on neighbouring

territory: they openly attacked such important and powerful cities as Basra and Kufa. Yet, in spite of these attacks, the Qarmatians were primarily conceived as a movement for reform and social justice. Such travellers as the Arab geographer al-Maqdisi found 'order and justice' in their state, while the great Persian traveller Nasir-i Khosraw observed that there were neither taxes nor tithes, that the poor or indebted were given assistance and that even foreigners were helped to earn their livelihood by being given the tools and materials necessary to practice their crafts.[17]

The Shi'a and the Fatimid caliphate (909-1171)

Perhaps the greatest of Isma'ili successes occurred at the beginning of the tenth century, when the sect was strong enough for the imam to come forward in North Africa and claim the caliphate with the title of al-Mahdi. The new dynasty which he founded was named Fatimid in order to emphasize the fact that they claimed descent from Fatima, daughter of the Prophet and wife of Ali. Such a claim, beyond its truth or falsity, was designed to provide a double legitimacy to their right to the caliphate.

The founder of this Fatimid dynasty was Sa'id ibn-Husayn (909–34), who was probably a descendant of the second founder of the Isma'ilis, Abdullah ibn-Maymun — who had organized the sect after the death of the original founder, the Imam Isma'il.[18] Sa'id went disguised as a merchant to north-western Africa and first became ruler with the title of Ubaydullah al-Mahdi in Tunisia. Within a few years he controlled the North African coast from Morocco to Egypt, plus Sicily, and his fleet carried out frequent raids throughout the Mediterranean. His immediate successors raided France, Italy and Spain, while it was the fourth caliph, Jawhar, who in 973 established his new capital in al-Qahirah, the site of modern Cairo.

The Fatimid dynasty reached its zenith under Caliph abu-Mansur Nizar al-Aziz (975–96). During his reign Cairo was embellished with new mosques, palaces, bridges and canals. At the same time his tolerance towards people of other faiths, including Christians, was notable.[19] This great caliph's son Al-Hakim (996–1021) founded the celebrated House of Science, or Al-Azhar, for the teaching and propagation of Shiite doctrine. Presided over by the Chief *Da'i*, this foundation was endowed with funds for copying manuscripts and repairing books. Subjects such as astronomy and medicine were taught in addition to theological topics. From this great centre of Isma'ili doctrine, missionaries and agents went out to preach and to organize the faith in Iraq, Persia, Central Asia and India. [20] Al-Azhar and other mosques and city gates still survive to testimony the quality and historical importance of Fatimid architecture.

The Fatimid empire was recognized as a powerful and well-administered state. The government was organized with a State Chancery (*Diwan al-insha*), Bureau of the Army (*Diwan al-Jaysh*) and a version of the modern concept of ombudsman in the Bureau of Verification (*diwan al-Tahqiq*). Behind this bureaucratic apparatus, the administration of the law was carried out by the Chief Qadi, normally an Isma'ili, who administered the law according to Isma'ili doctrine. [21] Moreover, throughout the duration of the Fatimid dynasty, Isma'ili missionaries, or *da'is*, defended the *ta'wil*, the esoteric interpretation of the Koran, by public disputation and spread the doctrines through their written work. [22] The caliphs were themselves often learned men, and the emphasis on a book culture and libraries made Cairo the centre of Islamic knowledge. They preached their mission, or *da'wa*, which on the disintegration of the Fatimid empire became known to Isma'ilis as the 'old preaching'.

Sects: Druzes

Yet the *da'wa* was not universal, and new schisms occurred within the Fatimid state. One modern scholar has argued that it was the success of the Fatimids which brought the first serious conflicts to Isma'ilism. [23] One such schism occurred after the disappearance of the sixth Fatimid caliph, al-Hakim (996–1021), perhaps the last of the great caliphs. After his mysterious disappearance, the dynasty began its slow decline.

Al-Hakim's character was one which tended to excess, from excessive generosity to excessive severity. He was possessed of a religious zeal which easily turned to violence. Testimony to these aspects of his character was his decision, after thirteen years of sponsoring the arts and scholarship and living a life of great pomp and luxury, to renounce the glory and magnificence of his office:

He exchanged the gold caparisoned horse for the ass with a plain saddle and bridle of silver or iron. With a simple turban on his head, the caliph rode on this lowly animal to the mosque and made his vists to the *suqs* and his rounds among the people. He dressed simply, ate sparingly, and was abstemious in bodily pleasures.[24]

He then developed the habit of riding into the desert with minimal escort and giving himself up to contemplation. In February 1021 he disappeared during one of these night excursions. Although many people believed that he had been murdered, a document entitled 'The Suspended Proclamation' appeared on the mosques, describing al-Hakim's disillusion after attempts at reform and giving this as his reason for disappearing. This document stimulated the foundation of a new sect whose fundamental tenet was a belief in al-Hakim's divinity. Its members refused to recognize his successors as caliph and soon became known as the Druzes after their leader, al-Darazi.[25] Their faith makes them many ways the closest of the breakaway sects of Isma'ilism to the Assassins. But on more than one occasion they fought against the Assassins when the latter began to carve out their own territory in Syria, where the Druzes were — and still are today — most prominent.[26]

The Nizari Isma'ilis

The final, and from our point of view essential, schism occurred during the reign of the eighth Fatimid caliph, al-Mustansir (1036–94). Since the time of the last great caliph, al-Hakim, there had been a gradual process of militarization of the Fatimid state. This process culminated in 1074 when the Armenian general Badr al-Jamali travelled with his army from Syria to Cairo and took effective control. From that moment, the power of the caliph was extremely limited and the real ruler of the state was the commander-in-chief of the army. The last caliphs were little more than figureheads.[27] With the 'Isma'ili' state run by men who were often not Isma'ilis at all, the propagandistic aspect of the Fatimid state clearly diminished in importance. At the same time, it was natural that sooner or later these military leaders would seek to obtain religious and dynastic legitimacy for their *de facto* rule.

This next stage occurred when General Badr al-Jamali was succeeded as commander-in-chief by his son al-Afdal. On the death of the Caliph al-Mustansir in 1094, the new commander opposed the Caliph's own designation of his son Nizar as caliph and placed Nizar's brother al-Musta'li on the throne. Al-Afdal had first taken the precaution of marrying al-Musta'li to his own daughter, hoping thereby to obtain total control over the caliphate. But the Isma'ili leaders had already accepted Nizar as their future leader, and were unwilling to accept al-Musta'li. Thus the Isma'ili sect was divided by al-Afdal's imposed choice, and for some time it was impossible to know which faction would eventually dominate.

Unfortunately for al-Afdal, however, the decline of the Fatimid caliphate had coincided with what almost amounted to a renaissance of Isma'ili activity in Persia against the Seljuk sultans. The Isma'ilis in the East refused to acknowledge al-Musta'li and broke off relations with the dynasty in Cairo. At the head of this opposition was the Persian leader Hasan-i Sabbah, who had contributed much to the recovery of Isma'ili strength in Persia, and who had spent some time in Cairo when sent by the Chief *Da'i* in Persia some years before. It was Hasan who rallied the dispersed members of the sect and initiated a new period of doctrinal and political development of the Isma'ilis.

The dissenting group proclaimed their allegiance to the by-passed Caliph Nizar, and it is for this reason that members of the sect which became known to history as *The Assassins* were first known as the *Nizari Isma'ilis.* [28]

2

HASAN-I SABBAH

HASAN-I SABBAH was a revolutionary of genius who devised and put into practice the 'new' preaching or *da'wa* of the Nizari Isma'ilis, which was to replace the 'old' *da'wa* of the Fatimid Isma'ilis at Cairo.

It is likely that he was born around 1060 in Qom, one-hundred-and-fifty kilometres south of modern Tehran. Qom is the second most holy city of Persia, where Fatima, the sister of Imam Reza, died in 818 on her way to meet her brother in Mashad in north-eastern Persia. It has long been a centre of Shiite teaching, and has recently been the base for the ayatollahs who have taken over modern Iran from the Pahlavi dynasty. Local tradition also maintains that Hasan was born there. He was brought up in Ray, near Modern Tehran.

Of the two main biographers of Hasan, Rashid al-Din makes Hasan a descendant of the legendary Himyarite kings of Yemen, and states that his father had come from Kufa in Iraq, while Ata Malik Juvayni suggests that Hasan's father was the man who moved from Yemen to Persia via Kufa in Iraq.[1] Now, while it seems certain that he was Persian and this ancestry has been judged legendary, it is worth noting that Kufa had for centuries been an important Shiite centre. It was there that Muhammad the Pure Soul had started his rebellion in the eighth century, and the Brethren of Sincerity were also influential there in the following century.

Early life

Hasan wrote an autobiographical account of the early years of his life and how he became a member of the Isma'ilis. This work, called the *Sar-Guzasht-i-Sayyidna*, or *Adventures of our Lord*, existed in a manuscript in the library formed by Hasan himself at Alamut. When the fortress was taken by the Mongol Hulegu in 1256, historians were ordered to examine the material in the library before it was destroyed. The official historian of the conquest was Ata Malik Juvayni, who studied the *Sar-Guzasht* and 'copied whatever was to the point and suitable for insertion' from what he describes as that 'multitude of lying treatises and false teachings' into his history of Hasan-i Sabbah. [2] Another version of the same events was written a generation later by Rashid al-Din, who had other information available to him beyond Juvayni's account. Some historians believe that this later version is closer to the original Isma'ili sources. [3]

Hasan was brought up as a twelver Shiite by his father, that being the dominant religion in Ray in the eleventh century. He tells us that he desired from the age of seven to become learned in religion, and began from that moment to seek for knowledge through his studies of religion. He assumed that their doctrines were sound until he met an Isma'ili *da'i* or missionary called Amira Zarrab, 'the coiner', after the Isma'ili practice of taking a trade as a form of disguise and often adopting the name from it. This Zarrab, who Hasan tells us 'held the beliefs of the Batinis of Egypt' [4], attempted to undermine his religious faith. During their conversations and discussions he gradually introduced Hasan to new ideas, and it is fascinating to watch the Isma'ili method, later used by the *da'is* of Hasan himself, as Zarrab slowly draws his pupil away from orthodoxy:

Amira Dharrab was a man of good morals. When he first conversed with me he said, The Isma'ilis say thus and so. My friend, I said, Don't say what they say, for they are beyond the pale, and it is contrary to [sound] doctrine. In our conversation we had arguments and disputes with each other, and he disproved and demolished my doctrine. I did not yield, but those words had their effect. In the course of our conversation I said, whenever someone dies in that belief it is certainly said: this is the corpse of a heretic [*mulhid*]; upon such the people at large, as is their custom, pour out a great deal of lies and nonsense. I saw that the Nizari group was Godfearing, pious, abstinent, and anxious about drink; and I dreaded drink, for it is stated in the tradition [*khabar*]: 'The sum of foulness, and the mother of offences.' Amira said to me, At night when you are thinking on your bed [*dar khwab*] you know that what I say convinces you. [5]

The process continued as Hasan read the works of Isma'ili authors, which Zarrab presumably supplied like any good missionary. But the climax came during a 'severe and dangerous illness'.

This sickness forced Hasan to reflect upon the teachings of the Isma'ilis, as if it had been an omen. It appeared to him that God desired that his 'flesh and skin' should become something different: '"God changed his flesh to better than his flesh, and his blood to better than his blood" applied to me, I thought'.[6] The thought that he might die without being able to accept this new truth was sufficient to convert him and enable him to recover from the sickness. After his recovery he met another Isma'ili *da'i* called Abu Najm Sarraj, 'the saddler', who expounded their doctrine and initiated him into the abstruse points and secrets. Finally, a third *da'i* named Mu'min administered the oath of allegiance with a curious twist that can be read either as prophetic or as hagiographic hindsight. With a double play on the meanings of Hasan, both the son of Ali and 'good', the *da'i* replied to his request: 'Thy rank, since thou art Hasan, is higher than mine since I am but Mu'min. How then shall I administer the oath to thee?'[7] But after some persuasion, Mu'min relented and took the future leader's oath as an Isma'ili.

By his own account, Hasan must have been something of a prodigy as far as theology is concerned, and he rose quickly within the Persian Isma'ilis to a position of importance. At that time the Chief Isma'ili in Persia and Iraq was Abd-al-Malik ibn-Attash, a physician, fine calligrapher and man of letters who was born and lived in Esfahan but was accused of heresy and had to flee to Ray.[8] Mu'min himself had been appointed by Attash, and now it was to be ibn-Attash who provided perhaps the most important promotion in Hasan's short career. In his own words, 'in the year 464 [e.g 1071–2] 'Abd-al-Malik, the son of 'Attash, who at that time was the *da'i* in Iraq, came to Ray. I met with his approval, and he made me a deputy *da'i* and indicated that I should go to His Majesty in Egypt, who at that time was Mustansir'.[9] This was to be the beginning of two decades of mission and travel which only terminated with Hasan's establishment in the castle of Alamut.

Apart from these events, the most famous story concerning Hasan's youth involves his supposed friendships with two of the greatest men of his time, the astronomer and poet Omar Khayyam and Nizam al-Mulk. While Omar is known today through the versions of his quatrains by Edward Fitzgerald, Nizam al-Mulk was one of the greatest politicians of medieval Persia and will reappear later in Hasan's story as one of his most prominent victims.

The best-known form of the story is in fact that propagated by Fitzgerald in his introduction to the first edition of the *Rubaiyyat of Omar Khayyam*, published in 1859. In his *Wasiyat*, or 'Testament', Nizam relates how he had been sent from his hometown of Tus in Khorassan to school with a celebrated master in Nishapur, to the west of Tus and interestingly within an area later dominated by the Assassins. We shall allow him to tell the story of the legendary meeting in his own words as reported by Fitzgerald:

I found two others pupils of mine own age newly arrived, Hakim Omar Khayyam, and the ill-fated Ben Sabbah. Both were endowed with sharpness of wit and the highest natural powers; and we three formed a close friendship together. When the Imam rose from his lectures, they used to join me, and we repeated to each other the lessons we had heard. Now Omar was a native of Naishapur, while Hasan Ben Sabbah's father was one Ali, a man of austere life and practice, but heretical to his creed and doctrine. One day Hasan said to me and to Khayyam, 'It is a universal belief that the pupils of Imam Mowaffak will attain to fortune. Now, even if we *all* do not attain thereto, without doubt one of us will; what then shall be our mutual pledge and bond?' We answered, 'Be it what you please.' 'Well,' he said 'let us make a vow, that to whomsoever this fortune falls, he shall share it equally with the rest, and reserve no pre-eminence for himself.' 'Be it so,' we both replied, and on those terms we mutually pledged our words.

Edward G. Browne convincingly demonstrated that Nizam al-Mulk could not have been a school-friend of two such younger men. He does, however, assert in a note that there is 'good reason to believe' that Nizam al-Mulk was acquainted with Hasan-i Sabbah before the latter left on his visit to Egypt.[10] But it is also interesting that the story was also given by the 'reliable' historian Rashid al-Din in his history, and cited as being in the *Adventures of our Lord* quoted above.[11] So, although chronology would appear to make the story impossible, there is some factual basis for it.

That the Seljuks became one of the greatest dynasties of medieval Islam is largely due to Nizam al-Mulk, whose title in fact means 'Organization of the Kingdom'. The historian ibn-Khallikan relates that the Seljuk Sultan Malikshah had little to do but hunt and sit on his throne for twenty years while his vizier had all the power concentrated in his hands. [12] Nizam was a cultured and learned man, who wrote a celebrated treatise on the art of government. His most interesting achievement was the foundation of well-organized academies for higher learning, particularly that known as the Nizamiyah founded in 1065–7 in Baghdad. [13] His friendship towards and patronage of Hasan-i Sabbah would therefore argue for signs of particular brilliance or ability in the younger man. In view of Hasan's later writings, such a relationship is quite plausible.

Such a friendship — or at the least mutual esteem — would appear to be attested by the fact that it was with the help of Nizam al-Mulk that Hasan obtained some kind of post at the Seljuk Court. But if it existed, it was short-lived, since the only certain evidence from that period shows that something happened which forced Hasan to leave the Court. From that moment, the vizier was rather an enemy than a friend: the only reference Hasan himself makes is when he mentions that 'Nizam al-Mulk . . . was making great efforts to find me'. [14] One explanation of this change is that Hasan managed to gain influence over the Sultan and aspired to Nizam's position as vizier; or it may have been that Hasan's progress alarmed Nizam so much that he pre-empted the possibility of Hasan's taking over from him by discrediting him before it happened. This is something common in Persian history, and occurred even in this century when ministers of Reza Shah fought for power in the 1920s.

Moreover, the story sounds authentic, for Hasan-i Sabbah's force of character, ability and certainty in his own powers shine through many of the early stories of his life. Furthermore, since much of Persian history follows the borderline between fact and legend, and the legends often bear at least some relation to the facts, there is no reason to doubt the general lines of his character as they now appear. A further example will confirm this: when Hasan was forced to leave the Court he went to Esfahan to study Isma'ili doctrine under Ra'is Abu'l-Fadl. One day, he is supposed to have said to his teacher: 'Alas! had I but two men of one mind with me I should turn this realm upside down.' Abu'l-Fadl concluded that 'from much thought and fear and the undertaking of dangerous journeys Hasan had been attacked with melancholia'. [15] He prepared perfumed drinks and special foods to 'moisten' his pupil's brain. It was at this point that Hasan decided that it would be a good idea to leave Esfahan. Later, when the ex-master travelled to Alamut, Hasan was to ask him 'Does it seem now that I had melancholia or thou?'

Travels

On his way to Egypt, Hasan travelled through Azerbaijan, Mayyafariqin and Damascus, arriving in 1078 by sea from Syria. He stayed in Egypt for one and a half years, a period about which little is known. But although the accounts of this period of his life are often ambiguous or contradictory, it was a vital sojourn, since it was at that time that the seeds of the future Order of the Assassins were sown in his mind.

The caliph at that time was al-Mustansir (1035–94), but, as will be recalled, the military governor or Commander-in-Chief, Badr al-Jamali, was by that time the real power within the Fatimid caliphate. It was against the supporters of al-Jamali that opposition in Persia was leading to a renaissance of Isma'ilism in that country, and it was against al-Jamali's faction that the Isma'ilis chose the man he had cast aside — Nizar — as their leader. But although Hasan was later to be at the centre of the development of the Nizari Isma'ilis there is no evidence that he was in any way an opponent of Badr al-Jamali during his stay in Egypt.

But there are legends. The most noteworthy is that Hasan opposed al-Jamali whilst in Cairo and as a result was imprisoned and then thrown out of the country. This opposition, and al-Jamali's violent reaction, was based upon the idea that Hasan already at that time supported Nizar in his claim to the caliphate. But, as Bernard Lewis has pointed out, there was no dispute over the succession to al-Mustansir during the year Hasan-i Sabbah spent in Egypt.[16] The stories, as so often, appear to have been fabricated *a posteriori* in order to legitimize Hasan's defection from the Isma'ilis in Cairo and suggest that he had already developed his policies at this early moment. Hasan himself states that he conducted propaganda on behalf of Nizar in Cairo, and that was the reason al-Jamali was 'ill-disposed towards me and girded himself to attack me',[17] but this is not to say that he was a political opponent of al-Mustansir.

From Egypt Hasan returned — or escaped — to Esfahan. It is worth noting in passing, in view of the later history of the sect, that he stopped for some time in Aleppo during his journey. For it was to Aleppo that the first Assassin mission from Alamut to Syria later travelled. Then, in the service of the Isma'ili *da'wa*, he travelled for nine years throughout Persia, including Yazd and Kerman in eastern Persia, and Khuzistan.[18] Later, he spent three years in Damghan, where we may safely assume that he laid the foundations for that important centre of Assassin power and perhaps even took the castle of Girdkuh. It was from Damghan that he sent the first missionaries into the Alamut region,[19] and it was at this time that Nizam al-Mulk was making great efforts to find him.

As he travelled seeking and converting new members to the Isma'ili faith, it is clear that the idea of founding a permanent well-defended community was developing in Hasan's mind. Sources refer to his searching for a site for such a headquarters as the decade of the 1080s ran on and the number of supporters increased. The idea of founding an order such as that of the Assassins would appear to have evolved during this decade, although it is possible that it was already germinant in his mind during the years in Esfahan, as his remark to his teacher there suggests.

As the decade progressed, by a process we cannot trace, Hasan's attention gradually became concentrated on the area of north-western Persia which is dominated by the Alborz Mountains and corresponds to the modern provinces of Gilan and Mazandaran, roughly speaking between Tehran and the Caspian Sea (and corresponding in part to the area once known as Tabaristan). The Alborz Mountains, which rise to a maximum height of over six-thousand metres in the volcanic Mount Damavand, constitute a natural barrier between the Caspian and the vast gently tilting plateau which constitutes Central Iran. Although not distant as the crow flies from Tehran, this mountainous area has always been and still is remote. It was presumably for this reason that many shi-ite sects and fleeing Isma'ilis and other Moslem heretics had, as we have seen, for many centuries taken refuge in the mountain kingdom of ancient Daylam. Hasan had already sent *da'is* from Damghan, and as part of his plan to move into Daylam himself he travelled from Damghan to Qazvin sometime towards the end of the decade — perhaps to find a secure refuge from Nizam al-Mulk.

Headquarters at Alamut

Hasan relates how he took Alamut by means of a stratagem:

From Qazvin I again sent a *da'i* to Alamut, which was held by a Alid called Mahdi as a fief from Malik-Shah. Now Alamut is *aluh-amut*, i.e. 'the eagle's nest', and an eagle had its nest there. Some of the people in Alamut were converted by the *da'i* and they sought to convert the 'Alid also. He pretended to be won over but afterwards contrived to send down all the converts and then closed the gates of the castle saying that it belonged to the Sultan. After much discussion he re-admitted them and after that they refused to go down at his bidding.[20]

After this initial failure, Hasan spent some time moving around Daylam, converting many people by virtue of his extreme asceticism. Eventually he entered the castle in secret, hidden by his followers, and lived there at first under the name of Dihkhuda. When the owner of the castle discovered his existence, he was unable to do anything since Hasan's power already extended over most of the people resident there. It was the Alid himself, recounts Juvayni, who was *given permission to leave* and 'Hasan wrote a draft on the governor of Girdkuh and Damghan, the *rais*, Muzaffar Mustaufi, a secret convert of his, for the sum of 3,000 gold dinars as the price of the castle'.[21] This draft, much to the Alid's surprise, was later honoured by the *rais* who not only paid up instantly without question but even kissed the paper it was written on.

Once established in a secure and permanent base, Hasan sent *da'is* out from Alamut in all directions. At the same time he pursued a policy of territorial expansion, taking castles either by means of propaganda or by force, and building others. The main secondary base was established in the region of Quhistan, near modern Birjand in south-east Persia, where Hasan sent a prominent *da'i* called Husayn Qa'ini. But the numbers of the 'companions' were at first small, perhaps only sixty or seventy men at Alamut in 1092.[22] It was, however, true that forces could be increased in time of need by calling other men from Qazvin and the neighbourhood — as was the case during Malik Shah's failed assault of 1092.

Life at Alamut, and we may suppose in the other fortresses at this time, was characterized by extreme asceticism and severity. In the thirty-five years of residence at Alamut, nobody ever drank wine —

nor even, as Juvayni says, kept it in jars: 'Indeed, such was his austerity that a certain person having played the flute in the castle he expelled him therefrom and would not re-admit him.'[23] Hasan's personal asceticism is vividly emphasized by the fact that his time at Alamut was totally devoted to organizing the movement of *da'is* and *fida'is*, fasting, praying, reading and writing the doctrines of the sect. It was said that he only twice left his house on Alamut in those thirty-five years, and that was to go onto the roof.

Hasan's legendary severity may also be seen in the two incidents in which he put his own sons to death. The first, Ustad Husain, was executed because it was thought that he had been involved in the murder of the *da'i* Husayn Qa'ini — although it was later discovered that he had been innocent. The second son, Muhammad, was put to death after being accused of drinking wine.[24]

The rigour of his life was extended to other castles and to the organization of the sect as he approached death. When he had fallen so ill that he knew he would never recover he first summoned Buzurg' umid, one of his most faithful lieutenants who had ruled the nearby castle of Lammassar for twenty years, and announced that he would be the next leader. Then he chose a certain Dihdar Abu-Ali to be entrusted with the 'propaganda chancery'. He charged these two faithful supporters and the commander of the forces, Kiya Ba-Ja'far, to take charge of his kingdom and to act in agreement between them. Thus the transition of power was guaranteed. Shortly afterwards, on 12 June 1124, Hasan-i Sabbah died.

The policy of assassination

Political assassination was not unknown in Islam before Hasan-i Sabbah. Earlier sects had used murder as a political technique, and there is evidence that Muhammad himself disposed of his enemies by suggesting that they did not deserve to live — and hoping that faithful followers would take the hint. There had even been an extremist Shiite group known as the 'stranglers' after their preferred method of assassination.[25]

Within the Moslem world, authority was invested in the person who managed first to gain and then to keep it, whether by subterfuge, assertion of hereditary rights or usurpation. Even hereditary rights were dependent on the claimants' strength in asserting them, and a powerful empire often disintegrated as soon as its founder died — while his heirs and successors squabbled over division of the kingdom. Roles such as imam and caliph, where individual ability and authority were the key to maintaining power, were particularly susceptible to being at least temporarily weakened by the process of eliminating the individual who had managed, often after years of political manoeuvres, to attain them.

This fact made Islamic authority particularly vulnerable to a policy of assassination, since the removal of a single person could throw a situation into turmoil, and the whole process had to begin again. This is one of the reasons why Assassin techniques proved to be of limited success when used against Christians in the Holy Land. Military authority in crusading forces was hierarchical, so that assassination could not undermine or unbalance it. If a Master of the Temple were to be murdered, for instance, it would make no difference whatsoever since a new Master would immediately take his place.

Yet the weapon of assassination seems to have been used without clear criteria. Under the rule of the first three Grand Masters of Alamut, from 1092 to 1162, Rashid al-Din provides three lists which comprise seventy-five victims. Of these victims, perhaps half may be described as murders which could potentially destabilize the Seljuk enemy, while those of scholars and minor dignitaries are less obvious in their scope.[26] But these records are not necessarily accurate or complete, and the number of assassinations seems to have varied according to the whims and enthusiasm of a single Master rather than according to some long-term and precise strategy. This is complicated by the fact that, as Hodgson observes, an apparent epidemic of assassinations might simply derive from an author's interest in collecting the names.[27] As time went on, the assassinations became in Persia more and more a matter of retaliation or defence based upon local territorial needs: a ruler who threatened Isma'ili possessions, local leaders or religious leaders who attacked their doctrine, or specific retaliation for some offense given or action taken against Isma'ilis elsewhere.

Although it is possible to credit Hasan-i Sabbah with the first *systematic* implementation of political assassination, it may also be the case that the 'policy' of assassination was evolved by chance. When the first Assassins were seeking to establish themselves, and Malik

Shah was trying to extirpate them before they became too powerful, we have seen that Hasan was constantly menaced by Nizam al-Mulk. That statesman was obviously perceived by Hasan-i Sabbah as a major threat, so in 1092 an assassin called Bu-Tahir, disguised as a Sufi, killed the old vizier as he was being carried 'from the Sultan's audience-place to the tent of his harem'.[28] He was, therefore, the first person to be killed by the *fida'is*. Could it be that the success of this early political assassination, ridding Hasan-i Sabbah of a dangerous opponent, suggested the possibity of using such a weapon regularly and preparing men specifically for that task?

Hasan did not invent assassination, but he created from the idea of assassination a political tool which struck horror into the hearts and imagination of his contemporaries. It is for this that his sect became known and feared in the West and generated legends. Whatever the merits or demerits of the policy, it seems just that echoes of its origin have survived in the modern European variants of the word assassin.

Yet the fact that Hasan's main legacy survives in the etymology of this word is extremely unjust, since he was much more than a simple murderer or organizer of murders. He had a fine mind, an excellent knowledge of theology, and evidently possessed the phenomenal strength of will necessary to pursue his ideal for so many years. The power of Hasan's personality is undeniable. It was by his personal asceticism and good example that he won converts to his preaching, and he was clearly skilled in the arts of verbal persuasion, just as his own mentors had been. We can imagine him converting the people of Daylam just as he had himself been converted, by patiently digging away at a potential proselyte's religious doubts until they were strong enough to admit the possibility of an alternative. Above all, perhaps, the austere planner and philosopher living for so many years isolated in his remote castle at Alamut inspires a curiosity to know more about a man who must have been very remarkable indeed.

ALAMUT AND
THE PERSIAN CASTLES

THE difficult terrain and harsh climate, together with the practice of destroying castles once taken, have resulted in the surviving castles of the Assassins being today little more than heaps of rubble. As a historian of modern Iran has remarked, 'taken together, Iranian geographical and climatic conditions produce a fine balance between subsistence and the lack of it'.[1] When the political and economic conditions for the existence of a fortress or city cease to exist, so does the fortress or city — as artefacts of a moment of subsistence. This is as true for the sites of the Assassins as for the cities which Alexander the Great founded — such as Balkh, or Alexandria-the-Furthest, in northern Afghanistan — or the literally uncountable ruined cities in the desert south-east of Tehran where Persia, Pakistan and Afghanistan meet and where now arid conditions belie the great fertility of ancient times.

Beyond the natural erosion of wind, sand or rain, and human borrowings, most of the Assassin castles are sited in an area of high seismicity. Studies of the historical seismicity of the country have demonstrated how often earthquakes have devastated human settlements and destroyed architectural features of great importance. Yet for the remote and inaccessible areas such as the Alborz Mountains less evidence is available. What does exist suggests that most of the castles suffered considerably: at Samiran, for instance, parts of the main castle can be clearly seen to have slipped down towards the river which runs past the site. Such damage is typical of the dislodgements caused by earthquakes.

In a study on the historical seismicity of north-central Iran, N.N. Ambraseys has provided interesting information on the possible effects of earthquake damage which is pertinent to a study of Assassin castles.

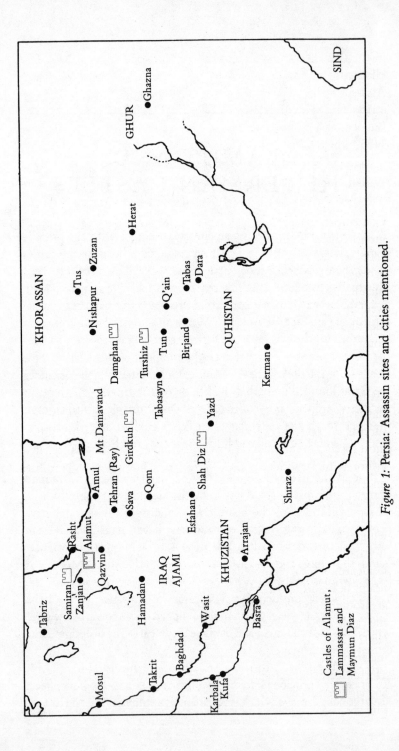

Figure 1: Persia: Assassin sites and cities mentioned.

In the Qazvin area, which loosely comprises Alamut (about fifty kilometres north-east of Qazvin as the crow flies) and other major Assassin castles such as Lammassar and Samiran, destructive earthquakes were recorded in 1119 and 1176 during Assassin residence. But of much greater importance was the major earthquake of 14 August 1485, which:

... devastated the districts of Eshkevar, Alamut, Talekan and upper Shahsevar. Within an area of 10,000 square kilometres all houses and public buildings were either destroyed or damaged beyond repair and many people were killed. [2]

Contemporary records speak of after-shocks which continued for two months after the main earthquake. Other earthquakes in 1639 and 1808 — besides those likely but unrecorded — compounded the damage, while many recorded castles remain nothing but names. Even such important sites as Alamut were only recognized for what they were in the nineteenth century, while Lammassar was convincingly identified only in 1962 by Peter Willey. These problems must be constantly borne in mind during any discussion of Assassin castles.

Alamut

We have already seen the site of Alamut and the difficulties in reaching the castle even today. Although few walls or architectural remains survive, the position of the castle on its rock still renders Alamut the most spectacular of the Assassin castles, and provides the imaginative visitor with a succinct and powerful framework against which to understand the life of Hasan-i Sabbah and the success of his organization.

The very site led to the choice of Alamut as ideal when religious refugees from the Abbasid caliphs built the original castle around 860-1. It was extended and largely rebuilt in the early years of Hasan-i Sabbah's residence, together with the construction of irrigation systems for nearby fields. Problems in ascertaining to what extent surviving remains are from the period of the Assassins are compounded by the fact that the castle was rebuilt yet again during the Safavid dynasty of Persia (1502-1736), with fortified living quarters, mosques, gardens, stables, underground storage rooms and refinements which are associated with a fortified city rather than a bleak mountain fortress. In the seventeenth and eighteenth centuries the castle was used as a royal prison. [3] The French traveller Jean Chardin relates in his *Voyages* that Alamut

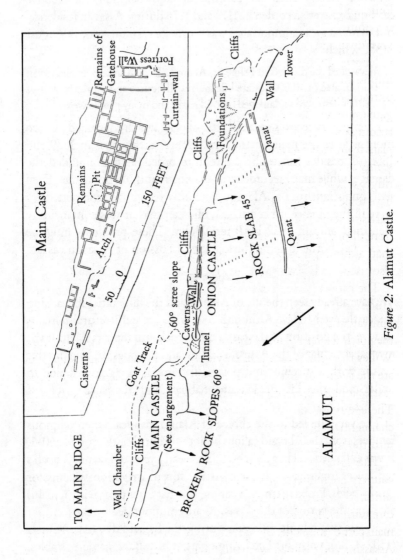

Figure 2: Alamut Castle.

was used as a prison for prisoners of the same blood as the kings 'whom they wished to get rid of without excessive scandal'.[4]

The castle stands on a narrow ridge, about four-hundred metres long, and varies in width from a minimum of a few metres to a maximum of thirty-five metres. The part of the castle once inhabited was much smaller, the same width but only about a hundred metres in length. On both sides the almost sheer rock would render attack impossible, and on the north side loose scree renders it almost unreachable today. Within the main castle, the layout of entrance, gatehouse and buildings may be discerned, and the surveyor who accompanied Peter Willey on his 1962 expedition made recognizable plans from the broken-down remains (see Figure 2). The main entrance seems to have been at the saddle between the two main parts of the ridge, where the only path still reaches today. Thus any attack would have to be made up a sixty degree scree slope against a well-defended garrison which could presumably fire down on the attackers' flank from the gatehouse and walls lining the approach path. Lockhart noted that, although the main building material was stone, burnt brick was also used, and that the quality of the mortar was excellent.[5]

The most striking feature of Alamut is its water storage system. Huge cisterns were cut into the solid rock at several points to collect rainwater off the catchment area of the slopes beneath the castle. At the north-western point of the castle is one cistern which may possibly, Willey thought, have a well providing water.[6] More remarkable still are the *qanats,* or water channels, which run parallel to the lie of the castle along the smooth southern rock slopes where there is no scree. These were designed to collected rainwater from the slopes, then channel it at a slight gradient along the side of the mountain and into the underground cisterns.

This attention to detail concerning the provision of water in a country and climate where water is of vital importance in the arid summers (even at that height) is perhaps the best indication of the care with which the whole fortress was built. If the buildings in the main part of the castle, the apartments of Hasan-i Sabbah, other leading Assassins and visitors, were built with equal care and with the fine building materials noted on the site, then it may well have been a magnificent residence worthy of visitors' impressions. It is evident that the famous garden — the 'taste of paradise' which authors mention

— also required liberal quantities of water. It is noteworthy in this context that our word paradise derives from the Persian word for garden, *ferdows*, for the water-filled, shady, pooled garden that a traveller met after weeks of desert travel at up to fifty degrees centigrade was indeed meant to be perceived as paradise. The Persian garden, such as those of Esfahan, Shiraz or the wonderful shrine of Mahan, still functions in this way.

But it is also necessary to examine a concept of space prevalent to Persia which may indicate a completely different notion of the function of Alamut. Jean Aubin has shown convincingly in a study of urban agglomerations in Persia that the name of a town, village or castle often implies a much greater area. Thus Kerman, in south-eastern Persia, was once called *shahr-i Kirman*, meaning 'the town [chief place of the province] of Kerman', but then became simplified to Kerman without changing its original meaning. What Aubin describes as this 'tendency of the Persian language not to distinguish between the territory and its principal locality' reminds us that a single name often means both the town itself and the district.[7] Evidence concerning Alamut, including Ivanow's observation that the people of the area only use the word 'Alamut' to describe the whole valley and never the castle,[8] suggests that we should consider Alamut in the same way — as a complex of castles, outlying observation posts and villages, the central point of which was the rock which western sources call Alamut.

Given its spectacular and inaccessible site, the obvious care with which it was constructed, and the intelligence and power of the man who resided there, it is not surprising that, even today, ruined by time, earthquakes, souvenir and treasure hunters, Alamut remains one of the most inspiring and memorable of all castles.

Samiran

The site of Samiran, more easily reached by car by travelling north from Zanjan, one-hundred-and-eighty kilometres further along the Tehran–Tabriz road than Qazvin, covers a much larger area. Samiran was once the capital of a Daylamite prince, and the ruins cover the area of an entire town. A fine surviving octagonal tomb tower and other pieces of wall and buildings which have recently been washed away, after the building of a dam further down the Qizil Uzun River, suggest the size and wealth of that town. The Uzun River drains into the Sefid Rud (river) almost exactly opposite the Alamut Rud.

This explains the strategic importance of Samiran, Alamut, the modern town of Rudbar, and other castles further north along the Sefid Rud as it drains into the Caspian Sea. These rivers and their tributaries provide the only routes through and along the Alborz Range between Tehran (the Karaj valley) and the road north from Miyaneh to the Caspian. If we imagine the rectangle Tehran–Miyaneh–Rasht –Chalus with this river system as an inverted 'T' pointing north towards the Caspian, then we shall have a clear idea of the area within which the Assassins held their greatest power from the taking of Alamut by Hasan-i Sabbah (see Figure 3). The total area is roughly thirty-four-thousand square kilometres.

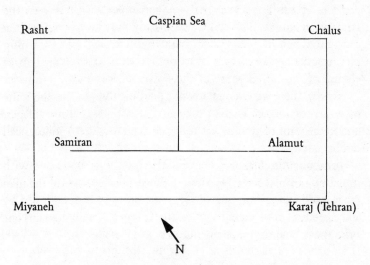

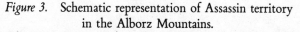

Figure 3. Schematic representation of Assassin territory in the Alborz Mountains.

The castle and octagonal tomb tower are the most impressive and interesting ruins, the castle itself being, as Sylvia Matheson remarks, 'very Norman in appearance'.[9] In 1838, Sir Henry Rawlinson described it as being 'on an isolated and most precipitous hill . . . immediately overhanging the river'.[10] In fact, the scree slope to the south of the castle, dropping into the Gizil Ukun river, appears once to have been cut into a series of terraces, parts of which have literally slipped down the side of the hill into the river. Where the terraces finally end, the slope turns into an almost vertical rock face down to the river. The drop is of perhaps a hundred metres, and in spring the river below is a rushing torrent. The castle was originally surrounded by a triple wall, only one of which remains in brief fragments, although traces of the other walls can be seen amongst the scree and rubble which cover the site. It is clear that with fortified terraces, the river and its cliffs providing a natural boundary on one side, and slopes of forty-five degrees on the other three sides, the castle was relatively easy to defend.

When the Persian writer Nasir-i Khusraw visited Samiran in 1046 on his way as a pilgrim to Mecca he observed the triple wall and also stated that the garrison was of one-thousand men.[11] This testimony provides a plausible estimate of its size and importance in the Assassin's strategic economy. The castle was already in ruins in the thirteenth century when the historian Yakut visited it and described it picturesquely as a 'mother of castles',[10] another expression which eloquently conveys a sense of the power of Samiran.

Nearby, there were several towers, mausoleums and mosques, most of which disappeared when the valley was flooded in the 1970s to create the dam. One interesting tower reported by Willey, with a double spiral staircase so that men climbing and descending the staircase at the same time would never meet, has thus disappeared. The remaining tomb tower, standing on a small hill across the dry valley (that is, when the dam is not full) to the north of the castle, has long since seen its roof collapse onto the floor. But it has fine quality brickwork, and some interesting pieces of stucco remain attached to the upper part of the tower, with inscriptions in kufic script.

Lammassar

Although Alamut has the most spectacular site, the castle which created the greatest resistance when the Mongol leader Hulegu, grandson of Ghengis Khan, eventually destroyed the Assassins as a 'political' and religious power was Lammassar. Their resistance was possible because of one particular feature that in turn was facilitated by the peculiar topographical position of the castle.

Little is known of the history of Lammassar until it was captured in 1102 by Buzurg'umid, the vizier to Hasan-i Sabbah who later became his successor. The occupants of the castle had refused to be converted to Hasan-i Sabbah's new preaching, so he sent Kiya Buzurg umid with some men from Alamut, who 'climbed up by stealth in the night', killed the inhabitants and took over the castle. In a way which reminds us of Hasan himself and presumably inspired his faith in this leader, Buzurg'umid 'resided in that castle for 20 years and did not come down until he was summoned by Hasan'.[13]

Some sixty kilometres down the Shahrud valley from Alamut, almost due north of Qazvin, the castle of Lammassar stands on a strange truncated hill, like an upturned and tilted table looking down onto the valley. The interior ground of the castle rises up this tilted plane in a series of terraces away from the river valley. This peculiarity gave great importance to the southern, or lower, entrance to the castle, which could only be approached across a narrow neck of land. Beside the entrance, and on both the eastern and western sides of this castle, the land falls away at about forty-five degrees as at Samiran. But the entrance is its unique feature.

This entrance stands between two towers, and is closer to the dimensions of a domestic doorway than a castle entrance: about six feet high and three feet wide. This, as Willey observes, 'must have caused packhorses difficulty'.[14] But it must have caused even greater difficulty to any attacking force, since the only feasible way to gain entry to the castle would have been through this gateway. The only other entrance, no larger, led from the north or top of the castle to the ridge which rises behind it and certainly does not offer an easier route to enter the castle for an attacking force from below. The entire side is protected by natural cliffs which were surmounted by walls. Thus, Lammassar is the most obviously impregnable of Assassin castles. The detail of the tiny entrance provides a much greater insight into the castle building mentality and defensive strategies of the Assassins than any account of the mere size of their castles.

The castle was apparently never used again after the defeat of the Assassins, and Freya Stark records that when she visited Lammassar in 1931 the rooms in the southern part of the main keep, towards the top of the castle, still had their doors intact.[15] From a tower built onto the eastern wall of the castle a covered path, presumably once with steps cut into it to enable men to climb the steep slope more easily, fell several-hundred metres to the tributary of the Shah Rud far below, providing a secret protected entrance and safe access to water — although, as on Alamut, there were cisterns to catch rainwater as it ran off the castle walls.

Maymun Diaz

The Arab chronicler Mustawfi stated that Maymun Diaz was the strongest of fifty castles that belonged to the Assassins,[16] but it belonged to them for a short period. Juvayni has left a vivid account of its construction by Ala-ad-Din, penultimate Grand Master of the Persian Assassins:

Now the history of that castle is as follows. At the time when that people were at the height of their power, 'Ala-ad-Din . . . had instructed his officials and ministers to survey the heights and summits of those mountains for the space of 12 years until they chose that lofty peak which confided secrets to the star Capella; and on its summit, which had a spring of water on its top and three others on its side, they began to build the castle of Maimun-Diz making the ramparts out of plaster and gravel. And from a parasang away they brought a stream like the Juy-i-Arziz and caused the water to flow into the castle. And because of the extreme cold it was impossible for beasts to find a home in that place from the beginning of autumn till the middle of spring. On this account Rukn-ad-Din thought it impossible for human beings to penetrate to the castle and lay siege to it, since the mountains intertwined and the very eagles shrank back from the passes whilst the game animals at the foot sought some other way round.[17]

Although part of this description might be aimed at glorifying the feats of Hulegu Khan by his official chronicler, such as the eagles which 'shrank back', the precision of this account was sufficient for Peter Willey and his expedition to identify the site.

Maymun Diaz lies west of Alamut, and was taken by Hulegu immediately before proceeding to the Assassins' headquarters. Although it can be reached over a difficult pass from Alamut, the best route to approach or attack is from the south. Again, like Alamut and Lammassar, the site is spectacular and virtually impregnable in itself. The castle was built on a rock that stands five- or six-hundred

metres high above the river valley, again tilted towards the valley like
Lammassar. The top of the rock, on which the castle stood, is about
five-hundred metres long and one-hundred metres wide, although
it widens out at its base. Willey describes it as rising 'gradually above
a great saucer-shaped moat of a sufficient size to contain the Mongol
armies'. [18] The castle was well-fortified on its southern side, overlooking
the valley and most probable approach for any attacker. In fact Hulegu
did attack from this direction.

Shah Diz

The castle of Shah Diz is in a certain sense atypical, since it stands
on a mountain eight kilometres south of Esfahan far from the two
major concentrations of Assassin castles in the Alborz and in Quhistan.
Yet we have seen that Esfahan was an early centre of Isma'ilism and
that Hasan-i Sabbah himself went there when he returned to Persia
from Cairo. Although a legend reported by Ibn al-Athir suggests that
the castle was of recent construction, having been built by Malik Shah,
to whom Nizam al-Mulk was vizier, Minasian has convincingly argued
that it is much more ancient. [19] The key factor is that the fortress
was taken for the Assassins by ibn-Attash, Hasan's former mentor,
during the period of weakness in a dynastic squabble for power after
the death of Malik Shah in 1092. From that moment Shah Diz became
one of the most important Isma'ili centres.

The citadel, or fortress proper, is reminiscent of the great castles
of the Alborz in its dimensions and site: it stands on a rock rising
about eight-hundred metres from the surrounding plain. It is about
one-hundred-and-fifty metres long, and varies from fifteen to twenty
metres in width. Two sides of the rock beneath the castle, the north
and east, are vertical and thus offer natural protection, while the other
two sides were strengthened by stone walls which have largely
disappeared. A fine stretch of fifteen metres of well-dressed and
cambered stone together with the remains of two turrets still survive
on the southern side. Minasian has shown that the total area built
within the citadel was some three-thousand square metres, consisting
of rooms, a central hall, a temple and perhaps a small courtyard,
probably for the use of a royal household. Attached to the citadel was
what he describes as the 'grandees' quarters', which must have been

an impressive building built on terraces along the slope of the mountain, with a series of wide balconies on each level so that 'facing the Grandees' Quarters from the south, one can picture its original building as storied grand terraces with the citadel on its top, highly reminiscent of a ziggurat'.[20] It is interesting to speculate whether the terraces at Samiran were built for a similar function.

Two large barrack wings complete the main building units within the castle walls. As always, water supplies were of vital importance, and in this case provided by a well-protected dam which gathered water and spring snow for the summer. This huge fortress could be entered by five gates, each of about two and a half metres width.

Shah Diz provides one of the striking examples of the excellence of military architecture of the period, although we cannot claim that the Assassins were wholly responsible. Walls were massive, between one and nearly four metres thick, usually double and made with cut and dressed granite blocks. There were also regular turrets to provide both defensive power and architectural merit. The site was superb, and the attraction of such an ideal military and strategic site close to a major city is obvious. It was built as a stronghold: 'Almost every detail was carefully considered and worked out primarily for defensive purposes without sacrificing the offensive possibilities to those in the stronghold'.[21] Most interesting of all is the relative impossibility of making a direct attack, since the fortress was proof against the techniques of attack then in use (ramming, undermining, escalading, and any form of thrown weapon, arrow or catapult) because of its position. Direct assault was rendered impossible by the precipitous rocks beneath the fortress.

Yet Shah Diz did not long remain in Assassin hands, since it was taken in 1107 within Hasan-i Sabbah's lifetime by the only possible method of attack: siege. The dynastic squabbles which had caused the weakness in the state that enabled Shah Diz to be easily taken had resolved themselves with the decisive action of Sultan Muhammad. In 1105 he seized power after the death of his half-brother Barkyaruq, who had succeeded Malik Shah. One of Sultan Muhammad's prime objectives was to retake Shah Diz, although he had already been fighting the Ismai'ilis elsewhere in Persia.

Beginning in the spring of 1107, the siege lasted throughout that winter with the Isma'ilis playing for time by protracting negotiations.

One of the main requests was to divide the garrison into three parts with safe conduct to three other Isma'ili castles, Tabas, Arrajan and Alamut. Sultan Muhammad agreed and allowed the first two batches of Isma'ilis to depart — after which Attash reneged on his agreement to give up the fortress and began to attack the Sultan.[22] The end of the siege was ambiguous: one story has it that one of the Isma'ili chiefs betrayed his sect by providing Sultan Muhammad with information to enter the castle; another has it that ibn-Attash surrendered after a failed attempt to kill the Sultan.

Whatever may be the truth, Sultan Muhammad's subsequent action is interesting. As soon as he had captured this strong, and apparently comfortable, fortress he destroyed it completely, presumably out of fear that the Isma'ilis might be able to retake it in his absence. This fear was justified, since his father's vizier Nizam al-Mulk had recently been murdered by the Assassins. Similarly, the contradictory stories of betrayal and attempted murder at the fall of the castle suggest confusion and perhaps fear. In terms of a history of the Assassins the most striking fact is the powerful position from which ibn-Attash was able to negotiate with the Sultan as early as 1107 — even though he eventually lost the castle. It suggests that the organization had already gained a reputation which generated fear, and that the Assassins were already a power to be reckoned with — even by a king.

Other castles

Many of the castles, fortresses and other defensive positions of the Assassins have disappeared without trace for reasons explained at the beginning of this chapter. Those of Quhistan were in an area notorious for this phenomenon, where literally thousands of cities, villages and castles have come into being and then totally disappeared in historical times. Others, like Saveh, south of Tehran, have never been studied or excavated, and there is no contemporary evidence to make them of interest beyond their extreme picturesqueness.

The great castle of the Girdkuh was one of Hasan-i Sabbah's earliest bases when he was preaching in the area of Damghan, east of Tehran on the main road to Mashad and Afghanistan. It was mentioned by the historian Yakut,[23] and bears the distinction of a mention in the Persian national epic, the *Shahnamah* or *Book of Kings* by Firdawsi.

This was the castle of the *rais* Muzaffar who paid for the rock of Alamut. Once he had revealed his allegiance to the 'new preaching' he ruled from Girdkuh in Hasan-i Sabbah's name for forty years.[24] The ruins of his castle stand on the strange circular mound of Girdkuh west of modern Damghan and visible from the main Tehran-Damghan road. The base of the hill is surrounded by the remains of a double curtain wall built by the Mongols during their siege, and mangonel ammunition lies scattered around the site nearby. The usual water cisterns and fortifications can be found on top of the rock. Legend has it that this castle was so well provisioned that it was only taken when the defenders' clothes wore out.[25]

The now disappeared castles of Quhistan of which we have some record in the accounts of near-contemporary travellers or historians include: Muminabad (The Believer's Home), which was a day's march east of the modern city of Birjand, and was in the fourteenth century an important centre of saffron production;[26] Turshiz, in north-western Quhistan near modern Nishapur, which was taken from the Assassins in 1126 by the vizier of the Seljuk Sultan Sanjar, one of the other sons of Malik Shah; and four famous castles sited around Turshiz which Mustawfi mentioned, Kal'ah Mikal, Kal'ah Bardaru, Mujahidabad (The Champion's House), and Atishgah (The Fire Temple).[27]

Other castles elsewhere included the fortress of Ustunavand on the slopes of Mount Damavand, within a day's journey from the old Persian capital at Ray, and Tabas, a city which was considered Isma'ili in the late eleventh century, but which was besieged by Sanjar's army in 1102 and in part destroyed.[28] Tabas was celebrated for its dates, lemons and oranges, and provides an interesting example of potential earthquake damage in that the entire city was razed to the ground in 1978 during a massive earthquake that killed some thirty-thousand of its thirty-three-thousand population. Yakut further mentions the fine fortress of Kilat in the Tarum mountains between Qazvin and Khalkhad, which possessed a multi-arched masonry bridge and excellent markets,[29] while Mustawfi speaks of the two castles of Kal'ah Tighur and Diz Kilat, situated near Arrajan, later Bihbahan, on the Tab River in West Fars. He says that the Assassins used these two castles and bases for marauding and plundering Arrajan.[30]

There is no record of the Assassins as great builders, and Hasan-i Sabbah left no architectural monuments. Even though Islamic architecture at that time was at its zenith — with the fine mosques of Cairo, and the tomb towers of the Seljuk princes as evidence — the Assassins do not seem to have indulged in elegance or extravagance. That the men who built Alamut, with its water cisterns, and Lammassar, with its superb southern entrance, were excellent and skilled builders seems beyond doubt. But their labours were essentially utilitarian, in line with the austere personality of the Order's founder and the aims of the organization.

There is little today to remind us of the power of the Assassins, beyond a few walls and the images an imaginative traveller can create for himself from the ruins that lie scattered on the mountainsides of the Alborz. Perhaps, indeed, the most eloquent testimony to their power and aims is to be found in the *sites* of their castles — the secret, inaccessible nature of the places they chose not only for military defence but as lifetime residences in which their scholarly writings and political activities were conceived in isolation from the world.

THE ASSASSINS
AS A SECRET SOCIETY

ISMA'ILISM was from the first an 'underground' religion, with occulted imams, disguises and all forms of religious meeting or discussion carried out either in secret or in anonymity. Loyal adherence to a persecuted and officially heretical sect had always required strong faith and determination. That these should be characteristics of the Nizari Isma'ilis is therefore not surprising. When the sources refer to the Assassins as the *fida'i* or faithful they are but emphasizing the extent to which Hasan-i Sabbah was able to refine and hone the traditional qualities of the Isma'ilis.

The loyalty of the *fida'i*, and their readiness to obey an order even if it involved sacrificing their lives for an apparently futile reason, is the aspect which most struck such early western chroniclers as Marco Polo. It was one of the features which helped their sinister reputation to establish itself rapidly in European legend and language, but there is little mystery or magic about it. The essence of this loyalty was clearly their faith, strengthened by the reorganization of the traditional Isma'ili hierarchy into a system of initiation which enhanced the element of secrecy and of *belonging*, which in turn fuelled loyalty.

The origin of Assassin doctrines

Towards the end of the tenth century there appeared in Basra the eclectic school of philosophy known as *Ikhwan al-Safa*, or the Brethren of Sincerity. Their name derives from a story concerning a ringdove in which a group of animals managed to escape the snares of a hunter by acting as faithful friends — that is, as the *ikhwan al-safa*. Thus the term does not necessarily imply any kind of 'brotherhood'.[1] This strange and secretive Isma'ili sect aimed to overthrow the existing political order by undermining the predominant intellectual system and religious beliefs. Their doctrines, which were a synthesis of semitic and Neoplatonic ideas with leanings towards Pythagorean speculation, were expounded in a collection of fifty-one epistles known as the *Rasa'il*.

Fundamentally, the authors of these epistles formulated a doctrine which they believed led to God's favour and the attainment of paradise. They suggested that this path, in order to avoid the errors which had crept into orthodox Islam, led to perfection by means of a synthesis of Arab religious laws and Greek philosophy.[2] Neoplatonism underlies the harmony between revealed religion and philosophical speculation, while they drew on Aristotle for logic and Pythagoras provided their particular reverence for numbers. Thus the system represents a remarkable synthesis of monotheism, Greek philosophy, elements of Persian religion and Hindu mysticism.

Isma'ilis believe that the *Rasa'il* was written by Imam Ahmad, one of their hidden imams, although it seems more likely that it was written by several authors.[3] These epistles constitute an encyclopaedia of knowledge at that time. Al-Ghazzali, perhaps the greatest of all Islamic theologians, was influenced by the ideas of the Brethren and was himself a great influence on Dante and St Thomas Aquinas,[4] as well as exercising enormous influence throughout Islam. Their ideals also entered Christian scholasticism through the works of Avicenna (Ibn-Sina).

The two great Assassin Grand Masters, Hasan-i Sabbah and Rashid al-Din Sinan, both have close links with these epistles. We know that Rashid, chief of the Syrian Assassins and original 'Old Man of the Mountains', used the writings in the *Rasa'il* diligently,[5] while in the eighth epistle of the second section there is a spiritual portrait of the ideal man which is uncannily close to the person and ideals of Hasan-i Sabbah: this ideal man would be 'Persian in origin, Arab by religion, Iraqi by culture, Hebrew in experience, Christian in conduct, Syrian in asceticism, Greek by the sciences, Indian by perspicacity, sufi by his way of life, angelic by morals, divine by his ideas and knowledge, and destined for eternity'.[6] Furthermore, many of the ideas of Hasan and the very terminology of Assassin doctrines recall the ideas of these precursors.

In general, the subjects studied by the Brethren fall into two groups: the Macrocosm, or the development of the universe as the evolution of plurality out of unity (i.e. from God through intelligence, soul, primal matter, secondary matter, the world, nature and the elements); and the Microcosm, which represents the return from plurality to unity (i.e. Man). The aspirant 'brother' was first to be well grounded in the so-called mundane subjects (reading and writing; grammar; calculation and computation; prosody and poetics; omens and portents; magic and alchemy; trades and crafts; commerce; biography and narrative) and religious studies (Koranic knowledge; exegesis of the scripture; the science of tradition; jurisprudence; the commemoration of God, the ascetic life, mysticism and the beatific vision).

When this period of studies had been completed, the aspirant could begin the programme of philosophical studies in the *Rasa'il*, which comprised the following.

Epistles 1-13: Mathematics and logic. Number, geometry, astronomy, geography, music, arithmetical and geometrical relation, arts and crafts, diversity of human character; the categories; the interpretation of texts; and the application of algebra in geometry.

Epistles 14-30: Natural science and anthropology. Matter, form, space, time, and motion; cosmogony; production, destruction and the elements; meteorology; mineralogy; the essence of Nature and its manifestations; botany; zoology; anatomy and anthropology; sense perceptions; embryology; Man as the Microcosm; the development of the soul; body and soul; the true nature of psychical and physical pain and pleasure; philology.

Epistles 31-40: Psychology. The Understanding; the world-soul.

Epistles 40-51: Theology. The esoteric doctrine of Islam; the ordering of the spirit world; the occult sciences.[7]

The object of mathematics as studied at the beginning is to conduct the soul from the sensible to the spiritual, since the theory of number is divine wisdom expressed symbolically. First mathematics leads to astrology, which governs all human life as man comes under the influence of the planets. Yet since all men do not live long enough to allow the slow progress through planetary influence to wisdom, God has sent prophets whose teachings may be used by the initiated to speed up the process. Through a gradual process the aspirant is taught to philosophize about questions like the origin or eternity of the world, but this is impossible without renunciation of the world and righteous conduct.

At its highest level this system attempts a reconciliation between science and life, philosophy and faith. The religion of Muhammad is presented as having been rough and ready, simplified for simple desert folk, while additions from Christianity and Zoroastrianism rendered it more perfect as a system of revelation.

The ordinary man requires a sensuous worship of God; but just as the souls of animals and plants are beneath the soul of the ordinary man, so above it are the souls of the philosopher and the prophet with whom the pure angel is associated. In the higher stages the soul is raised also above the lower popular religion with its sensuous conceptions and usages.[8]

This argument leads to an elitist, ascetic and spiritual concept of man which often marks the various branches of Isma'ilism and especially reminds us of Hasan-i Sabbah.

This classification of philosophy introduced the concept of steps of graded knowledge. To each of the four sections of the *Rasa'il* corresponded a grade which was fixed by age — reminiscent of Plato's *Republic*. Young men of fifteen to thirty whose souls are completely submissive to the teachers form the first grade. In the second grade, between thirty and forty, these men are introduced to secular wisdom and receive an analogical knowledge of things. Then in the third grade, from forty to fifty, they are given access to the Divine Law of the world. Finally, over fifty years old and in the fourth grade, the aspirant will see the true reality of things, like the blessed angels. Then he becomes exalted above Nature, doctrine and law.[9] Although the grades increased, first to seven and then to nine, this is recognizably the basis of later esoteric forms of Isma'ilism including the Assassins.

Grades of initiation of the Nizari Isma'ilis

As far as we know, the Isma'ilis used grades of initiation from a very early date, perhaps from the period of the rise of the Qarmatians or even the Brethren of Sincerity. But in the late eleventh century these grades were reorganized and renamed by Hasan-i Sabbah as he established the sect known as the Assassins.

There were at first seven grades of initiation, the first of which, imam, was hereditary in that the imam was necessarily a descendant of Ali and Nizar. Furthermore, the remaining six grades may be divided into four groups according to the degree of initiation. Thus the hierarchy may be divided into the 'fully initiated', the 'partly initiated' and the 'uninitiated', as follows:

Group A: descended from Ali and Nizar	1 Imam
Group B: fully initiated	2 *Da'i 'd-Du'at* (Chief *Da'i*) 3 *Da'i 'l-Kabir* (Superior *Da'i*) 4 *Da'i* (ordinary *Da'i*)
Group C: partly initiated	5 *Rafiq* (comrade)
Group D: uninitiated	6 *Lasiq* (adherent) 7 *Fida'i* (self-sacrificer)

Of these last 'uninitiated' groups, the *Lasiq* had taken an oath of allegiance to the Imam. Both the *Lasiq* and the *Fida'i* had heard of the mysteries of the esoteric doctrines and aspired to them, but these two grades had no knowledge beyond the public, exoteric doctrines.[10]

The key figure in these stages of initiation is the *da'i*. This figure is in many ways a uniquely Persian one, similar to the missionary in some ways but greater in learning and knowledge of character — by which means he was able to impress the people he met and stimulate their curiosity to know more. His intention was to provide just enough information to 'hook' the potential proselyte, and then explain that the divine mysteries could only be disclosed to those who have taken an oath of allegiance to the imam, or God's present representative on Earth. We have seen how this procedure was used by the *da'is* of Attash to draw Hasan-i Sabbah into the nascent Isma'ili sect in Persia.

In his outline of the procedures of the *da'i*, based upon the writings of the historian an-Nuwayri, Silvestre de Sacy showed how by means of simple questions like 'Why did God take seven days to create the universe?', 'Why were the Heavens created according to the number Seven, and the Earths likewise?', the *da'i* would create interest in his listener. Then he would ask:

Will you not reflect on your own state? Will you not meditate attentively on it, and recognise that He who had created you is wise, that He does not act by chance, the He has acted in all this with wisdom, and that it is for secret and mysterious reasons that He has united what He has united, and divided what He has divided? How can you imagine that it is permissible for you to turn aside your attention from all these things, when you hear these words of God (*Qur'an*, li, 20–21): '*There are signs on the earth to those whose believe with a firm faith; and in your own selves; will ye not then consider?*'[11]

He goes on to give further examples from the Koran, indicating how an esoteric interpretation may be derived from the ambiguities and unanswered questions of that work.

The next stage of the *da'is* task was to obtain the oath of allegiance, the key part of which took the following form:

Bind yourself, then, by placing thy right hand in mine, and promise me, with the most inviolable oaths and assurances, that you will never divulge our secret, that you will not lend assistance to any one, be it who it may, against us, that you will set no snare for us, that you will not speak to us aught but the truth, and that you will not league yourself with any of our enemies against us.

The secret, heretical and political nature of the sect is emphasized by the repeated insistence on the fact that the neophyte should never act against the sect in any way.

Although the details of the stages of initiation from which these passages are taken derive from a historian writing around 1332 about the Druzes, we may assume that the procedures were not entirely dissimilar from those adopted by the Assassins up to about the same period. The major difference is that the degrees have here been increased from seven to nine, perhaps to agree with the nine celestial spheres, that is the seven planetary spheres plus the Sphere of the Fixed Stars and the Empyrean. It is worth quoting the whole passage from E.G. Browne's account:

Second Degree. The neophyte is taught to believe that God's approval cannot be won by observing the prescriptions of Islam, unless the inner Doctrine, of which they are mere symbols, be received from the Imam to whom its guardianship has been entrusted.

Third Degree. The neophyte is instructed as to the nature and number of the Imams, and is taught to recognise the significance in the spiritual and material worlds of the number Seven which they also represent. He is thus definitely detached from the *Imamiyya* of the Sect of the Twelve, and is taught to regard the last six of their imams as persons devoid of spiritual knowledge and unworthy of reverence.

Fourth Degree. The neophyte is now taught the doctrine of the Seven Prophetic Periods, of the nature of the *Natiq*, the *Sus* or *Asas* and the remaining six *Samits* ('Silent' Imams) who succeed the latter, and of the abrogation by each *Natiq* of the religion of his predecessor. This teaching involves the admission (which definitely places the proselyte outside the pale of Islam) that Muhammad was not the last of the Prophets, and that the Qur'an is not God's final revelation to man. With Muhammad b. Isma'il, the Seventh and Last *Natiq*, the *Qu'im ('He who ariseth'), the Sahibu'i-Amr* ('Master of the Matter'), an end is put to the 'Sciences of the Ancients' (*Ulumu'l-awwalin*), and the Esoteric (*Batini*) Doctrine, the Science of Allegorical Interpretation (*Ta'wil*), is inaugurated.

Fifth Degree. Here the proselyte is further instructed in the Science of Numbers and in the application of the *ta'wil*, so that he discards many of the traditions, learns to speak contemptuously of the state of Religion, pays less and less heed to the letter of Scripture, and looks forward to the abolition of all outward observances of Islam. He is also taught the significance of the number Twelve, and the recognition of the twelve *Hujjas* or 'Proofs', who primarily conduct the propaganda of each Imam. These are typified in man's body by the twelve dorsal vertebrae, while the seven cervical vertebrae represent the Seven Prophets and the Seven Imams of each.

Sixth Degree. Here the proselyte is taught the allegorical meaning of the rites and obligations of Islam, such as prayer, alms, pilgrimage, fasting, and the like, and is then persuaded that their outward observance is a matter of no importance, and may be abandoned, since they were only instituted by wise and philosophical lawgivers as a check to restrain the vulgar and unenlightened herd.

Seventh Degree. To this and the following degrees only the leading *da'is*, who fully comprehend the real nature and aim of their doctrine, can initiate. At this point is introduced the dualistic doctrine of the Pre-existent and the Subsequent, which is destined ultimately to undermine the proselyte's belief in the Doctrine of the Divine Unity.

Eighth Degree. Here the doctrine last mentioned is developed and applied, and the proselyte is taught that above the Pre-existent and the Subsequent is a Being who has neither name, nor attribute, of whom nothing can be predicted, and to whom no worship can be rendered. This Nameless Being seems to represent the *Zerwan Akarana* ('Boundless Time') of the Zoroastrian system, but . . . some confusion exists here, and different teachings were current amongst the Isma'ilis, which, however, agreed in this, that, to quote Nuwayri's expression, 'those who adopted them could no longer be reckoned otherwise than amongst the Dualists and Materialists.' The proselyte is also taught that a Prophet is known as such not by miracles, but by his ability to construct and impose in a kind of system at once political, social, religious, and philosophical . . . He is further taught to understand allegorically the end of the world, the Resurrection, Future Rewards and Punishments, and other eschatological doctrines.

Ninth Degree. In this, the last degree of initiation, every vestige of dogmatic religion has been practically cast aside, and the initiate is become a philosopher pure and simple, free to adopt such system or admixture as may be most to his taste.[12]

This passage clearly illustrates to what degree the Isma'ilis were heretical in denying the essential tenets of Islam. It also illustrates the degrees of initiation we may reasonably assume an Assassin adept was required to pass through.

The Chief *Da'i*, or 'Chief Propagandist', was the Grand Master, who became known as the 'Mountain Chief' through his more common title of Shayku'l-Jabal. From this title comes the incorrect form 'Old Man of the Mountains' which was adopted in Western Europe after its frequent use by crusaders and such writers as Marco Polo. In order to give some frame of reference Browne compared the *Da'i Kabir* to bishops, each of whom was responsible for a particular 'see'. The greater part of the initiated members were the *da'is*, but the greater proportion of the Isma'ilis as a whole belonged to the seventh group according to the Assassin degrees, the *fida'is*, translated variously as 'self-sacrificers', 'self-devoted ones', 'the destroying angels', whose legendary loyalty and ruthlessness inspired the legends. It was the *fida'is* who were the real 'assassins'.

Exoteric doctrine: the ta'lim

The fundamental doctrine of the *Shi'a* is based upon the *ta'lim*, or authorized teaching. The imam was responsible for this teaching, from which no deviation at all was possible. This is the basis of the authority of the Shiite imams, and informs their role as descendants of Ali, while *Sunni* Moslems argued that they themselves had chosen Mohammad's successor in Abu Bakr and that only their choice was valid. All religious knowledge came from the *ta'lim*, and all disputes could only be resolved by the person named by the last imam, whose authority therefore derived directly from the Prophet himself. Full acceptance of the *ta'lim*, with all its implications, was the necessary condition for being a member of the sect of Nizari Isma'ilis, and in itself would do much to explain the extreme devotion and loyalty of the *fida'is*.

Furthermore, the idea of *ta'lim* is vital for an understanding of the Isma'ili view of prophecy and the imamate, which 'was based on the belief in the permanent need of mankind for a divinely guided, impeccable leader and teacher to govern it justly and to direct it soundly in religion.'[13] This leader was clearly the imam, while the imamate was 'part of the prophetic chain which spans the history of man from the beginning to the end. This belief about the significance of the Imammate was part of the heritage which Isma'ilism carried on from the earlier Shi'a, but it transformed it into its own cyclical yet ultimately teleological view of history'.[14]

The essential division between *Shi'a* and *Sunni* is based upon the dispute between the mutually exclusive notions that authority may be explained by *ta'lim* or that it may be explained by means of reason and analogy. One of the few surviving writings believed to belong to the authentic canon of Hasan-i Sabbah, preserved by Shahrastani, deals, under the title the 'Four chapters' with this central problem. Thus we can see in his own words how Hasan dealt with the problem and even managed to increase his own power through his interpretation of this key point. The following discussion is based upon Hodgson's translation of the 'Chapters' and his detailed analysis of them.

The new teaching of Hasan-i Sabbah implied a new interpretation of *ta'lim*, in the course of which we obtain an interesting insight into the theological thought of Hasan and its subtlety. These arguments do much to stamp the personality of Hasan as a *religious* leader, and diminish the more conventional view — fuelled by misunderstanding and centuries of propaganda against the Isma'ilis. The elaboration of the new *da'wa* is far from the image of a bloodthirsty assassin, or even the co-ordinating mind behind the Assassins. In the first 'chapter' he wrote:

He who delivers opinions on the subject of the Creator Most High must say one of two things: either he must say, I know the Creator through reason and speculation alone without need of the teaching [*ta'lim*] of a teacher; or he must say, there is no way to knowledge even with reason and speculation except with the teaching of a trustworthy teacher.[15]

The dilemma is twofold, and unavoidable, since a believer must either accept a teacher or be unable to assert his own thoughts or speculations above anybody else's. In either case a teacher is implied, even if that teacher happens to be the person himself. The next move in the argument is to assert that either the teacher must have authority or any teacher at all will be sufficient:

If one says that every teacher is acceptable, he has no right to deny the teacher opposing him; if he denies, he thereby admits that a dependable, trustworthy teacher is required.[16]

This, comments Shahrastani, 'is said to refute' the Sunnis, since they claimed to be able to transmit their tradition through a large number of teachers.

Then Hasan repeats the argument contained in the first proposition, denying even the traditional version of *ta'lim*:

. . . if the need for a trustworthy teacher is established, is knowledge of the teacher required or not? — assuring oneself of him and then learning from him? Or is learning permissible from every teacher without singling out his person and demonstrating his trustworthiness? . . . He for whom it is not possible to follow the way without a leader and a companion, let him '[choose] first the companion, then the way'.[17]

Having refuted the Sunni position, Hasan has gone on to refute the *shi'a* itself, thus preparing his way for the conclusive demonstration that the way of the Isma'ilis, and especially the Nizari Isma'ilis led by Hasan himself, is the correct one.

He does this by first asserting that man must have a single authoritative imam in order to attain knowledge of God. This argument involves setting up and then demolishing a further paradox: without the imam any results derived from reason would be unintelligible, but at the same time reason is essential in order to recognize the imam. It was essential to affirm the authority of the teacher, however, and this he did by presenting a synthesis of the two halves of the paradox. In an interesting display of dialectical sophistry, he showed that reason provides us with recognition of the need of an imam, but since we can reason then we can know the imam, who himself confirms the reasoning. Reason and the imam together are impregnable, and the doctrine of *ta'lim*, in only a slightly different form, has survived. The imam himself is the proof of the fact that he is the imam; critics of Hasan observed that Hasan seemed to be saying, 'My imam is true because he says he is true'.[18] Hence this new, or revised, doctrine of *ta'lim* was modelled so that it formed the basis of all Isma'ili teaching.

This attempt to achieve a basis for the *da'wa* with universal and incontrovertible validity was in many ways a return to the beginnings of Islam when such a universality existed in the person and teachings of the Prophet Muhammad. But the teaching of the Isma'ilis was not an attempt to revive the certainty of the past, since the thrust of their beliefs and actions was always forward-moving, looking towards the last imam and the ultimate triumph of the sect. Perhaps without the severity and obvious sincerity of Hasan-i Sabbah, this thoroughgoing and authoritarian scepticism regarding both tradition and the emphasis on logic and reason as paths towards truth could not have been accepted. Hasan-i Sabbah moulded them to his own remarkable personality and created his, and his sect's, power from what might appear today to be a slender basis.

He was ruthless in the concentration of both power and understanding, confining philosophical speculation to the highest grades of his sect. As Shahrastani puts it:

Moreover he prevented ordinary persons from delving into knowledge; and likewise the elite from investigating former books, except those who knew the circumstances of each book and the rank of the authors in every field. With his partisans, in theology he did not go beyond saying, our god is the god of Mohammad.[19]

The demand for an absolute universal validity achieved by means of logic led Hasan-i Sabbah to place the entire weight of argument and proof on the imam, who is the only authority — even if it might appear that his only authority derives from what he accredits to himself. The imam is thus given even greater importance than in usual *shi'a* practice, so much so that, in Hodgson's words, '. . . it is finally not the rational content of the imam's truth that Hasan is interested in, but his sheer authority'.[20] If all authority is vested in the imam, and truth is to be found (according to a logical analysis) only in unity, then the power of Hasan and his followers is clearly based on a total group devotion. Hence the fanaticism of the *fida'i*, whose existence and role seem to be directly attributable to Hasan, and the ultimate origin of most of the legends about the Assassins.

But it is important to understand that this devotion was neither political nor probably based upon the use of drugs. Hasan-i Sabbah had managed through careful theological argument and relentless logic applied to the *Shi'a* doctrines, to create a powerful sectarian sense of community based on the traditional secrecy and conspiratorial nature of Isma'ilism. It was this achievement which enabled him to create terror throughout the world of the Middle East to such an extent that its echoes soon reached the West.

The esoteric truths (haqa'iq)

Once the validity of the imam is demonstrated, and the imamate in a certain sense guaranteed, the cyclical view of history held by the Isma'ilis is readily constructed and understood. The religious evolution of man was considered to have taken place in seven years under seven Messenger Prophets, the first six of whom were Adam, Noah, Abraham, Moses, Jesus and Muhammad. Each of these messengers revealed a religious law in exoteric form, which was readily interpreted even by the uninitiated: this is the *zahir* or external aspect. But each of these messages also contained an inner, esoteric truth which required interpretation by the small number of initiates capable of receiving them: this is the *batin*, or esoteric truth.

The esoteric truths themselves, *haqa'iq*, were explained by a successor of each of the Messenger Prophets known as the *wasi* (Legates) or by the *sami* (Silent One) whose task was to explain the *batin* of the Scriptures and Law. Each Legate was in turn followed by a series of seven imams, the seventh of whom became the next Messenger Prophet in the series. The last era would be marked by the *Mahdi*, who would make the inner doctrine public and inaugurate an era of pure spiritual knowledge.

Isma'ili theology was thus revelationary in character. The *haqa'iq* transcended human reason and ultimately derived from gnostic doctrines, considering the principles of spiritual and physical worlds in Neoplatonic terms. The gnostics held that the physical world had been created by an inferior deity, the Yahweh of the Old Testament, who was allowed a certain lassitude until God decided to send His son to inhabit the body of Jesus and free the world from false teachings. Certain gnostic notions passed into Islam when Muhammad adopted the gnostic idea that the body which was crucified was only a phantom which the Jews and Romans could not harm. This, in a memorable phrase of Bertrand Russell, was due to 'a strong class feeling that prophets ought not to come to a bad end'.[21] The essential point about the gnostics, in their many manifestations and sects, was their claim to special knowledge, *gnosis*, of an esoteric kind about God and the metaphysical structure of the universe.[22]

Isma'ili doctrine followed this lead in removing all attributes and names from God and accepting Him as a transcendent non-being.[23] In this, it in turn followed Neoplatonic doctrines which filtered into the Islamic world. The Druze faith, which mingled with that of other Isma'ilis through the teaching of Hakim, had incorporated Neoplatonic ideas: in a melange typical of many of these 'heretical' sects of Islam, they revered Hermes, Pythagoras, Plato, and Plotinus — evidence of whose system appears in the Druze Scriptures.[24]

Kindi (Abu Yaqub ibn Ishaq al-Kindi, c801–70), who lived in Baghdad and had translated works of Greek philosophy into Arabic, including those of Aristotle, first introduced into Islamic philosophy the doctrine of the Spirit or Mind which characterized much medieval Moslem philosophy. This doctrine states that higher reality belongs to the Spirit, and that physical reality must dispose itself in conformity with this Spirit. Mid-way between the two is the Soul of the world which first called into being the Spheres and also emanated the Human Soul.[25]

Now while this scheme clearly provides a theological justification for astrology, and Kindi was known as an astrologer, it led to a further elaboration in the thinking of al-Farabi (d.950), known as the 'second Aristotle'. Al-Farabi assimilated the apparently discordant doctrines of Plato and Aristotle, who he described as the imams of philosophy, to Islam. Everything that exists was for al-Farabi either a necessary or a possible thing. The necessary Being was the first cause and therefore unprovable and undefinable, but man attempts to name this most perfect Being, using names that refer to his nature or names which describe his relation to the physical world. What is interesting is that al-Farabi insists on these names being understood only metaphorically. It is in this sense that the Isma'ili idea of removing all names from God derives from the attempt to synthesize Neoplatonic thought and Islam. Above all, al-Farabi insists on the fact that creation, or the *emanation* of the world, is an eternal and intellectual process:

By the first created Spirit thinking of its Author, the second Sphere-spirit comes into being; while, by the same Spirit thinking of itself and thus realizing itself, there proceeds from it the first Body, or the uppermost celestial Sphere. And so the process goes on in necessary succession . . .[26]

To this well-known Ptolomeic sphere-system process, which was later the basis of Dante's cosmogony in *The Divine Comedy*, the Isma'ilis made a significant change. In the words of Madelung, Isma'ilism 'described the Universal Intellect not as proceeding from the One by emanation but as brought forth through his divine Order (*amr*) or Word (*kalima*) in the act of primordial, extratemporal Origination (*ibda*)'. This is an extension of the Islamic concept of *tal'im* to Neoplatonic philosophy. Hence the gnostic and neoplatonic cosmology was given a peculiarly Moslem stamp by the Isma'ilis, who in turn were attracted to Neoplatonic theology by its insistence on the oneness and transcendental nature of God. Isma'ilism does not require proofs of God, and therefore contradicts orthodox Islam and the thought of such great philosophers as Ibn-Sina — whose father had been converted to Isma'ilism but who was not himself an Isma'ili — who used the doctrine of God as a necessary Being as the basis of his proof of the existence of God.

It was against the rationalism of Ibn-Sina that Hasan-i Sabbah wrote the 'Four chapters' mentioned in the section on *tal'im*, since rationalism represented a real threat to Isma'ili doctrine. It was for this reason that Isma'ilis were often known as the believers in *tal'im* or *ta'limiyya*.[27]

The heart of the Isma'ili *haqa'iq*, which consists in their denial of rationalism and forms the basis of their 'heresy', lies in the denial that God is the first cause. For them, the first cause was the Order or Word of God, which became united with the Universal Intellect. Hence the idea of the Order is at the heart of their esoteric doctrines, and achieves their synthesis of Neoplatonic philosophy and Islam. Wilfred Madelung has explained this complex doctrine as follows:

The Order was, however, addressed to the whole universe, and the Intellect contained the forms of all things in the spiritual and physical worlds which were thus originated all at once in the *ibda* [origination]. They were all directly related to God in their origination, though they were manifested only gradually in the process of emanation and causation proceeding from the Intellect in accordance with the divine ordination. The Intellect was called the First Originated Being, since the Order, though logically prior to it, became united with it in existence. God, by his primordial act, could be called the Originator. [28]

This, in the view of the Isma'ilis and in particular of Hasan-i Sabbah, emphasizes the authority of the imam's truth, and thus the authority of the imam himself. Mohammad himself is merely a link in this chain of being which necessarily ends with the most recent imam. The end result of this severe, revelationist esoteric doctrine is what Marshall Hodgson called a 'dehistoricized, absolute imamate'. [29] The power of Hasan-i Sabbah himself, and the fanatical devotion of the *fida'i*, ultimately derived from this categorical insistence on the transcendental nature of God. Such an absolute God, and absolute imam, demands absolute faith and obedience.

Numerology

One of the most obvious approximations of the Isma'ilis to what are today known as the occult sciences lies in their use of number magic. The use of numbers throughout Islamic mysticism is of great importance: numbers were used mystically to form words belonging to the *'ilm Wifd* or science of calculation, which was used for invocations and prayers. [30] Use was also made of a *tasbih*, which was a rosary consisting of ninety-nine beads representing the ninety-nine names of God.

Mathematics and the science of numbers were of particular importance in the *Rasa'il* or the Brethren of Sincerity. In that work arithmetic does not investigate numbers as such but deals with the significance of numbers; things are explained in accordance with a system of numbers. The theory of number *is* divine wisdom precisely because things are formed after the pattern of numbers, so that the absolute principle of existence is the number one. At the beginning, middle and end of philosophy the science of numbers is always present. Arithmetic is the true and pure science, while geometry is easier for beginners to understand because it provides visual examples. But even geometry is divided into the study of lines, surfaces and solids on the one hand, and a spiritual form which deals with the properties such as length, breadth and depth on the other. [31] The occult knowledge and understanding of those early Isma'ilis was constructed upon a foundation of numbers.

As we have seen, the number seven was of sacred importance to the Isma'ilis, and their gnostic cosmogony consisted of seven steps. There were seven imams, and seven grades of initiation. Although, as in so many features of their thought, it is impossible to provide precise evidence, it seems likely that the Assassins believed in and practised a form of cabalistic *gematria*, which asserts a 'geometrical' and thus occult connection between two persons whose names have the same numerical value. An example of this is the often cited case of the numerological significance of the name of Alamut. If the total of the numbers attributed to each of the Arabic letters of the name of the fortress in its Arabic form *Aluh-amu't* is added $(1+30+5+1+40+6+400)$ the total is 483, which in turn is the Arabic date, 483 AH, from the hejira, of the taking of the castle, AD 1090–1. [32] This provides an interesting instance of the way in which *gematria* might have been used by the Assassins.

Hashish

Now that the commonly accepted etymology of the modern English word 'assassin', and its European equivalents, derives from the use of hashish by members of the Nizari Isma'ilis (as we shall see in a later chapter), it remains to be seen what truth there is in the Assassins as hashish takers, or eaters, and to what extent the use of hashish contributed to their doctrines, fidelity and efficacy as Assassins.

Hashish has an ancient and accepted importance in the history of Persian mysticism, where it has traditionally been used not as a stimulant but as a 'spiritual soporific' producing a quiescence of soul which is known as *keyf* or *kaif*, which translates as intoxication, carouse or placid enjoyment. [33] The plant from which the drug is derived is correctly called hemp, *Cannabis sativa*, but has many other names: in India it is known as *bhang, charas* or *ghanja*; in Egypt and the Middle East hashish; in North Africa *keyf*, and in Western Europe marijuana. In his study of the Egyptians written in 1860, Edward William Lane describes popular story-tellers recounting the life of Ez-Zahir, which was based on the life of Sultan Baybars. In this story the fedayeen were always described as using *beng*, or hemp, and henbane, mixed with hashish. Lane records that even at that time it was a common practice.[34] Other writers confirm this use of a mixture of hashish and other drugs, and one author on oriental spiritualism explains this use for the effect of 'raising the imagination until it attained to a beatified realisation of the joys of a future world'.[35]

One of the greatest of Persian scholars, Edward G. Browne, in an address to the doctors of St Bartholomew's Hospital, London, also stressed this use: '. . . not as a therapeutic agent, but as the inspirer of the wildest pantheistic speculations, the most disordered metaphysical phantasies, and the most incredible visions and ecstasies.[36] He quotes verses by one of Persia's greatest mystic poets, Hafez, in praise of hashish: 'O Parrot, discoursing of mysteries, may thy beak never want for sugar'. These lines are reminiscent of the parrot symbolism in a Sufi author reputed to be near to the Isma'ilis as many Sufis were: Attar, in his *Conference of the Birds* has her arrive 'with sugar in her beak, dressed in a garment of green, and round her neck a collar of gold'. He then observes that the hawk 'is but a gnat beside her brilliance; earth's green carpet is the reflection of her feathers, and her words are distilled sugar'.[37]

Much of the well-known mystical symbolism of Sufism, often best known through the *Rubaiyyat of Omar Khayyam*, was taken over by the Isma'ilis. They joined Sufism and Shiism in a peculiar and unique blend, often appearing as a particular group of Sufis with their own *shaykh*. It may be that members of the sect came in from and went out to similar Sufi groups, since it is often difficult to distinguish their ideas from those of the Sufis.[38] It is in this sense that Ivanow suggests that the ground was prepared for the introduction of Isma'ilism by the prior popularization of Sufic ideas. It would not therefore be surprising if the use of hashish and other drugs for achieving mystical ecstasy was also carried over from the Sufis.

Many scholars have argued, and demonstrated convincingly, that the attribution of the epithet 'hashish eaters' or 'hashish takers' is a misnomer derived from enemies of the Isma'ilis and was never used by Moslem chroniclers or sources.[39] It was therefore used in a pejorative sense of 'enemies' or 'disreputable people'. This sense of the term survived into modern times with the common Egyptian usage of the term *hashasheen* in the 1830s to mean simply 'noisy or riotous'.[40] It is unlikely that the austere Hasan-i Sabbah indulged personally in drug taking. Yet the use of hashish as an agent of mystical visions is well attested, and it would be remarkable if there were not some truth in the Assassins using the drug just as other contemporary sects did. In the context of twelfth century Persia there is no real mystery, nor any particular dishonour, to be attached to this usage. But the above survey of Assassin doctrine and the consequent fidelity of the companions suggest that hashish was not necessary in order to inculcate discipline and loyalty.

Transmigration

The doctrine of rebirth, or more correctly transmigration, is central to many eastern faiths — in particular to Jain, Hindu and Buddhist teaching. In the Hindu version, the soul is born again and again so that it may gradually acquire more understanding and then attain perfect knowledge or freedom. When the name and form, *nama-rupa*, dies, life, *jiva*, continues to live: in the picturesque example of the *Brihadaranyaka Upanishad*: 'The embodied self separates itself from the gross body as a fruit separates itself from its stalk.'[41]

Such ideas were widely accepted in Persia, and evolved in the particular Moslem form of belief in the *Mahdi*, the 'one guided by God to the truth'. The Isma'ili version of these ideas consisted of two schools of thought: first, a belief in Ismail himself as immortal, and consequently that he is the *Mahdi*; second, some believed that Muhammad, son of Ismail, was the *Mahdi* who would not die until he had conquered the world.[42] Either way, this concept lies at the root of Islamic Messianism.

The Druzes accept reincarnation as one of the chief distinguishing principles of their religion: their founder and apostle Hakim is held to have possessed the soul of the twelfth imam, and it is from this fact that his authority derives.[43] Druzes, about whom we have more information than the Assassins and whose doctrines are usually almost identical, believe that all human souls were created together and that their number is fixed. As in the Hindu concept cited above, souls progress through a series of transmigrations to a higher degree of excellence. One of the Druze Epistles states that the virtuous progress in their knowledge of religion until they attain the imamate.[44]

Several of the anecdotes written about 1324 by Abu Firas and reported by Guyard concern reincarnation in its particular form of metempsychosis. One of them tells the story of how Rashid Sinan was travelling with some Assassins after a certain Fahd had killed the usurper Khodjah 'Ali. Sinan had been ordered by his superiors at Alamut to throw public blame on the rebels who had attepted to take over the sect. During the journey, they saw a snake and Sinan's guard immediately went to kill it. But Sinan stopped them, saying: 'Don't touch it. It is Fahd. This metamorphosis into a snake is his purgatory and we must not deliver him from it'.[45]

On another occasion reported by Abu Firas, the Assassins noticed that their leader Sinan often went alone from the camp during the night. They believed that he went to bury treasures and jewels in some secret place. Then one night one of his followers surprised him in conversation with a green bird. Sinan argued that this bird was Hasan-i Sabbah, who had come from Alamut to pay him a visit.[46] This story illustrates the way in which legends become compounded and confused, since the green bird almost certainly represents the parrot, which we have seen represents in turn hashish. These two anecdotes serve however to illustrate an attribution of belief in metempsychosis to the Assassins.

The problem of Isma'ili doctrine

Scholars have established the main lines of the exoteric doctrines of the Isma'ilis, and have shown how the main thrust of esoteric ideas developed from Islam and Neoplatonic sources. But the details of the esoteric aspects can only be discussed in general terms and with a certain degree of supposition. Even within the Isma'ili faith there have been many divergent sects, perhaps differing in a single important concept or interpretation. Recent research on Isma'ili writings and doctrines which have emerged in Syria and India will not necessarily tell us much about the practices of Hasan-i Sabbah. And while the Druzes do possess a more precise written record of their doctrines, which may be presumed close to early Isma'ili doctrine, even that parallel should not be pushed too far.

The real problem of the Isma'ilis in general, and the Nizari Isma'ilis or Assassins in particular, is that they were always considered heretical and persecuted by official Islam, except for the period in which

Isma'ilism was the official religion under the Fatimid caliphs of Egypt. The consequence of this is that no comprehensive formula of the Assassins' creed was ever generally recognized.[47] Their doctrines were maintained in secrecy by the Assassins themselves, while their enemies were content to dismiss them as heretical without studying or reporting them.

AFTER HASAN-I SABBAH

ALAMUT remained the headquarters of Assassin activity in Persia from the moment Hasan-i Sabbah took the fortress in 1090 to the capture and destruction by the Mongol Hulegu in 1256. The sequence of the lords of Alamut was as follows:

1090–1124	Hasan-i Sabbah
1124–38	Buzurg'umid
1138–62	Muhammad ibn Buzurg'umid
1162–66	Hasan II
1166–1210	Muhammad II
1210–21	Hasan III
1221–55	Muhammad III
1255–6	Khwurshah

Until 1094 Hasan-i Sabbah had in theory been an agent of the Isma'ili Chief *Da'i* in Cairo. In that year the Caliph al-Mustansir died, and the Persian Isma'ilis separated from their co-religionists in Cairo by declaring allegiance to the caliph's son Nizar. It was at this moment that the lords of Alamut became rulers of an independent Isma'ili state. As we have seen Hasan-i Sabbah managed during his rule to extend the lands controlled by the Assassins in the absence of Seljuk authority over the country.

Buzurg'umid 1124-38

During the early phase of Assassin expansion Kiya Burzug'umid had been sent to capture the castle of Lammassar, where he remained as commander until the death of Hasan. From 1102 onwards he had controlled the entire Rudbar area from this castle. In the absence of a direct heir, Hasan chose Buzurg'umid to succeed him as Chief *Da'i*, presumably as a reward for his long-time loyalty. He sent for him to come from Lammassar in the spring of 1124 when he had fallen into a sickness which was to lead to his death.[1] Bernard Lewis suggests that many people must have believed that the state founded and expanded by Hasan-i Sabbah would undergo the customary crisis subsequent to a great individual's death, and that it would be taken by enemies or friendly opportunists.[2] But Buzurg'umid managed to maintain the strength of the Assassin territories even after a renewed attempt by the Seljuks to attack their mountain stronghold. It was during his rule that the 'pattern of Nizari revolt eased almost imperceptibly into one of a permanent Nizari state with a fixed, though scattered, territory'.[3]

It must be remembered that the Assassins stood out like sore thumbs in a map of the Middle East that the Seljuks had forced into Sunni orthodoxy over the previous half-century. Assassin territory in Persia at the time of Hasan-i Sabbah and Burzug'umid consisted of three small areas: Rudbar, based on the fortress at Alamut; Girdkuh, just south of Damghan, perhaps a single fortress; and Quhistan, where they held several fortresses and perhaps had the greatest territorial control.[4] But the distance from Alamut to Girdkuh was one-thousand kilometres, while the centre of Isma'ili influence in Quhistan lay a further fifteen-hundred kilometres south-east from Girdkuh unless the direct desert route was taken.

That this small *Shi'a*, and therefore heretical 'state', divided into even smaller parts scattered over a vast area should have survived repeated attempts to destroy it by one of the greatest of all Moslem dynasties is something of a miracle that can only be explained by the fundamental disunity of the Seljuks.

When Seljuk, a Turcoman perhaps of Nestorian Christian origins, converted to the Sunni faith and established himself in Bokhara, most of Persia was firmly Shiite. Seljuk's grandson Tughril (1037–63) occupied Khorassan in eastern Persia and conquered the Ghaznavids of Afghanistan, taking the northern city of Balkh and also Ghazna, and then moved west to conquer Esfahan and Baghdad. His nephew Alp Arslan (1063–72) presided over an Empire which included Persia, Syria, Iraq, Afghanistan and much of modern southern Russia. Alp

Arslan's own son Malik-Shah (1072–92) fought in campaigns from Antioch to Samarkand, while his brother Tutush (1094–1117) ruled over Syria. It was partly as the result of Malik-Shah's successes in Byzantium and Asia Minor that the first crusade was launched. One of the men responsible for the organization and efficiency of Malik-Shah's reign was his vizier Nizam al-Mulk, first friend then enemy of Hasan-i Sabbah.

The Seljuk achievement was notable. The concept of the *madrasseh*, or theological school, which propagated religious orthodoxy and lasted as the main educational institution of Islam until the nineteenth century, was invented by Nizam al-Mulk and may have served as the model for the idea of universities. This institution strengthened Sunni orthodoxy, and ought to have rendered the new preaching of the Isma'ilis more difficult than it was. The Seljuks were also responsible for some of the greatest Islamic architectural monuments; tomb towers, mosques and *madrasseh* were adorned with fine brickwork and stucco decorations. One of their most interesting innovations was the complete covering of the domes of mosques with glazed, coloured tiles, a feature which has come to be associated with Islamic architecture as one of its main features. Poets, philosophers, astronomers and scientists were patronized and flourished. It is remarkable that the Assassins found space and recruits for their new preaching, and that they not only survived several violent attempts at repression but appear to have prospered. Here it is worth noticing that it was probably a traditional opposition to the Sunnis which made their *Sh'ia*-based doctrines attractive.

Sultan Sanjar, the greatest of the Seljuk opponents of the Assassins, became Sultan in 1117 and reigned until 1157. But he had already ruled Khorassan since 1096, and in the midst of fraternal dynastic controversy was the *de facto* enemy of the Assassins for sixty years. The focus of Seljuk power shifted back from the Middle East and Baghdad to Khorassan, where the Isma'ilis were well established in Nishapur, Tus and Zuzan. Nearby, two of their main areas of influence — Damghan in eastern Mazandaran, and the towns and castles of Quhistan to the south — also threatened the Seljuk state.[5] For half a century Sanjar defended this empire from threats from the east, while the smaller empire established within his empire by Hasan-i Sabbah remained a constant thorn in his side.

For many years the Assassins under Hasan-i Sabbah had established what appears to have been a kind of truce with Sanjar. This may have been out of respect for the Assassin leader, or simply a pragmatic recognition of the impossibility of taking his mountain fortresses. Assassins continued their missionary activity within Seljuk realms, but were left alone within their own lands. Stories do exist of threats to Sanjar, but, since the same legends exist with regard to Saladin in Palestine much later, it is difficult to give them too much credence. The most celebrated variation is that of the Assassins planting a knife beside the sleeping Sanjar, with the obvious implication — and perhaps an explicit message — that if he did not desist from attacking the Assassins they would be equally capable of planting a knife in his heart.

It may then be the case that a renewed Seljuk offensive against the Nizari state two years after Buzurg'umid took power was a test of his leadership and of the strength of the Assassins after their founder's death.[6] As if to emphasize the futility of such an enterprise, the Assassins increased their hold over the Rudbar area by building the great fortress of Maymun Diaz. Attacks on a dependent castle of Alamut and against Lammassar failed during this period.

Sanjar's vizier Mu'in al-Mulk led the attack against Tarz and Turaythith in Quhistan, south of Nishapur, with troops from Khorassan, apparently killing several Isma'ilis and looting their property, although the expedition seems to have made no permanent difference to Assassin strength in that area. The Seljuks also attacked Rudbar soon afterwards. Then Mu'in al-Mulk was murdered by two Assassins posing as grooms, as if to show that threats against Sultan Sanjar had been justified. After this the Assassins raided Sistan in the south-east. Mahmud, Sanjar's brother and ruler of Esfahan, invited an ambassador from Alamut to discuss peace terms, but when the ambassador was killed he refused to accept responsiblity. Buzurg'umid ordered a reprisal to be carried out on Qazvin, just south of their main territory, where it was claimed that they killed four-hundred people. Mahmud's attempted counter-reprisal was a failed attack on Alamut. At this time, 1126–9, the Nizari Isma'ilis also carried out successful assassinations of important political figures in Esfahan, Qazvin, Hamadan and Tabriz, all in western Persia.[7]

The most important assassination carried out during the rule of Buzurg'umid was that of the Caliph al-Mustarshid of Baghdad in

1138. After the death of Sanjar's brother Mahmud, his successor
Mas'ud had been at war with Baghdad since the caliph had joined
an alliance against the Seljuk leader. Mas'ud captured al-Mustarshid
near Hamadan in south-western Persia and took him to his camp.
At this time a large band of Assassins managed to enter the camp,
whether with the explicit purpose of murdering the caliph or for some
other reason we cannot tell. But the idea of killing a Sunni caliph
would have been too hard to resist. Some authors believe that Mas'ud
was deliberately negligent, and others that Sanjar himself ordered the
murder. Whatever the truth of this assassination, the Assassins at
Alamut are said to have celebrated the caliph's death for seven days
and nights. [8]

But generally, in the rule of Buzurg'umid there were fewer
assassinations and less recorded activity than in that of Hasan. This
may be because he was a less able and less dynamic leader than Hasan
had been, though loyal. But Lewis has also suggested that he was
a local man from the Rudbar area who had spent most of his life as
the administrator of an Assassins' castle. [9] His had not been a life of
covert journeys to Cairo, years as a secret agitator and founder of the
Order. Yet his rule had been valuable, since he was an authoritative
and loyal follower of the founder who for twenty years continued
the original policies. [10] When he died peacefully in 1138 — or, as
Juvayni more picturesquely expresses it, 'when he was crushed under
the heel of Perdition and Hell was heated with the fuel of his carcasse' [11]
— enemies of the Assassins once again hoped that the problems of
succession would cause the sect to lose some of its power and impetus.
But Buzurg'umid thwarted them by nominating his own son
Muhammad as Grand Master a few days before his death, thus initiating
a hereditary principle which continued down to the fall of Alamut.
It is to Buzurg'umid, not Hasan-i Sabbah who left no direct heir,
that the present Aga Khan implicitly claims descent as leader of the
Isma'ilis today.

Muhammad ibn Buzurg'umid (1138-62)

The new rule opened spectacularly with the assassination of al-
Mustarshid's son and successor the new Caliph Rashid, who, once
again as the result of disputes with the Seljuks, had been deposed

from his throne by an assembly convened by Sultan Sanjar and forced
to travel from Baghdad to Esfahan. Some Assassins murdered him
there, and once again there were seven days of celebration at Alamut.
But this murder resulted in violent local reprisals against Ismai'ilis
in the Esfahan area. [12]

Although there were at least thirteen other important political
murders attributed to them during the rule of Muhammad, the sect
of the Assassins slowly began to lose its thrust and perhaps its
enthusiasm. The *da'wa* seems to have been forgotten as the Assassins
occupied themselves more and more with the acquisition of new castles
or positions near their main centres of power. Raids were aimed at
such towns as Qazvin, within fifty miles of Alamut, rather than at
more distant targets; local treaties with Sunnis and Seljuks suggested
an acceptance of things as they were in contrast to the missionary
fervour of an earlier generation. Under the rule of Buzurg'umid traces
of the original idea of a religio-political campaign against Seljuk and
Sunni predominance still remained; under that of his son, many
Isma'ilis began to feel that this original motivation had disappeared.
Nostalgic memories of the strong faith and adventure of Hasan's times
led some members to seek new leadership. [13]

It was Muhammad ibn Buzurg'umid's son and heir Hasan who
drew the focus of discontent into a fresh force, and brought about
a 'restoration of the more personal and occult aspects of Isma'ilism'. [14]
Since he was already considered the legitimate heir to the lordship
of Alamut, no disruption in leadership was caused. He seems to have
studied the works of Hasan-i Sabbah and other earlier Isma'ili authors,
the Islamic philosophers such as Ibn-Sina, and the Sufi mystics. [15] He
was an intellectual, but also a courteous and friendly young man
possessing qualities of eloquence denied to his father. As a result he
soon attracted followers, who 'not having heard the like discourses
from his father began to think that here was the Imam that has been
promised by Hasan-i Sabbah'. [16] Thus the people's enthusiasm for him
increased, and encouraged him. 'Soon he began to preach a spiritual
interpretation of Isma'ilism which strikes us as far removed from the
rigorism of his father and grandfather, but to which the people of
Alamut now responded warmly.' [17]

Muhammad feared this popularity and judged Hasan's behaviour
to be at odds with the rigid principles which he had learned from

his father and ultimately from Hasan-i Sabbah. He publicly denounced his son, arguing that Hasan could not possibly be an imam since he was not the son of an imam: 'I am not the Imam but one of his *da'is*.'[18] He reacted as ferociously as we might imagine an Assassin Master to react: it is said that he tortured adherents to Hasan's cause and once killed two-hundred-and-fifty of them at Alamut. The corpses were then bound to a further two-hundred-and-fifty men condemned on the same charges, who were exiled from the fortress and forced to carry their executed companions down from the mountain.[19] But it was only a temporary stay of the new forces, lasting until Muhammad ibn Buzurg' umid's own death in 1162.

Hasan II (1162–6): the Qiyama or Resurrection

Hasan II's short rule marks an important point in the succession of the lords of Alamut, at which a fresh impulse of enthusiasm and doctrine was added in order to provide new impetus to a stagnant situation. It is doubtful whether during Muhammad's rule the lord of Alamut really commanded more than the immediate territories of Alamut, maintaining relations with rather than command over a series of independent Assassin fiefdoms, each of which had evolved its own hereditary leadership much as Alamut. The dramatic proclamations of Hasan II mark a vital shift at roughly mid-point in Assassin history, bearing out, as it happens, the perceptive Arab philosopher of history Ibn Khaldun's theory that 'prestige lasts at best four generations in one lineage' unless a strong leader comes along to renew the starting point of that prestige.[20]

Two years after the beginning of his rule, Hasan II introduced his reform in a singular and dramatic manner which was as astonishing as the announcement itself, as a contemporary Isma'ili source recounts. Hasan is referred to as 'Ala Dhikri-hi s-Salam, or 'upon his mention peace', which became a kind of blessing:

The lord 'Ala Dhikri-hi s-Salam, wearing a white garment and a white turban, came down from the fortress about noon, and came to the pulpit from the right side; and in a most perfect manner mounted the pulpit. He said greetings three times: first to the Daylamites [in the centre], then to the right hand [those from Quhistan], then to the left hand [those from Iraq, e.g. Iraq 'Ajami in western Persia]. He sat down for a moment; then rose up again

1. The Assassin castle of Samiran, showing how the castle has slipped down the slope.

2. Samiran: note the similarity to a Norman castle.

3. Samiran: the tomb tower on its hill seen from the castle.

4. Samiran: the tomb tower.

5. Samiran: detail of Kufic script (i.e. the formal Arabic script used for religious writings in Persia) on the tomb tower.

5. Samiran: the only surviving stucco, inside the tomb tower.

7. (*Above*) Samiran, showing the sheer rock face to the south and how the terraces could have slipped into the river.

8. (*Below*) Samiran: looking down towards the river.

9. (*Opposite*) Samiran: an example of building technique, using the sheer solid rock for foundations.

10. (*Opposite*) Samiran, seen from across the river.

11. (*Above*) Alamut: the rock, with the castle just visible, seen from the road up from Shotorkhan. Note the strong horizontal line to the right: this is an artificial channel cut to catch surface water on the rock.

12. (*Below*) Alamut: looking up from the saddle to the west end of the castle. Note the wall/bridge protecting the only practicable entry point.

13. Two views of the Assassin castle of Saweh, near Qom, south of Tehran.

and baring his sword said in a loud voice: O inhabitants of the worlds, jinn, men and angels![21]

Then he announced the message which had come to him from the hidden imam, with its three essential points. He declared himself to be the caliph and divinely appointed ruler, abolished the ritual law which Nizari Isma'ilis had followed, and finally proclaimed the resurrection of the dead. Those who believed and accepted him would rise to immortal life, while those who refused to accept him were judged and therefore banished into non-existence. As Hodgson remarks, 'Hasan had either to be laughed at or adored'.[22]

The apocalyptic and antinomian nature of this extraordinary proclamation is underlined by the reverse ritual employed just as worshippers of the occult and witches in western heresies reversed the official liturgy of the Church. The ceremony had taken place during Ramadan, the month of solemn fasting. The historian Rashid al-Din commented that 'Ever after that the Malahida [heretics] called the 17th of Ramadan the Festival of the Resurrection; on that day they used to show their joy with wine and repose, and used to play and make entertainment openly'.[23] In fact, on the same day, in the middle of Ramadan, the announcement was followed by a feast that had been prepared by Hasan. Similarly, the position of Hasan's audience was of vital importance, since they had their backs turned to Mecca. Messengers were sent from Alamut to other strongholds of the Assassins, both in Persia and Syria, where the same ceremony was performed by local leaders.

This new doctrine of resurrection, *Qiyama*, marks an interesting shift in Assassin history, with Hasan claiming for himself a spiritual imamate. He presented himself as the Judge of the Resurrection. This judge, or *qa'im*, is one of a line of imams whose task is to introduce Paradise on earth, and, following Hasan's second proclamation, ritual law would be abolished. The way had been prepared by the *hujja*, in this case Hasan-i Sabbah, and now the true cosmic sabbath could be introduced, after which there would be neither work nor sickness. Thus Hasan II presented himself as fulfilling the prophecies of the earlier Hasan.[24] Men could now see God directly with their spiritual eyes, and achieve the promised resurrection that would be the culmination of the ages.

It was a bold and dramatic claim, which meant that the Assassins had now set themselves up as a truly alternative faith, no longer following the basic laws of Islam but in fact refusing to accept such laws. The declaration of *qiyama* sets them apart, but also makes them unacceptable and definitively heretical. Henceforth they were always referred to as the heretics, and these events may be interpreted as an admission of defeat in the attempt to take over Islam at large.[25] The original missionary purpose, of converting the Sunni religionists to the new faith, was forgotten in the drama of this new claim. Such a proclamation, in its accept or die severity, could not conciliate but only separate, pushing the Assassins out beyond the pale. Thus, after three quarters of a century of existence, the fundamental theories of Hasan-i Sabbah were radically altered and the new preaching he had developed came to an end.

Hasan II's task in implementing his proclamation was facilitated by the fact that it was the people themselves who had insisted upon his imamate and pushed him towards the decision. But not all the Assassins readily accepted such a dramatic overturning of tradition: it was not easy to deny laws that men had followed since their birth, and many chose exile rather than face the death sentence for continuing to obey the *shari'a*. One and a half years after the announcement of the *qiyama*, Hasan II was murdered by his brother-in-law Husayn-i Namawar inside the castle of Lammassar. But the opponents, and party of this Husayn, were thwarted in any attempt to restore the old ways by the speedy action of Hasan's son, who became the new lord of Alamut as Muhammad II at the age of nineteen.

Muhammad II (1166–1210)

Muhammad elaborated and propagated the *qiyama* introduced by his father throughout his long rule. He asserted that both his father and himself were descendants of Nizar and therefore imams. But it is noteworthy that his long reign made almost no impact on the world outside Alamut and received no mention in Sunni chronicles of the time. It was only when the documents of Alamut's library were studied by historians in the train of Hulegu that these events became known. For half a century the Assassins of Persia lived in relative obscurity and unimportance, with few assassinations, no dramatic events, and almost no mark on the course of history. It was at this time, as we shall see later, that the Assassins began to develop their reputation and achieve a certain notoriety in the Holy Land, though their doctrines and ideas were completely ignored by those who visited them or wrote about them. From an external point of view, Muhammad II's rule was a lengthy interim.

But in terms of Isma'ili doctrine as it continues to this day, Muhammad's work was of vital importance since it crystallized his father's ideas into a clear gospel of the *qiyama* which 'became the definitive spiritual ideal for the Isma'ilis which it afterward remained'. [26] In two ways, this elaboration was particularly important. First, Muhammad *was* an imam and not merely the representative of the imam. This decisive change clearly provided greater spiritual authority for Muhammad himself and his successors. But even more important for Isma'ili worship was the move by which he asserted that there was an association between the moment when believers see God in Paradise and the imam. Thus God was actually present in the physical person of the imam, Muhammad himself.

This step was carried out by an ingenious and apparently invented history. It was said that a grandson of Nizar, from whom the Assassins derived their fuller and more correct name, was taken as a baby to Hasan-i Sabbah and brought up at Alamut. His son, who only *appeared* to be the son of Muhammad ibn Buzurg'umid, was Hasan II. Thus Muhammad II had managed to demonstrate a direct lineage from the line of Ali, via the Fatimids, which further strengthened his claims. Muhammad and his successors would never again be merely the *da'is* of Alamut. [27] Now the Isma'ili faith concentrated on the imam, their leader, who is himself a revelation of God and in a sense independent of the Prophet. This spectacular culmination — maintained today in the person of the Aga Khan — was in many ways the logical outcome of Hasan-i Sabbah's reasoning.

Hasan III (1210–21)

The dispensation of the *qiyama* in the long term prevented friendly relations with the Sunnis who surrounded the Isma'ili territories and rendered peaceful co-existence and trade difficult. Thus the *qiyama* gradually became in the course of Muhammad II's long rule 'no longer an answer to a historic crisis, but rather at best a spiritual luxury' [28] which many Isma'ilis did not accept as necessary. Even within his own family, in the person of his own son and heir, Muhammad saw the signs of this move away from total acceptance of the *qiyama*.

In a reversal quite as spectacular as Hasan II's declaration of the *qiyama*, his grandson Hasan III rejected altogether the beliefs of his ancestors by accepting the Sunni faith and re-instating the *shari'a*. Perhaps he was persuaded by the new circumstances and balance of power throughout the Middle East and Persia. As the Seljuk dynasty gradually lost its importance, two new centres of power, between which the Assassin territories lay, developed in Baghdad and Transoxiana. To the north-east, Muhammad Khwarazmshah, whose ancestors had been vassals of Sanjar in northern Transoxiana (which included Samarkand, parts of modern Russia and Afghanistan), had accepted the task of achieving a universal monarchy over the Islamic lands. At the beginning of the thirteenth century he took much of Persia and began attacking Assassin positions both in Quhistan and at Alamut. To the south-west, the Caliph Nasir in Baghdad had again made that office a major centre of power, and attempted to revive the concept of a caliphate as the central religious and political institution of Islam.

Between these opposite threats, Hasan III was evidently tempted by the security of the Sunni faith. In Hodgson's words, 'Taking advantage of the notoriety of his ancestors, Hasan moved from an anomalous position on the margin of Islamic society to an almost equally anomalous position in the spotlight'.[29] He built mosques for the new forms of worship and became in effect one of many minor Sunni vassals. It was only, however, with difficulty that he managed to convince his previous enemies of his sincerity. It is said that he invited some Sunni scholars to visit Alamut, study the books in the library there and burn any that they might consider heretical.[30]

One of the most extraordinary facts about the Assassins must remain the alacrity with which they followed their leaders in any change of direction and doctrine, however dramatic. Clearly the perception of the *da'i* as imam contributed much to this acceptance, but purely practical considerations must often have weighed heavily in favour of such decisions. As an example, one practical consequence of this reversal by Hasan III was the assistance of the emir of Aleppo. This occurred when the Syrian Assassins were seriously threatened by a

Christian army which attacked them in 1214, after they had murdered
the son of the lord of Antioch. [31]

Muhammad III (1221-55)

Yet in the end the break with the *qiyama* remained in a sense a personal
phenomenon, since during the rule of Hasan III's son Muhammad
the *qiyama* received a new interpretation which responded to the needs
of the time but still accepted much of traditional Isma'ili doctrine.
Although outwardly the Assassins in the early years of Muhammad
III's rule conformed to the Sunni doctrines which his father had
embraced, there were increasing signs that they gradually began to
return to the *shar'ia*. [32] A new doctrine was in the process of formation:
that known as the doctrine of *satr*, entailing an interpretation of the
traditional Isma'ili faith which met the needs of that time. This was
because it 'explained the polices of Hasan III and his son as a return
to that *satr*, occultation, which had preceded the appearance of Hasan
II in the Qiyama. In the name of the *satr*, the new doctrine toned
down the Qiyama system to the point where it could be lived with
by ordinary people, in ordinary times'. [33] In other words, it was another
example of the essential flexibility of Assassin doctrine once the rigid
asceticism and purity of Hasan-i Sabbah were forgotten. Once again,
the doctrine was adjusted to suit present needs.

Muhammad presided over the last phase of Assassin independence
in Persia, when the sect paid lip-service to the concepts of *satr* and
qiyama but seemed to have lost the thrust of their faith and mission
with the demise of their Seljuk enemies. There were no new
developments, but the Assassins remained an independent and
individual sect:

. . . although their life might bring forth no striking new departure, it
remained distinctive, and to that extent great: holding fast to its assurances
of special divine guidance, its own persistent social integration, its own
traditions of dedication to a community which (even tucked away in its
own mountains, now) could still face the rest of the world on equal terms. [34]

But already under his rule, the power and authority of the Assassins
in Persia was coming to an end, although ventures well beyond the
frontiers of Persia — as far as India in the East and Britain in the West
— promised a certain continuity of intent. Muhammad himself seems

to have represented the classical syndrome of the ruler of a decaying sect: already the ruler at age nine, he bled himself in treatment of what was probably nothing more than a melancholy frame of mind, seems to have drunk excessively, and had a particularly nasty temper which could transform him into a violent tyrant at the slightest hint of bad news. [35] Thus, clearly, like many tyrants before and since, he was only fed good news and probably could never rule properly as the result of lack of information about the problems of his state and territories. He kept concubines and had homosexual affairs, and became a symbol of decadence.

Clearly this was not the man to oppose the immense force of the Mongol advance which began to threaten the Middle and Near East towards the end of his reign. Both his son Khwurshah and many Assassin notables seem to have recognized this fact. As Muhammad descended further into madness — marked amongst other things by his insistence that they would be able to defy the oncoming Mongol attack — it was obvious that something must be done. Khwurshah first considered leaving Alamut and fleeing to Syria or another Assassin fortress, but was convinced by the notables to accept a position as regent while Muhammad was put quietly aside from his responsibilities.

But the plan was never put into action, and with hindsight it appears that it would actually have made little difference. Muhammad was murdered by Hasan Mazandari, who had once been his lover and who had received one of the Master's concubines as his wife. Thus the penultimate Grand Master of the Persian Assassins died ignominiously, slaughtered with an axe by the hand of a former homosexual lover.

Khwurshah and the fall of Alamut (1255-6)

Khwurshah was still in his twenties when he became the last lord of Alamut, facing the immediate prospect of attack by Hulegu, brother of the Great Mongol Khan Mongke. The Mongols had entered Persia in the same year, and had already established themselves within the old Assassin territories of Quhistan.

The small and frightened Nizari state found itself a pawn in the way of the Mongols' plan for world conquest. In 1251, Mongke, grandson of Ghengis Khan, had become the Great Khan after a long series of dynastic disputes. He had then launched an ambitious campaign which was designed to extend his power from China to Egypt. While Mongke himself planned to lead the attack against China, his brother Hulegu would lead that against Persia and the Middle East. In the intervening years smaller Mongol armies had established themselves in Persia, and had apparently informed Mongke that of all their enemies the two most obstinate and difficult were the caliph in Baghdad and the Assassins in Alamut.[36]. From the Mongol point of view, the survival of independent powers whose members venerated leaders in place of the Great Khan was unacceptable. The Mongol advance was not a crusade against Islam, as many Christians believed, but simply a political war designed to achieve total loyalty and devotion to Mongke as Great Khan.[37] Since Ghengis Khan's sweep through Transoxiana and Khorassan in 1219–24, the Mongols received nominal allegiance from many local rulers; this new attack was an attempt to complete the political and bureaucratic control of the region and assert supreme authority.

In the spring of 1253 an immense army departed from the Khan's capital at Karakorum, the ruins of which lie two-hundred-and-twenty miles west of the modern Mongolian capital Ulan Bator. Hulegu himself departed in October of the same year. After a slow march across the Central Asian steppes the army crossed the River Oxus somewhere between Balkh (now in northern Afghanistan) and Bokhara on New Year's Day 1256, thus entering Persia. Agents and engineers preceded this great army, repairing or building bridges, preparing supplies of flour and wines, requisitioning land for grazing, and holding boats in readiness for river crossings. A thousand teams of Chinese engineers also accompanied the army, their function being to work siege engines and flame-throwers. The total force consisted of two out of every ten soldiers in the entire Mongol fighting force. Other contingents joined this army as it made its slow but determined way across the steppes of Central Asia and down into Persia.

Khwurshah attempted to negotiate and play for time. Responding from a position of enormous strength, Hulegu demanded his submission. But the Grand Master refused and attempted to improve the conditions of his surrender, apparently hoping to force negotiations through the summer of 1256 in order to gain respite through the winter — when a campaign against such castles as Alamut would be impracticable. But Hulegu's patience ran out, and he began his attack, first against Maymun Diaz, providing an illustration of the efficiency and thoroughness of Mongol campaigns.

The attack began with a preliminary bombardment of three days with mangonels, or huge catapults, set up on surrounding hills. After a failed direct assault on the fourth day, siege engines were brought into action against the castle, while immense crossbows with a far greater range than anything in Assassin hands launched javelins dipped in burning pitch into the castle. Then Hulegu launched a final bombardment, which Juvayni has described vividly:

As for the mangonels that had been erected it was as though their poles were made of pine-trees a hundred years old (as for their fruit, 'their fruit is as it were the heads of Satans'): and with the first stone that sprang up from them the enemy's mangonel was broken and many were crushed under it. And great fear of the quarrels from the crossbows overcame them so that they were utterly distraught and everyone in the corner of a stone made a shield out of a veil, whilst some who were standing on a tower crept in their fright like mice into a hole or fled like lizards into crannies in the rocks. Some were left wounded and some lifeless and all that day they struggled but feebly and bestirred themselves like mere women. And when the heavens doffed the cap of the sun and the earth raised the curtain of night from the soil up to the Pleiades, they withdrew from battle. [39]

It must of course be remembered that this eye-witness account was written by the official historian of the conqueror, but the passage is nonetheless an eloquent reminder of the fact that no castle was immune to such a well-planned attack by a powerful, patient and well-equipped army as that of Hulegu. The Assassin castles had remained impregnable up to that time because there was no concerted opposition to them by a power militarily strong enough to attempt the enterprise of rooting them out from the Rudbar district by sheer force of arms.

Although some fanatical Assassins attempted a last ditch defence and refused to surrender, this battle was followed by the formal submission of their leader. Alamut followed suit, its defenders cowed by the sight of a vast force surrounding them. Three days after the surrender of Alamut, the castle was sacked and burned while its library was made available to the Mongol's historian Juvayni before he too burned the documents and books.

Khwurshah himself was treated as an honoured prisoner, allowed to take a Mongol wife, given gifts of camels by Hulegu and allowed to accompany the Khan on further expeditions. But, as Lewis suggests, this was clearly for the political advantage that Hulegu derived from having the Isma'ili imam by his side. Although outlying areas and such vital castles as Lammassar did not submit, Khwurshah was useful to him in trying to persuade other Isma'ilis to do so; when his usefulness ended, there was little doubt that Khwurshah would be cast aside: 'The surrender of most of the castles made [Khwurshah] unnecessary to the Mongols; the resistance of Lammassar and Girdkuh showed that he was useless'.[40]

The Isma'ilis themselves were more concerned with the fate of Khwurshah's son and heir, so that the Master's situation could be considered by that time a more or less personal affair between him and Hulegu. The Isma'ili succession had to be guaranteed for those who remained faithful, and in fact it was later claimed that his son was spirited out of sight to safety so that the line of imams were preserved.[41]

To a modern observer, this campaign against the Assassins might appear an unnecessary effort, given the rapidly diminishing importance of the Order under their last three Masters. But the shrewd political strategies of the Mongols perceived it as more than the mere defeat of a small, heretical sect. As a modern historian of the Mongol Conquests has remarked, they were always cunning in their exploitation of the feuds and quarrels of their enemies: 'By proclaiming war against the hitherto invincible Assassins, they engaged the sympathy of Sunnite Islam . . .'.[42] That they then destroyed Sunnite power in taking Baghdad, thereby 'engaging the sympathy' of Shiites and Christians, simply emphasizes the quality of the enemy which the Assassins unwittingly found descending upon them. Herein lies the reason for Hulegu's thoroughness, against which Khwurshah had never had the means to resist, a motivation which the Assassins themselves probably did not appreciate.

When Assassin power and possessions were completely destroyed, Khwurshah asked to be able to meet the Great Khan. His desire was given Hulegu's consent and he travelled to Karakorum. Mongke refused to see him on the grounds that the last Persian castles of Lammassar and Girdkuh had not yet surrendered, and he was ordered to leave that city. But there may be another and much more simple reason for this refusal: fear of an Assassin plot against the Great Khan's life. William of Rubruck relates that when he arrived at Mongke's court in May 1254 he and his host were summoned by the Khan's vizier and interrogated concerning the purpose of his visit to Karakorum. It transpired that the reason for this suspicion lay in a rumour that forty Assassins 'had entered the city under various guises' in order to murder Mongke.[42]

However that may be, during the return journey, Khwurshah, humiliated and no longer able to inspire authority in his own diminishing train, was kicked to pulp by his guards and then finished off with the sword. Thus, ignominiously, ended the line of 'Grand Masters' that had ruled the state of the Assassins in Persia for over a century and a half.[44]

PART II: THE SYRIAN ASSASSINS

INTO SYRIA, 1103-62

THE Persian Assassins began to extend their activities into Syria at the beginning of the twelfth century, within a decade of taking Alamut. The same crisis in Seljuk power that enabled the First Crusade to achieve a solid foothold in the Holy Land in 1099 allowed the Assassins to move into Syria. There were several reasons for their interest in expanding into Syria. For many centuries, northern Syria had been a refuge for Isma'ilis of various kinds, and the Druzes were well established there together with other Shiite 'heretics'. Hasan-i Sabbah had himself stopped in Aleppo on his way back from Cairo to Persia, and may have developed personal contacts from that time. Syria could offer mountainous and inhospitable terrain similar to that in which the Assassin tactics had developed, and above all perhaps it offered the possibility of a headquarters nearer to the seat of Fatimid power in Cairo.

The gradual process of the acquisition of power in Syria had four main phases: the establishment of an Assassin centre in Aleppo (1103-13); a base in Damascus, with the acquisition of early castles in the Jabal as-Summaq, the mountain range between Aleppo and Hama east of the Orontes River (1113-29); the foundation of bases in Central Syria in the Jabal Bahra, the mountains west of the Orontes in which the main later Assassin castles were situated (1131-62); and the rule of Sinan Rashid al-Din (1162-92/3).

The Assassins in Aleppo (1103-13)

The way was facilitated by a long history of connections with Shiism and Isma'ilism in their many forms. At the time of the Fatimid caliphate of Cairo, Syria had occasionally fallen within the Isma'ili sphere of influence. Communities of dissenting sects of the Isma'ilis, such as the Druzes, had long been established in the area, while other non-Isma'ili Shiite sects were open to Isma'ili ideas and doctrines. Syria was at that time a particularly unstable and fragmented country, caught between the Seljuks to the north and north-east and the recently arrived crusaders who had just established Christian states to the east in Edessa and to the south in Tripoli.

The Seljuk dynasty of Syria began with the advance into Asia Minor and Christian Armenia by Alp Arslan (ruled 1063–72), nephew of the great Seljuk Tughril and father of the Malikshah we have seen combatting the Assassins in Persia. Alp Arslan held Aleppo from 1070, but the Seljuk dynasty of Syria was founded by his son Tutush in 1094. After the death of Malikshah in 1092, however, the civil wars between his sons — and consequent minor rebellions throughout the Seljuk-held lands — led to the progressive breaking up of Seljuk power. Jerusalem fell to the Fatimids, and then to the Christians; Edessa was lost to the crusaders of the First Crusade. When Tutush died in battle in 1095 his possessions in Syria followed the same pattern as the result of rivalry between his two sons: Ridwan made his capital in Aleppo, and ruled that city from 1095 to 1113; Duqaq took Damascus, which he ruled until his death in 1104. It may be said that hostilities between these rival brothers formed the central event of their reigns.[1]

It is in this context that we may understand the invitation and patronage offered to the Assassins by Ridwan, and the ready acceptance of their doctrines. Their history as staunch opponents of the Seljuks must have made them appear attractive. So in a moment of great uncertainty and fear many people rallied to the sect which 'seemed to offer the only effective challenge to the invaders and rulers of the country'.[2] It is often suggested that Ridwan was the sincere convert of a local Isma'ili astrologer, al-Hakim al-Munajjim, but most scholars seem to agree that his real motivation in welcoming the Assassins to Aleppo was fear of his rivals, and the increased safety such renowned warriors would bring.[3] From about 1103 Assassins began to move into Aleppo and a 'House of Propaganda' was built for their preaching activities. They lived openly in the city, and were accused of arrogant behaviour in the streets and committing such crimes as robbery and murder as often as they could.[4]

The early leaders of the Syrian Assassins were Persians sent from

Alamut by Hasan-i Sabbah specifically to install an Assassin state based on the Persian Model. Their task was the same as that of the Assassins in Persia: to undermine Seljuk authority both militarily and religiously and create an independent power in their midst. They soon began their operations with the 'official' assassination of one of Ridwan's enemies, the ruler of Homs Janah al-Dawla in May 1103. In typical Assassin fashion, he was killed in a mosque during Friday prayers by three Persians disguised as Sufis. No attempt was made by the *fida'i* to escape, so they too lost their lives in the resulting confusion.[5] But it was a slow and difficult process, requiring over thirty years of patient activity before the Order began to acquire fortresses in the Syrian mountains to use as permanent bases.

A few weeks after that murder, al-Hakim al-Munajjim died, and was succeeded by the second Syrian leader. This man was another Persian, abu-Tahir as-Sa'igh, known as the goldsmith. It was under his leadership that the Order acquired their first castle in Syria in 1106, at Afamiya south of Aleppo, where local Isma'ilis were powerful enough to seize the citadel. But within a year it was lost to Tancred, a Norman from Sicily, who had first taken power in Tiberias as vassal of Godfrey of Bouillon and then become Prince of Antioch.[6] In the course of the battle many leading Assassins, including abu-Tahir, were captured and later ransomed. It seems that Tancred also took other castles from the Assassins in 1110, but already before that the slow and uneven progress of Isma'ili power had suffered other setbacks. Between 1105 and 1107 Sultan Muhammad Tapar launched several campaigns against the Assassins in Iraq and Persia in order to check their advance, at the same time as his brother Sultan Sanjar was attacking the Persian Assassins in Quhistan. This was also the time of the siege of Shah Diz near Esfahan. These attacks, and the consequent diminuition of Assassin strength in Persia, had negative consequences for the Syrian branch of the Order.[7]

In 1110 another incident of interest occurred: after the Assassins had murdered a wealthy Persian traveller and enemy of the Isma'ilis in Aleppo, Ridwan found it impossible to prevent a general massacre of Assassins in the city. This and the above episodes first of all indicate the difficulty with which the Assassins in Syria began to operate, without the safe refuges of the huge mountain ranges and remote valleys of northern Persia. But they must also have emphasized to the

Assassin leaders the need for stronger independent bases for their operations. [8] It may have been for that reason that a future leader of the Assassins, Abu Muhammad, arrived from Alamut at about this time.

Assassins in the Jabal as-Summaq (1113-29)

After Ridwan's death in 1113, his son Alp Arslan at first continued the policy of protecting and patronizing the Assassins in Aleppo. But he was soon encouraged by Sultan Muhammad in Baghdad to end such tacit support and destroy them. On the demand of both the Shiite and Sunni leaders, the Isma'ilis in Aleppo were either banished or arrested at this time. Several fortresses that Isma'ili leaders held nearby were given up as they attempted to establish new centres of propaganda. Their major base ceased to be Aleppo, although they continued to play a role both in the city and in its neighbourhood. [9] The initiative in 1124 was taken by the commander of the militia, who arrested and executed Abu Tahir and other Isma'ili leaders, altogether some two-hundred. Their property was confiscated, many were thrown to their deaths from the citadel of Aleppo, and others fled from the city. [10]

The area of the Jabal as-Summaq, south-west from Aleppo, was a logical place to attempt a recovery since Isma'ilis had been resident there for centuries and a hidden imam had once resided there in the ninth century. [11] Abu Tahir's place was taken by another Persian, Bahram, who according to an Arab historian went underground for some time: 'he lived in extreme concealment and secrecy, and continually disguised himself, so that he moved from city to city and castle to castle without anyone being aware of his identity'. [12] In this classical Isma'ili way he slowly began to pick up the pieces and lay the basis for a solid Assassin power in Syria.

In this period the Assassins once again gained a foothold in an important city when the ruler of Damascus, Tughtugin, offered them protection and used their services, perhaps because his vizier was sympathetic to Isma'ili views. As in Aleppo a decade earlier, they were given a building to use as a 'House of Propaganda' for their headquarters. [13] The Atabeg Tughtugin had formerly been a slave of Tutush, and later regent to the young Duqaq, after whose death in

1104 he himself took over the government of Damascus. It seems that the Assassins by then had achieved a reputation for their courage in battle, since in 1126 Tughtugin, perhaps in exchange for the permission to build a headquarters in Damascus, invited them to join his troops in an important battle against the Christian forces. Although the result was disastrous for the Moslems in general, and presumably for the Assassins, it does mark their presence as an important fighting force at that time.

In May of that year, in the midst of a complex series of gains and losses between several opposing forces — Beduins, Christians, Ortoqids, and local emirs — a Moslem alliance captured the Christian fort of Kafartab and laid siege to Zerdana. King Baldwin II of Jerusalem marched to save Zerdana with an army of eleven-hundred horsemen and two-thousand foot soldiers. They met the Moslem army at Azaz, north of Aleppo, where the Moslems attempted a hand to hand battle confident in their superior numbers. But Frankish armour and training were sufficient to win the battle, which was 'one of the most bloodthirsty battles in the history of the Crusades'.[14]

Possibly as a result of this allegiance to Tughtugin, the Assassins were in the same year given the castle of Banyas, on the coast north of Tortosa, the northernmost city of the County of Tripoli. But even this must not appear as a disinterested gift, but rather the allocation of an important frontier fortress which the Assassins were expected to hold against the crusaders of the Holy Land.[15] However, Bahram took advantage of this unexpected gift and immediately made the city and stronghold his base. The Damascus chronicler Ibn al-Qalansi describes how 'when he had established himself in Banyas, he set about fortifying it and rebuilding what was in ruins or out of repair'.[16] From this first Syrian headquarters Bahram sent raiding parties and missionaries out into the surrounding country. It was said that the Assassins terrorized their Sunni neighbours from this fortress, and Bahram was accused both of highway robbery and of slandering reputable men. On one occasion he was suspected of luring a local chief from the Valley of Tayyim into his hands and then killing him. This episode had unexpected consequences, since the man's brother swore revenge for the murder and Bahram had to lead an expedition into the valley to crush the resulting rebellion. Unfortunately, he was taken by surprise by this emir and the raid ended with his own death.[17]

Again, as in Aleppo, Assassin power and stability depended ultimately on the benevolence of a powerful local lord, and their usefulness in his personal political strategies. When Tughtugin died in 1128 there had been another backlash, with Isma'ilis being killed or exiled from Damascus. The tenure of Banyas must have taught them that a similar fortress was essential to their survival, and it was in the next phase of Assassin development in Syria that they began acquiring or capturing further castles. Within three years of Bahram's death, his successor Isma'il offered Banyas to the Franks in exchange for safe conduct for the Assassins to leave the city. The Assassins in Syria once again found themselves with no base.

Assassins in the Jabal Bahra (1129–62)

The move of the Assassins into the Jabal Bahra mountains of Syria, just to the north of the crusader County of Tripoli and today known as the Jabal Ansariyya, was facilitated by a gradual weakening of the crusader state. These weaknesses were exacerbated and exploited by the great Moslem leader Zengi, Imad-al-Din, 'the pillar of faith' (1084–1146). Zengi was the son of a Turkish slave of Malikshah but had managed to carve out for himself a principality including Aleppo, which survived until 1262. He was the first of the great series of 'anti-crusaders' which culminated with Saladin and was later to recapture the County of Edessa for Islam. But he was only one element of a complex situation which included wars with the Moslems in the south and the Armenians to the north. After three decades of rule a power vacuum was developing within the territories held by the County of Tripoli, which had lost its defences to the east and Cilicia to the north. It was an open country in which any man with military support could carve out for himself a territory. In 1131, a Turkoman adventurer had taken the castle of Bisika'il in the south, and in the same year the Franks lost the important castle of Qadmus to the emir of Kahf, Saif ed-Din ibn Amrun. It was this emir who sold Qadmus to the Assassins in the following year, while Kahf itself was sold to them by the emir's son in 1135[18].

Thus the Syrian castles came to the Order either by gift or by acquisition, not by conquest. Until this time the Assassins had been an underground religious sect seeking to establish themselves. It was with the acquisition of Qadmus in 1132 that the Assassin 'state' began to develop as a permanent feature of the complex geography of emirates and feudal groups of Syria. After the failed attempts to establish themselves in such important cities as Aleppo and Damascus, they at last began to set up an organization based on several strong mountain fortresses which echoed more precisely their strategy in Persia.

From the taking of Qadmus to about 1140 the Assassins acquired by various means eight to ten castles in the area of the Jabal Bahra. The local rulers who had sold Qadmus and later Kahf to the Assassins apparently did so to prevent them falling into the hands of their own relatives. Masyaf was gained by a murderous stratagem: it had first been sold by its local owner to the Munqidhites of Shayzar, but the Assassins killed their representative and held the castle from then on. Later, the castle of Khariba was taken from the Christians[19]. These castles were held for many years against both the local Moslem rulers and the Christian forces to the south. In the County of Tripoli, and to the north, in the principality of Antioch. We shall see in a later chapter some examples of the relations which the Assassins maintained with these 'enemies' and neighbours.

Although there were still small groups of Isma'ilis in the northern Syrian towns such as Aleppo, Bab and Raqqa, and some in the Jazr, it was from this time that they became the inhabitants of a small mountainous area waging their own religious and political war against the peoples surrounding them. This early phase of the history of the Syrian Assassins may be said to have ended about 1162, when Rashid al-Din Sinan was sent to Syria by his friend and mentor Hasan II of Alamut. It was under the rule of Sinan that this branch of the Assassins developed its own partly autonomous character in the second half of the twelfth century.

Role of the Assassins in Syria

The establishment of an Assassin state created a new balance of power between the Moslem forces whose aim was to reconquer the holy city of Jerusalem. As we shall see, all the great anti-crusaders had to deal with them in one way or another, including Saladin, who after two failed attempts on his life reached a *modus vivendi* which enabled him to get on with his more important task. Yet it was rare that a

Moslem leader was strong enough to threaten the Assassins: the Seljuk Sultan Muhammad had managed to keep them in check in the second decade of the century[20], and Saladin achieved the same result by means of a truce. But between these two rulers, for a period of over fifty years, the Assassins were relatively free to negotiate, acquire castles and gradually strengthen their own position.

The murders carried out by the Syrian Assassins in the twelfth century were ironically clearly advantageous to the Christian crusading forces in destabilizing the delicate equilibrium between Moslem rulers in the area. The only exceptions might be the murders of two important Christian princes, but in any case the list of most important murders in the twelfth century is eloquent:

1103 Khalaf Ibn Mula'ib, Emir of Apamea	Apamea
1113 Mawdud, general to Sultan Muhammad	Damascus
1121 Al-Afdal, vizier to Fatimid Caliph Al-Amir	Cairo
1126 Atabeg Aqsonqor il-Bursuqi	Mosul
1130 Al-Amir, Caliph	Cairo
1131 Taj al-Mulk Buri, atabeg of Damascus	Damascus
1135 Abbasid Caliph Murstarshid, in exile	Azerbaijan
1152 Raymond of Tripoli	Tripoli
1174 Attempted murder of Saladin	Aleppo
1176 Attempted murder of Saladin	Aleppo
1192 Conrad of Montferrat	Tyre
1213 Raymond, son of Bohemond Count of Tripoli	Tortosa

These murders cover a wide geographical area, and each of them had a precise political scope and serious consequences. Even in the case of the Christians: in 1192 Conrad of Montferrat was recognized by most crusaders as the ideal man to oppose Saladin and recapture Jerusalem. Sir Steven Runciman described his death as a 'serious blow to the renascent Kingdom of Jerusalem'.[21] It was in fact a blow from which the Christian forces never recovered, and as a result of his murder a perfect chance to recapture Jerusalem was lost. Thus in at least one case the political assassinations listed above had far-reaching consequences that perhaps the Assassins themselves did not understand.

Their role within the complex map of power in twelfth century Syria was of fundamental importance. A modern historian of the crusades has argued that 'but for the Assassins, the long survival of the Crusading States in the Levant would be inexplicable. The Franks confronted an enemy who was forced to fight with one hand tied behind his back'.[22] This was the true legacy of the Assassins' attempt to establish themselves in Syria, and illustrates how their tenacity in following the strategy originally elaborated by Hasan-i Sabbah came to have consequences which influenced Western Europe.

MASYAF AND THE SYRIAN CASTLES

A MODERN historian of crusading castles has observed that the strongholds of the Assassins in the Jabal Nusairi 'owed their comparative impregnability to their remote situation rather than to strong construction'.[1] This seems to be even more the case in Syria than in Persia, since there is little evidence of castle building on the part of the Assassins, and most references are in fact made to an impregnability which depends more on their site than their defences. Today the castles of the Assassins in Syria are rendered even more inaccessible to the traveller than those of Persia, since they lie close to the frontier between modern Syria and Lebanon. The principal castles of Banyas (which the Assassins only held for a short period), Qadmus and Masyaf lie within close reach of one another on an almost straight line inland towards the city of Hama.

This position made them of major strategic importance, since they lay *within* the Frankish crusading states: due south of Masyaf within a day's journey lay the Hospitaller fortress of Krak des Chevaliers, perhaps the greatest of all Christian fortresses in the Holy Land, while along the coastal route south of Banyas were the Templar castles of Chastel Blanc, Tortosa and Chastel Ruge (Qala'at Yahmur). To the north of the mountain range on which they stood was the Principality of Antioch, with the Templar castles of Baghras, Darbsak and Roche Roussel guarding the route south from Turkey. Mukaddari wrote in 1185 that 'The Lebanon Mountains are full of the castles of Ismailis. This range [i.e. the Jabal Lubnan] is the boundary between the Muslims and the Franks, for beyond them to the north lie Antakiyyah [Antioch] and Al Ladhikikiyyah, and other towns, which are in the hands of the Christians'.[2] Thus the area which came to be recognized as Assassin territory lay practically on the northern border of the

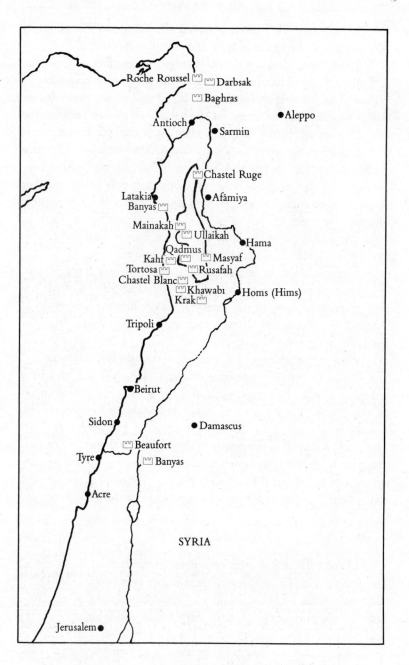

Figure 4: Syria: Assassin sites and cities mentioned.

crusader County of Tripoli, between the Christian Kingdom of Jerusalem and the much older Principality of Antioch.

This delicate situation, in a situation of permanent flux where castles and cities changed hands according to the temporary exigencies or power of local rulers and interest or disinterest of the more distant rulers whose policies influenced the balance of power, explains the odd alliances which the Assassins were often accused of making. It also emphasizes the need to establish a *modus vivendi* with local Christian forces. Rulers such as the Seljuk Sultan of Turkey, Mas'ud ibn Kilij Arslan, and the Emperor John of Constantinople often found it convenient to make what appear to modern eyes to be impossible alliances. To the north the rulers of Cilician Armenia controlled the vital overland route to the Holy Land from Europe, and constituted another important link in the balance of power.

Neither could the Assassins depend upon their Moslem neighbours, whose needs and alliances shifted similarly. The Seljuks of Ma'sud and of Baghdad were clearly their enemies, while the local emirs of Aleppo, Damascus and Homs – each only a short journey from the Assassin castles – could never be entirely trusted. Their support varied according to the whims or real needs of successive rulers throughout the period of Assassin presence in Syria. We shall see later how complicated relations were with Saladin, the greatest of the Arab leaders of this period. The Fatimids of Fustat and Sultan of Egypt were also always present and ready to take advantage of any weakness. Only the innate strength of the positions they chose to occupy and defend, together with the reputation which was fast developing and creating an aura of fear around them, enabled the Assassins to set up their small 'state' in the midst of such territorial confusion.

Some Syrian castles

One of the earliest and most complete descriptions of the castles of the Assassins in Syria is that of the chronicler Dimashki (1256–1327), who gave what Le Strange called a 'jejune description of his native land'[3], but who provides interesting information about the country and the best contemporary list of the Assassin castles in Syria. His main account of the castles is interesting on two points: first, the statement that the 'chief' of the Assassins generally is the Grand Master at Alamut; and second, for his reference to the Assassins being celebrated for their impiety. He begins as follows:

The castles of the Assassins (Kila ad Dawiyah) belong to the districts of Tarabulus. These have been lately built by Rashid ad Din Muhammad, the disciple of 'Ala ad Din 'Ali, who holds the fort of Al Alamut in Persia near Kasvin. He is the chief of the Assassins, whose sect is celebrated for its impiety. They are called Ismailians also.

After this brief introduction, Dimashki goes on to list eight castles belonging to the sect, although it must be remembered that he was writing some time after their decline. He does, however, include some fascinating details and legends:

Among their castles are *Hisn al Khawabi; Hisn al Kahf,* where there is a cavern in which Rashid ad Din, it is said, once took refuge, and now lies buried; or, as others say, has only disappeared, and will return again according to the belief of his people; *Hisn al Kadmus,* where during the months of Tammuz and Ab numbers of serpents appear in a certain hot bath. *Hisn al'Ullaikah, Hisn al Mainakah, Hisn ar Rusafah* lie on the spurs of the Taraz (Mountains) towards Damascus. Also *Hisn Abi Kubais* [Bokebeis of the Crusading Chronicles] and *Thughr Masyaf.* The Assassins chosen are sent out thence to all countries and lands to slay Kings and great men. [4]

This list was in part confirmed by the celebrated Arab traveller Ibn Batutah, who in 1355 visited Hisn al Masyaf, Hisn al Kadmus, Mainakah, Ullaikah and Kahf. [5]

The chief centre of Assassin activity in Syria was Masyaf, which was described by the Arab historian and author of an epitome of universal history, Abu-l Fida (d.1331). He visited Masyaf at the end of the thirteenth century and gave the following account:

Masyaf is a beautiful place, with a small river coming from a spring. It has gardens; also a strong fortress. It is a centre of the Ismailian Doctrine, and lies on the eastern flank of the Jabal al Lukkam, about a league south of Barin (Mons Ferrandus), and a day's journey west of Hims. [6]

He provides accurate information concerning the location of the main Assassin castles, together with the distances between them, when he writes of the Jabal Sikkin:

This is the mountain chain where the Ismailians have their chief quarters and their fortresses, such as Masyaf, Al Kahf and Al Khawabi. These fortresses lie in the mountains that run down the coast over against the country between Hims and Hamah. Masyaf makes a triangle with Hims and Hamah; the east point is Hamah, the north-west is Masyaf, and the south-west is Hims, they being about a day's journey the one from the other.[7]

The Hims referred to here is usually known as Homs, midway on the road north from Damascus to Aleppo. Although Abu-l Fida's use of the cardinal points is not particularly accurate, the triangle he describes is easily discernible just north of the modern frontier with Lebanon.

Yaqut b. Abdullah (1179–1229), a Greek-born slave who gained freedom in Baghdad and became the greatest of Moslem geographers,[8] provided a description of al-Khawabi in his *Geographical Lexicon*. This account is noteworthy since he uses the name 'Assassin' and curiously mentions the fact that the sect *does not* believe in resurrection after death. Speaking of Hisn al Khawabi (The Fort of the Ewes), he states: 'This fortress lies 15 miles south of Antarsus, by land. It is situated on a high mountain, and is an impregnable place. Its people are the Hashishiyyah, who are misbelievers in Islam, and believe naught of the Last Day, nor of the resurrection after death – Allah curse their unbelief'.[9]

One of the castles with the most detailed historical information is that of Banyas, locally known as Qal'at al-Numrud[10]. This is precisely because it changed hands so often and was therefore mentioned and described by several historians. The first description was that of the Damascus chronicler Ibn al-Qalansi, who related that it was given to the Assassins in 1126 by the ruler of Damascus, Tughtugin. As we have seen, the then Chief *Da'i* in Syria, Bahram, 'set about fortifying it and rebuilding what was in ruins or out of repair'.[11] Three years later Bahram's successor Isma'il 'the Persian' offered the citadel and town of Banyas to the Franks in exchange for asylum for himself and his followers. King Baldwin II of Jerusalem accepted the offer, the town was occupied, and there followed a massacre of the Isma'ilis resident there. From that moment, Banyas became an important Christian base for attacks against Damascus until it returned into Moslems hands after a siege by Nur al-Din in 1164.

This fortress is, however, of interest since it seems that it was the Assassins who built the walls which were later used and described by Christian sources. It therefore gives us some idea of their methods of castle building.

Banyas was less fortified naturally than the other Assassin castles. It stood at a vital point on the main road from Damascus to Tyre and had been the site of a fortress since ancient times. Just as Alamut was rather an entire fortified valley than simply a castle, so on the evidence of this fortified village most of the Assassin properties in Syria contained large living areas. The enclosed area of Banyas was about two-hundred-and-eighty metres square, surrounded by a moat and guarded by a heavily fortified wall with eight towers at regular intervals. At the most vulnerable point was the especially strengthened citadel. Although the town was only in Assassin hands for three years, it seems that no new building was done or additions made after their period of control. The later crusading forces, including the Hospitallers, who at one time held half the town, simply repaired and made good the fortifications which they found. [12]

The form of Assassin strongholds

It seems likely on the evidence of Alamut and the relative infrequency with which even the Syrian 'castles' were attacked that it is probably more correct to speak of fortified towns than of castles. In particular when the Assassins at the time of Sinan possessed an area which could be referred to as a state, each 'castle' must have had its own economic and social structures beyond a simple walled fortress.

The best model for a hypothetical reconstruction of one of these fortified towns is probably the generalized model of the Islamic city as a specialized urban form. The picture of a 'typical' Islamic city provided by Albert Hourani will serve as a basis on which to develop an imaginary Assassin fortified town or village. Hourani divides this 'typical' city into five parts, which will be followed here with divergences allowed for the size, function and religious differences which the particular features of Assassin communities would have presented. [13]

The first aspect, clearly pertinent to an Assassin centre, was the citadel, usually sited on a defence work. Cities such as Aleppo and Damascus, near the Assassin state, were themselves based upon such natural strong points. If we accept Archbishop William of Tyre's estimate of the Isma'ili community in Syria as consisting of about sixty-thousand members in the second half of the twelfth century

– under the leadership of Sinan – then it is clear that many of these people must have lived in dwellings which sprang up around the original citadels such as Qadmus and Masyaf.

The second normal feature of an Islamic city was a royal enclosure or quarter, either developed within an existing city by a new ruler or dynasty or itself the nucleus for a conglomeration of buildings as the power of the ruler or dynasty grew. In this case, the most likely hypothesis for the Assassin town would be the latter. This enclosure or palace need not have been the same as the citadel: in the case of Alamut, it was obviously within the walls on top of the rock; in Syria, it appears more likely that Sinan had a separate palace which could well have been built beside or near the original castles. The basis of truth in accounts such as those of William of Tyre and Joinville would suggest this hypothesis. Such a leader as Sinan would need a separate 'quarter', with barracks for guards and administrative offices in addition to his own residence.

Thirdly, most Islamic cities had a central urban complex consisting of mosques, religious schools and markets. Again, this would be most likely in the major Isma'ili centres, since so much value was placed upon religious training and preparation for both the *da'wa* and assassination missions. We have seen that the first step in developing an Assassin centre was the building of a 'House of Propaganda', which would presumably be beside a mosque or place of worship — just as the *madrasseh* is situated beside a mosque with interconnecting doors, passages or even cloisters. Again, as in Moslem cities today, the markets or bazaars, however small, would have been grouped around this central complex.

The fourth aspect would be a 'core' of residential quarters, in which soldiers, merchants, peasants and nomads settled in precise and compact groups. Again, we have no knowledge of the social organization of the Assassins, nor of the way in which the seven grades, from companion to Master, were organized in living quarters. But it would seem reasonable to assume a similar pattern: initiated members of different levels of the Order concentrated at the centre, with perhaps the lower levels divided between barracks within the citadel and more or less random distribution in the 'core' of the town.

Lastly, there were the outer quarters and suburbs, including areas where nomads and caravans might be found. It again must be assumed that a community of perhaps six-thousand people — William of Tyre's figure distributed among ten major centres — would on occasion offer hospitality to friendly caravans or nomads. Furthermore, such a large community would necessitate contact with merchant caravans and other travellers who provided the goods they needed. Unaffiliated peasants, women and parasitic families must also have existed around such communities.

If there is indeed anything in the idea, forwarded by Hammer-Purgstall as we shall see, that the Templars modelled their hierarchy and organization on the Assassins, then we might infer *a posteriori* that these communities were arranged like Templar properties. In that case, the large numbers of attendant workers, labourers, cooks and 'serving brothers', estimated at about ten to each knight [14], would presumably find an equivalent in Assassin communities. On this hypothetical model, these would be the people who inhabited the 'outer quarters', and it would be feasible to estimate perhaps six-thousand *fid'ais* at the highest point of Assassin power in Syria.

The territory controlled by the Assassins in Syria was much smaller than that in Persia. The religious mission never had the success that the *da'wa* had in the early years of Hasan-i Sabbah's rule in Alamut, with its conquest of large homogeneous areas of Quhistan, Khorassan and the Alborz Mountains. In a more fluctuating political situation such as that of Syria, such long-term territorial holdings would have been impossible for a relatively small force of fighting men. It appears from the few documents available that the total Assassin strength varied from eight to ten castles with the villages and lands belonging to the feuds. There was no single headquarters to equal Alamut, but rather a series of castles which leaders used according to temporary need. In fact this mobility and lack of a permanent centre is one of the main characteristics distinguishing the Syrian Assassins from the parent Order in Persia.

THE OLD MAN
OF THE MOUNTAINS

ALTHOUGH the term 'Old Man of the Mountains' was used of many Assassin leaders, including those of Alamut, it is properly used of Rashid al-Din Sinan, Grand Master of the Syrian Assassins from about 1162 to his death in 1193. This period coincides with the period of greatest power and fame of the Syrian Assassins.

Sinan was born in a village near Basra in the south-east of modern Iraq. He has been described as a schoolmaster and an alchemist, and is portrayed as a fine poet and prose writer by his biographer Kamal al-Din.[1] The same source describes him as 'an outstanding man, of secret devices, vast designs and great jugglery, with power to incite and mislead hearts, to hide secrets, outwit enemies and to use the vile and the foolish for his evil purposes'.[2] As a young man he became interested in Shiism. After a dispute with his brothers about which we have no details, Sinan apparently left home with neither money nor a horse and travelled to Alamut, arriving during the rule of Muhammad ibn Buzurg'umid. At Alamut, he 'trained himself in the sciences of the philosophers and read many of the books of controversy and sophistry, and of the Epistles of the Sincere Brethren and similar works of the philosophy that persuades and is put forward but not proved'.[3]

There is some confusion about how and when Sinan became leader of the Syrian mission. According to Kamal al-Din, Muhammad treated him as equal to his own sons Hosein and Hasan: 'He put me in school with them, and gave me exactly the same treatment as he gave them, in those things that are needful for the support, education, and clothing of children'.[4] When young Hasan succeeded his father as Hasan II in 1162, he ordered Sinan to travel to Syria, providing him with letters of introduction to Assassin companions along the route. His destination was the castle of Kahf, where he stayed until the Syrian leader Abu Muhammad died. Following his death the position of leader of the Syrian Assassins was usurped by a certain Hwaga Ali b. Mas'ud until he was murdered in a conspiracy. It was then that Sinan himself became the Chief *Da'i* in Syria, in or about 1162. At that time he was based in the castle of Kahf.[5]

An alternative hypothesis is that Sinan was already a supporter of Hasan at the time when he formed a group of friends dissatisfied with Muhammad's leadership and first formulated the ideas that were to lead to the *qiyama*. According to this version, Sinan had been forced to flee from Alamut by Muhammad, had spent time in hiding in one of the Syrian castles, and had then been made leader of the Syrian mission when his friend Hasan became Grand Master at Alamut.[6] This story accords well with the Isma'ili penchant for concealing true identity until the correct time comes to reveal it. What appears to be beyond dispute is that Sinan became Chief *Da'i* of the Syrian mission on direct orders and authority from Alamut, and that he had enjoyed an intimate friendship with Hasan II during their years of study together.

Sinan as the 'Old Man of the Mountains'

The term 'Old Man of the Mountains' is purely Syrian, and was in fact first used by western travellers in the Holy Land — so that Marco Polo's use of the term to describe the Grand Master in Alamut was derived from Syrian usage. Since Sinan's rule in Syria lasted for thirty years, c. 1163–93, and was that most often referred to by both Arab and western chroniclers, it is with reference to him that the term is properly used. The first recorded use of the term was by Benjamin of Tudela, who described the Assassins in 1167 as living in high mountains and obeying the Old Man 'in the land of al-Hashishin'.[7] This usage clearly refers to Sinan, and will hereafter be used exclusively of him.

The 'Old Man' appears in various forms in western sources, as 'vetus', 'vetulus de montanis', 'segnors de montana', 'li vius de la montaigne', 'veglio de la Montagna'. Curiously, the Arabic name *shayk al-jabal* seems to be a back formation translating the misunderstood western form into Arabic. Lewis has suggested that this phrase may have been a rendering of a popular Arabic expression which finds no equivalent in the literary sources: 'In all probability, ''Old Man of the Mountain'' is based on a misunderstanding of the Arabic word shaykh, frequently used of the Isma'ili chief, and fortuitously linked with the mountains in which he lived'.[8]

The first ten years or so of Sinan's leadership were mainly concerned with reasserting Assassin power in Syria. He had to 'order his diplomacy, his intervention in Muslim affairs or his conciliation of their rulers, cleverly enough to hold off the threatening Muslim powers; and meanwhile to consolidate the most defensible area held by the Isma'ilis into a firmly controlled block of territory, buttressed by strategic strongholds'.[9] The first step was to strengthen the castles already in their possession, especially ar-Rusafah and al-Khawabi. Then he captured the additional fortress of al-Ullaiqah. The anecdotes of Abu Firas suggest that he ruled by force of personality, and did not travel with personal troops or bodyguard. Neither did he make a permanent base in any of the castles controlled by the Assassins — especially the great castles of Masyaf, Qadmus and Kahf. He was in fact at the same time asserting his authority over many Isma'ilis who lived in scattered communities often side by side with the Sunni population, but owed allegiance to the Chief Da'i in Syria. It was also necessary to assert some control over Sunni vigilante bands known as Nubuwwiyya which were formed in such Sunni centres as Damascus in order to harrass members of the Shi'a. It seems that it was quite common to send Assassins against the leaders of these bands in order to weaken them.[10]

The hagiographic anecdotes of his life present Sinan as a man who was loved by all, and noted for his tenderness towards the villagers under his power. Abu Firas provides an instance of his gentility in circumstances in which he could easily have acted arrogantly:

A companion relates that the lord Rashid al-Din entered a village called Madjdal on his way to Masyaf. Immediately the inhabitants offered him some food, and the village headman personally brought some dishes covered by a dust-sheet. Rashid al-Din ordered that the food should be put aside and that no one should uncover it. When he rose to mount his horse, the headman asked, 'Sire, why did you not give me the pleasure of eating the food that I offered you?' Rashid al-Din took him aside and said, 'In her haste, your wife forgot to gut the chickens. I wished no one to see that, since it would have brought shame upon you.' The headman went to check what he had said, and things were as the lord had said.[11]

Apart from his obvious concern, this anecdote attributes almost miraculous powers of perception to Sinan.

He evidently had a powerful personality which enabled him to exercise authority over his followers, and this fact together with the fanatical loyalty we have already observed in the Assassins must account for the awe in which he was held by those who visited him. But beyond this he seems to have used what we would describe as 'magical' tricks to impress people, using such techniques as telepathy and clairvoyance. This personality was enhanced by deliberate use of spectacular techniques which are reminiscent of television and public relations-influenced politicians today. He practised statuesque positions and gave the impression of being a superhuman character by speaking very little and never eating in public. In Hodgson's words: 'With such prestige, Sinan proceeded to impose a one-man show upon the Syrian esoteric tendencies, permitting some to develop freely when they could support a loyalty to himself, but keeping anything within bounds that threatened ultimate dissolution of the group'.[12]

Sinan and the Qiyama

The position of Sinan with regard to Alamut was ambiguous. Although nominally subject to the decisions at Alamut, he was in fact an independent ruler in Syria for thirty years. It seems that he exercised this independence in such a way as to cause ill-feeling with the Grand Masters of Alamut, who on at least two occasions are supposed to have sent Assassins from Persia to kill him.

Yet Sinan had first been sent to Syria by the Masters at Alamut, and had maintained a close personal relationship with Hasan II. After the resurrection announced by Hasan in Alamut and other Persian strongholds, the ceremony of breaking the Ramadan fast was also carried out in Syria.[13] The biographer of Sinan reports in language which echoes that used to describe events in Persia after the declaration of Hasan that 'he allowed them [i.e. the companions] to defile their mothers and sisters and daughters and released them from the fast of the feast of Ramadan, and they called themselves Sincere'.[14] There is evidence, however, that Sinan over-stepped his loyalty, either from his own volition or in meeting the demands of his followers, in being accepted as an imam or direct representative of God.

Some of his own thoughts on the matter have been preserved in a brief but remarkable fragment published in the nineteenth century in French translation by Guyard. After reviewing the six previous ages from the creation of the world to the present he proclaims himself as supreme and divine leader, not only the latest prophet in the series but the incarnation of God himself:

> But religion has been perfected for you since I have appeared to you in the form of Rashid al-Din. Those who wish to acknowledge me have acknowledged me, and those who wish to deny me have denied me; but truth will follow its course, and those who proclaim it will continue their work: which is established for all cycles and all ages. I am the master of creation. The world is not empty of eternal seeds. I am the witness, the guardian, the dispenser of mercy, at the beginning and at the end.[15]

From this brief passage we can understand how Sinan attributed to himself the kind of powers which Hasan II had himself recently proclaimed, and might wonder whether he in some sense perceived himself as the true successor of his friend. If so, it would be sufficient to explain the rumoured attempted assassinations on the part of Muhammad II. Hodgson has suggested that this distinctly Syrian version of the *qiyama* marks the beginning of a divergence which has continued to the present day amongst Syrian Isma'ilis.[16] Sinan goes on to establish his authority as follows: 'Whoever knows me intimately possesses the truth, and no one can know me completely if he deviates from my commands'.[17] Supported by his unusual and powerful personality, such claims were the basis of Sinan's power over the Syrian Assassins for three decades.

It would appear likely that at first Sinan faithfully interpreted Hasan's doctrine of the *qiyama*, but that after his friend's death — within three years of Sinan's taking power — was less willing to accept the elaborations and commands of Hasan's son and successor Muhammad II, who outlived him. Thus it was that, for the period of Sinan's highly personalized rule in Syria, the Assassins there developed a certain autonomy which reverted to subjection as soon as Sinan died. However, about ten years after Sinan had come to power, this autonomy was for a time severely threatened by the parallel rise to power of one of the greatest of Moslem leaders.

The rise of Saladin

Saladin was the third in the series of anti-crusading heroes, following Zengi and Nur-al-Din and preceding the Mamluk Sultan Baybars who eventually destroyed the Assassin state in Syria. His full name was Al-Malik al-Nasir al-Sultan Salah-al-Din Yusuf, his name being Yusuf and his title Salah al-Din, 'rectitude of the faith', providing his usual name. Born in 1138 in the city of Baalbek (east of Beirut near the modern frontier with Syria), where his father was the Governor, he spent the first twenty-four years of his life studying the Koran, Arabic, rhetoric, poetry and indulging in the sports and pastimes suitable for the scion of such a prominent family: hunting, riding, chess and polo. Later his father, Job, 'Najm-al-Din' or 'Star of the Faith', was made the military commander of the city for Nur-al-Din, while Saladin's uncle, Shirkuh, was a general in the Sunnite king's army.[18]

Saladin's military experience was gained on campaigns with his uncle Shirkuh in the years 1164–9; in the latter year Shirkuh became vizier to the Caliph al-'Adid in Cairo. The holder of that office was generally known as the 'Sultan' and when Shirkuh died soon after his promotion, Salah took his place. From that moment he began a rapid rise to power. Within two years he overthrew al-'Adid and became ruler of Egypt; he also began to initiate drastic changes in the Fatimid Shiite army, for he himself, of Kurdish origin, was a member of the orthodox Sunni faith. What is most interesting in his career is the fact that he was from the beginning of his 'sultanate' fully conscious of a mission as the successor to Nur-al-Din. The concept of Holy War, *jihad,* as the often-cited diploma of investiture as vizier emphasizes, was part of his policy as early as 1169. Saladin is perceived as the embodiment and prime instigator of *jihad:*

As for the holy war, thou art the nursling of its milk and the child of its bosom. Gird up therefore the shanks of spears to meet it and plunge on its service into a sea of swordpoints . . . until God give the victory which the Commander of the Faithful hopeth to be laid up for thy days and to be the witness for thee when thou shalt stand in his presence.[19]

This prophetic passage informs Saladin's battles and campaigns of the next twenty years. He first consolidated his power as a ruler of the Moslem world, then slowly strangled the crusading states using a strategy against which they could offer little resistance. Saladin was by all accounts a man of simple tastes, with no interest in personal wealth or power, whose life was dedicated to the idea of *jihad*.

In 1174 Saladin took Damascus, and in the following year managed to supplant Nur-al-Din's son al-Malik al-Salih, who had opposed his leadership but was routed at his northern stronghold at Hamah. Saladin became effectively ruler of Egypt, Nubia, al-Maghrib, Arabia, Palestine, and Syria. Then, from Damascus and from Cairo, he began to operate a crushing pincer movement against the Christian states. In 1182 he finally conquered Mosul, which had been the last stronghold of Izz-al-Din, Caliph al-'Adid's brother, and in the following year took Aleppo. From that moment the destiny of the Frankish kingdoms was sealed and from the next year he began to use the title 'Sultan of Islam and the Moslems'.

Attempted assassinations of Saladin

Clearly such a powerful Sunni leader was a direct threat to the Assassins, and they seem to have been only too willing at that time to accept commissions to assassinate Saladin. It was during the siege of Aleppo at the beginning of 1175 that the first attempt was made, on the promise of rewards and estates by Sa'ad ad-Din Gumushtakin, ruler of Aleppo.[20] The appointed Assassins managed to enter Saladin's camp in disguise, but were recognized by a local emir who had dealt with them in the past. When this emir questioned them about their presence in Saladin's camp, they killed him and in the subsequent general fracas many of the people present were killed. Saladin, however, was unhurt.

The second attempt took place just over a year later, during the siege of Azaz, where the Assassins had fought for Tughtugin fifty years before. Assassins disguised as soldiers in Saladin's army attempted to kill him on 22 May of that year. This time they were closer, and did manage physically to attack their target, but Saladin's armour saved him from serious injury. The Assassins were themselves killed by the emirs attendant on Saladin, several of whom also died in the struggle. From this moment Saladin became far more cautious, 'sleeping in a specially constructed wooden tower and allowing no one whom he did not know personally to approach him'.[21]

Saladin's reprisal came two months later with an invasion of the Assassin state. On 30 July 1176 he laid siege to Masyaf. But this siege came to nothing, much as the two assassination attempts had done, although the reason is not clear. Perhaps it was, as some sources suggest, due to the intercession of Saladin's uncle, or because Saladin's presence was required elsewhere as the result of a Frankish advance. Yet another version suggests that Saladin was frightened by the supernatural powers of Sinan, and begged to be allowed to withdraw safely. [22] Kamal al-Din tells a remarkable story which hints both at some supernatural power and the skill of the Assassins at working undercover in disguise:

My brother (God have mercy on him) told me that Sinan sent a messenger to Saladin (God have mercy on him) and ordered him to deliver his message only in private. Saladin had him searched, and when they found nothing dangerous on him he dismissed the assembly for him, leaving only a few people and asked him to deliver his message. But he said: 'My master ordered me not to deliver the message [except in private]'. Saladin then emptied the assembly of all save two Mamluks, and then said: 'Give your message'. He replied: 'I have been ordered only to deliver it in private'. Saladin said: 'These two do not leave me. If you wish, deliver your message, and if not, return'. He said: 'Why do you not send away these two as you sent away the others?'. Saladin replied: 'I regard these as my own sons, and they and I are as one'. Then the messenger turned to the two Mamluks and said: 'If I ordered you in the name of my master to kill this Sultan, would you do so?'. They answered yes, and drew their swords, saying: 'Command us as you wish'. Sultan Saladin (God have mercy on him) was astounded, and the messenger left, taking them with him. And thereupon Saladin (God have mercy on him) inclined to make peace with him and enter into friendly relations with him. And God knows best. [23]

It is, in fact, most likely that some kind of a truce was agreed upon, especially since after this episode there are no records of further attacks against Assassin castles.

Sinan and Saladin

These three violent encounters within a brief space of time in fact suggest cat-like manoeuvres between two powerful personalities which could either have materialized into long-term opposition or have evolved into some kind of *modus vivendi*. Furthermore, they suggest a pattern in the relationship between these two great men. Both Saladin and Sinan had come to power a decade earlier, and had needed the intervening time to establish their own spiritual and military authority.

In 1175/6 they were at the height of their powers; Sinan consolidated as the Old Man of the Mountains and Saladin having taken Damascus and on the verge of becoming the chief ruler of Islam. Clearly the confrontation needed to take place, and with hindsight it may be seen to have resolved itself with benefit for both sides.

In Christian terms, the truce which Saladin and Sinan appear to have reached and then maintained until the end of their respective careers nearly twenty years later was tragically vital. Saladin himself had once said that his chief enemies were the Franks, the rulers of Mosul and the Assassins. By achieving the truce with Sinan in 1176 or thereabouts he was freed of one enemy to concentrate on Mosul, which he took in 1182. Thereafter freed of potential enemies and assassination attempts from within the Moslem world, Saladin needed only five years before he achieved his principal aim in retaking Jerusalem. That the truce continued is in no doubt: when Saladin later made a further truce with Richard I of England in 1192, he specifically included the Assassin territories in its terms.[24] That it was vital to Saladin's efforts towards re-establishing Moslem hegemony over the Holy Land seems equally clear.

These episodes illustrate the profound differences which developed during Sinan's rule when compared to the situation in Persia. Whereas in Alamut the remoteness of the Rudbar and its fortresses rendered an independent existence possible, and enabled the Assassins to maintain their identity as religious missionaries propagating the Isma'ili faith, in Syria activities were constantly influenced by local exigencies. The Holy Land in the twelfth century was in an extraordinary state of flux, with powers and territories constantly changing and disputes even within the two main contending parties, Christian and Moslem. In such a melting pot of faith and ideas it was inevitable that there should be cross-fertilization and profound exchanges of ideas: it was then that many eastern concepts, including magical and heretical ideas, passed the 'frontier' into western thought in processes that cannot now be discerned or explained. Thus it was also inevitable that the Assassin creed should be tinged with new ideas and varying doctrines.

In another sense, Sinan's leadership illustrates perfectly the perspective from which the Assassins viewed their strategic policy of murder: their own organization was an excellent example of dynamic and personalized rule by a single man. Had an enemy wished to weaken or destroy the Syrian Assassins, there would have been no better method than assassinating Sinan. The fact that this was never attempted, and that he ruled with such success — although wavering slightly from the Alamut line — emphasizes the power of his personality, and places him only second in consideration among the great men of the history of the Assassins after Hasan-i Sabbah.

The Syrian Assassins after Sinan

A sect such as the Assassins, reflecting the Moslem law on which its own premise of eliminating a threat by eliminating its leader was based, required a powerful personality in order to function. It seems that the Masters who followed the long and successful leadership of Sinan were unable to match his skill and authority. We have the names of some of them, but no precise dates and very little information about their activities. [25]

In fact, the most notable event in the years immediately following Sinan's death was a temporary reversion to the orthodox faith between 1210 and 1212. This also illustrates that the control of the Syrian Assassins was fully in the hands of Alamut at that time, even though under Sinan there had perhaps been a certain autonomy. For it was on orders from Hasan III at Alamut that this return to the 'signs of Islam' was carried out in Syria just as in Persia. The books of his predecessors were burnt and recognition given to the Abbasid Caliph an-Nasir. This demonstration of loyalty to Alamut at such a late date is of great importance. In fact it seems that the leaders in Syria came from Alamut, or were at least Persians, to the end of Assassin power. [26]

In 1213 the last celebrated assassination took place. The eighteen year old son of the ruling Prince Bohemond of Antioch, Raymond, was murdered in the cathedral at Tortosa. Bohemond had usurped the Principality of Antioch in 1201, and as the result of hostility between Leo of Armenia and Bohemond — and the eternal conflict between the Hospitallers and the Templars — the Hospitallers had sided with Leo against the Prince of Antioch. It appears that the murder of his son was carried out at the instigation of the Hospitallers, who at that time paid tribute to the Assassins. [27]

One of the consequences of this murder was that Bohemond attacked the Assassin castle of al-Khawabi together with a contingent of

Templars. Faced with a more powerful force, the Assassins appealed to az-Zahir, the ruler of Aleppo, for help. After a failed attempt to relieve the besieged garrison, az-Zahir in turn carried out negotiations to the effect that the siege of al-Khawabi was lifted.[28] This incident emphasizes two aspects of Assassin power in Syria at that time: first, that under any real threat from an armed force they were unable to defend themselves; and second, that the 'castles' which they held were in fact fortified positions to be used as attacking positions rather than for prolonged defence.

But this incident also appears to be a sign of Assassin decline, since no further political assassinations and no events of great importance occurred during the next half century or so.

Baybars and the end of Assassin power in Syria

The end of the Assassin power in Syria coincided with the destruction of Alamut, although there was no direct connection. Ironically, in fact, the Arab leader who eventually took the Syrian castles and subjugated their owners was the same man who defeated Hulegu and thus saved Damascus from Mongol invasion.

Baybars, who had been a general of the Mamluk Sultan Kutuz, in 1260 murdered the Sultan and usurped the Mamluk throne. In Baybars the Assassins met their match in more ways than one, since he was a decisive and often brutal man who created terror amongst Arab nobles as a result of the violent acts he sometimes committed.[29] Earlier that same year he had defeated Hulegu at the battle of Ain Julat near Nazareth. Now he was to remain Sultan until 1277 and become the last of the great anti-crusaders who definitively smashed crusader power in the Holy Land. He made his capital in Cairo, which became the seat of Islam, and quickly consolidated his empire in a series of moves which demonstrated his speed of action, resolution, courage, shrewdness and determination.[30]

It was this consolidation, with the strengthening of fortresses in Syria and the organization of communications between Cairo and Damascus, which provided for Islam the ideal conditions for dealing a series of crushing blows against the Christians in the East. The Assassins found themselves in the midst of these operations, with no hope of combatting on equal terms the general who had broken the Mongol armies.

Baybars could not tolerate the idea of an independent and potentially dangerous sect living freely within Syria, and he was powerful enough to act towards them as no ruler had done before. In 1260 he assigned land belonging to the Assassins in fief to one of his generals, and in 1265 he began collecting taxes on tributes received by the Assassins. The next stage was for the Assassins to pay tribute directly to Baybars, so that in fact it was he who commanded them: neither the Grand Master in Alamut, now that fortress had been taken by Hulegu, nor the Master in Syria. For a time this situation continued, but in the early 1270s Baybars increased the pressure and began seizing Assassin strongholds. [31] From 1271 to 1273 the castles fell to him one by one. Finally, during one of his expeditions into northern Syria, Baybars took all the Assassin castles and destroyed forever their claims to be more than a minor religious sect. [32] On 9 July 1273 the last independent outpost of the Assassins was lost when Kahf fell to Baybars.

In the same period Baybars took all the northern castles of the Knights Templar — Beaufort, Baghras, Roche Roussel and Chastel Blanc — and nullified their military importance. Thus these two orders, both proud and widely feared, were destroyed by a single man.

From that moment the Nizari Isma'ilis lost all religious and political importance in Syria, surviving as a minor heresy. From the fourteenth century onwards the Syrian Isma'ilis no longer recognized the same imams as their Persian counterparts. [38] Thenceforth there was no further contact between the successors of the Assassins in Syria and Persia.

ASSASSINS
AND CRUSADERS

IT WAS in Syria, and especially during the rule of Sinan, that the Assassins came into contact with Europeans. For over a century, from their first military action against a crusading army under Tughtugin in 1126 to their eventual demise in the mid-thirteenth century, they held a state within crusader territory and had dealings with the Franks resident in the Holy Land. It was in this period that their name became known in the West, and the legends that later writers were to elaborate were born in Syria.

While the Assassins were in the process of establishing their power in Syria, they appear to have ignored the existence of the crusading states. Their enemy had always been the *Sunni* faith and its representatives, and apart from sporadic fighting in the armies of other Moslem leaders they appear to have done little to antagonize their Christian neighbours. In the course of the first century of their existence, only one murder concerned a Christian. This was Count Raymond I of Tripoli, who was murdered by them in 1152. This murder was in itself fairly meaningless, the by-product of one of the many minor frontier wars which characterized the twelfth century in Syria. [1] But the consequences were both interesting and important: the Christian forces retaliated violently, massacring non-Christians in Tripoli and fighting relentlessly against the Assassins themselves. Furthermore, it was as a result of this incident that the Assassins found themselves weakened and obliged to pay a tribute to the Knights Templar.

Assassins and the Knights Templar

One of the first and most interesting contacts, although it has been used to prove ideas beyond its real scope as we shall see in a later chapter, was that with the Knights Templar. That an organization renowned as early as the 1130s for 'courage and gallantry'[2] amongst the Arabs should encounter a Christian organization later described by the Arab historian Ibn Alathir as 'the fiery heart of France' ('les charbons de France' in the French translation),[3] is not surprising. Moreover, as stressed in Chapter 7, some of the nearest castles to the Assassin 'state' as it developed were the Templar castles of Tortosa (granted to the Templars in 1152) and Chastel Blanc. While it is clear that few European chroniclers or soldiers understood the underlying religious purpose of the Assassins, and thus misunderstood the nature of their fanatical loyalty to their leader, it has been suggested that the Templars understood them better.[4]

So much so that the Assassins appear to have exercised some influence on the Templars. This point was first made by the controversial nineteenth century *History of the Assassins* by the Austrian orientalist Joseph von Hammer-Purgstall, whose work remained the principal study of the Assassins for over a century and influenced other reliable oriental scholars such as Edward Granville Browne in their discussions of the Assassins. While a more detailed discussion of von Hammer-Purgstall's work will be given in a later chapter, his ideas concerning relations between the Assassins and the Templars are pertinent here.

When the Knights Templar were founded in 1118/19 in Jerusalem, it was as a 'poor order' whose primary function was the protection of pilgrims along the main routes between the coast at Jaffa and the inland city of Jerusalem. But an important transformation took place when this nascent Order came under the patronage of St Bernard of Clairvaux, nephew of André de Montbard, one of the founding group of the Templars. Until his conversion at the age of twenty, St Bernard himself had been destined for a knightly career, and when he came to patronize the Knights Templar that Order was imbued with the ideals and convictions of the knightly class of Burgundy. In 1128 St Bernard himself probably provided the first version of the *Rule* governing Templar life and resuscitating the Order of Chivalry to its original purity.[5] The austere and spiritual Templars, looking back to some imagined form of lost perfection, an exalted and nostalgic idea of an ideal order of chivalry, conscious themselves of their courage, loyalty and religious purpose, cannot have failed to recognize the goals and methods of the Assassins as close to their own. The same kind of men, not great noblemen but men from modest country manors who would have no role in the non-religious context, appear to have joined the Assassins and the Templars. They were essentially new men whose success derived from their search for personal and spiritual identity reinforced by the tight religious structure, rules and hierarchy of the two orders.

Certain parallels are striking: Nowell, following von Hammer-Purgstall, observes that the lay brothers, sergeants and knights of the Templars duplicate the *lasiq* (layman), *fida'i* (agent) and *rafiq* (companion) of the Assassins, while the knightly equivalent within the Assassins, the *rafiqs*, wore white mantles trimmed with red which correspond to the white mantle and red cross of the Templars.[6] But it must be observed here that the white habit was just as likely based upon the Cistercian robes of their patron. St Bernard had saved the Order from possible dissolution as the result of difficulty in obtaining vocations due to its harsh standards when he joined it at Citeaux. He had then reformed and strengthened the Order, becoming Abbot of Citeaux and almost simultaneously sponsoring the Knights Templar.[7] It would not therefore be surprising if they based their formal dress on Cistercian practice.

Similarly, the right to wear a red cross was granted to the Templars in 1147 by Pope Eugenius III — ex-monk at Clairvaux and protégé of St Bernard — at a Templar chapter in Paris.[8] The higher ranks of both orders, with priors, grand priors and Master, are also strikingly similar: prior, grand prior and Master correspond to *da'i*, *da'i kabir* and the Grand Master.[9] In this context it is worth observing that while St Bernard provided the *Rule* of the Templars, the hierarchical structure seems to have come later and evidently from some other source.

One of the most interesting ways in which influence might be discerned would be in the adoption by the Knights Templar of Assassin strategies based upon the possession of castles. We have seen how Hasan-i Sabbah began missionary activities by establishing secure bases in remote mountain fortresses from which military raids or propaganda raids would then be carried out. This use of castles was echoed by the Templars, for whom a castle was far more than a mere fortress. As R. C. Smail has written of the crusading castles:

The crusaders' castles protected the Latin settlement against external attack, and in that defence the frontier castles had a special part to play; but that is neither the whole nor even the most important part of the matter. The castles were also the instruments of conquest and colonisation, and continuously embodied part of the force on which Latin dominion rested. [10]

Thus, Smail argues implicitly, the Templar method was a development of a peculiarly eastern use of the castle. Assassin castles usually consisted of a walled compound with a keep built at its weakest point, designed as a fortified base for operations rather than to defend territory. Before sophisticated siege warfare, such as that used by Hulegu against Alamut over a century later, they were in Syria relatively small and without the natural defence of remoteness of the Persian castles. It is this strategic, colonizing function of the castle which the Templars and other crusading orders may have developed from the Assassins, with no thought of territorial control, and no qualms about letting enemies pass between the castles.

So much is hypothetical: plausible, but without evidence. But the Templars and the Assassins were certainly in frequent contact, as the fact that the Templars exacted a yearly tribute of two-thousand gold byzants from the Assassins clearly demonstrates. Later in the century, the Templars' rival crusading Order of the Hospital also managed to exact tribute, since they from 1142 commanded the most powerful of all crusading castles, Krak des Chevaliers, within a day's ride due south of Masyaf. [11]

It was a dispute over the payment of tribute that led to one of the best known episodes concerning the Assassins and the crusading orders, when Sinan attempted to gain release from his obligation to the Templars. The story is recounted in detail by Archbishop William of Tyre, who was always willing to tell a story against the Templars. [12] It offers a unique example of Sinan's duplicity and willingness to accept any offer of alliance if he deemed it would strengthen the position of his Order. He sent a messenger named Abdullah to King Amaury I of Jerusalem offering to convert his faithful to Christianity if the Templars would forsake their tribute. Amaury was apparently so delighted by this extraordinary offer that he sent Abdullah back with his acceptance. On the way Abdullah's party was attacked by a group of Templars, one of whom, a certain Gautier du Mesnil, personally killed the Assassin envoy. This murder was probably carried out in

fear of the Templars losing their annual tribute, although as a matter
of fact Amaury I had guaranteed the tribute from his own purse as
the result of his pleasure at Sinan's offer. He arrested and imprisoned
Gautier du Mesnil in spite of an attempt to protect him by the Templar
Master Eudes de Saint-Amand.

This tale of Sinan renouncing his faith in favour of Christianity
smacks of improbability, especially since there is no other mention
of such a decision and a single murder would hardly have changed
a sincere and serious decision of the kind. But Nowell has pointed
out that there is a connection between William of Tyre's story that
under Sinan the Assassins had abolished their fasts, begun eating pork
and drinking wine, and torn down their places of worship, with the
recent events at Alamut, when Hasan II had introduced his resurrection
and ordered the breaking of the fast of Ramadan by a great feast.
In this version, therefore, the filtered account of the events at Alamut
had been merged with more local events. [13] If so, it would make another
interesting example of the frequent compounding of stories from Persia
and Syria. But it may also be the case that Sinan had made such an
offer in the hope of strengthening his own position in Syria after the
recent changes at Alamut had left him out on a limb.

The murder of Conrad of Monferrat

After the fall of Jerusalem to Saladin in 1187, a new crusade left Europe
in an attempt to reconquer the Holy City, led by King Richard I
of England and King Philip Augustus of France. The violent contrasts
between these two European kings, and of Richard with Conrad of
Montferrat, who was at that time Prince of Tyre and titular King
of Jerusalem, came to a head with the assassination of Conrad in the
streets of Tyre. Although the needs of propaganda and intrigue were
clearly behind explanations of this murder that attributed it variously
to Richard or to Saladin, the one thing which is both clear and
undeniable was that it was the work of the Assassins.

The attack occurred as Conrad walked through Tyre with the Bishop
of Beauvais after dinner. The poet Ambroise, who travelled with
Richard's army, describes it as follows:

> . . . two youths lightly clad, who wore
> No cloaks, and each a dagger bore,

Made straight for him, and with one bound,
Smote him and bore him to the ground,
And each one stabbed him with his blade,
The wretches, who thus wise betrayed
Him, were of the Assassin's men . . .[14]

Two main versions of the incident exist: in one, one Assassin was killed instantly, while the other escaped, but came out of hiding to finish off Conrad, whose still-breathing body had been carried into the church where the Assassin was hidden; the other version states that at least one of the Assassins survived to confess that he had been sent by the Old Man of the Mountains.[15]

Moslem sources state that Sinan had been asked by Saladin to murder both Conrad and Richard for the fee of ten-thousand gold pieces, and that he had accepted in the case of Conrad. It would contradict the accusation of Richard I being implicated, since the two Assassins had apparently infiltrated Conrad's entourage some six months earlier and gradually gained his confidence. Yet this fact of operating in disguise in preparation for the murder has the benefit of concurring with known Assassin methods.

In fact, the charges against Richard were made after he had left the Holy Land disguised as a Templar knight and was imprisoned in Austria. So it would seem most likely that the charges were invented by his arch-enemy Philip Augustus, and in fact most of the accusations against Richard came from French sources. As so often in the case of Richard I, his life engendered legend, so that the connection between the Assassins and the English King remained fixed in the popular imagination. More than a century later the French poet Guillaume Guiart wrote a historical poem in which *English* boys had been trained by Richard to perform assassinations using the methods of the oriental sect. They had even been given the same guarantee of entry to an eternal paradise as their reward.[16]

Assassins and Louis IX (St Louis) of France (1214-70)

The relations between Louis IX and the Assassins contain the usual blend of fact and legend. But they are more interesting than relations with other Europeans because they lasted for a period of several years. Moreover, they opened with the only reliable and well-attested case

of Syrian Assassins being sent to operate beyond their normal sphere
of action. While the King of France was only twenty-three years old,
in 1237, the Old Man in Syria seems to have heard that Louis was
thinking of going on crusade. He therefore sent two *fida'is* to France
to murder the King. But almost immediately after dispatching them
he changed his mind and sent two further, higher-ranked Assassins
to prevent the murder taking place.

It has been argued that this change of heart may have been due
to Templar persuasion,[17] and in fact the French Templars were always
close to Louis. When the King did eventually decide to go on crusade
in 1244 it was they who organized the finances of the expedition that
was in fact the last whole-hearted attempt to retake Jerusalem. Much
of the finance for this crusade came from the traditional Templar
recruiting ground of Burgundy, and they were instrumental in
providing for the departure of the crusade from Aigues-Mortes in
the Camargue. They provided the advance guard for his attack against
Cairo, and paid his ransom when the French King was captured.[18]
Thus the Templars would certainly have been interested in avoiding
the assassination of Louis; in any case, the incident offers further
suggestive evidence of close relations between the two orders.

The two original Assassins were found in Marseilles. Not only were
they stopped from carrying out their mission, but they were even
sent back to Syria laden with gifts from the French King. Since several
independent versions of this story exist, there are strong grounds for
accepting it as true. If that is the case, then it is indeed 'the most
convincing evidence we have that the Assassins sometimes operated
in Western Europe'.[19] This generous treatment of his potential
murderers may also account for the way in which relations between
Louis and the Assassins continued. In 1249 Louis departed from Cyprus
to attack Egypt. The first attack against Damietta at the mouth of
the Nile delta was successful, and then his army defeated the forces
of Turanshah at Mansourah. But after a winter of stalemate, the Sultan's
forces attacked and decimated the Christian forces in the spring of
1250, capturing the King of France. After the payment of a huge
ransom Louis was released from captivity and travelled to Acre, where
he was visited by agents of the Old Man of the Mountains.[20]

This embassy consisted of one high-ranking member of the Order
sent to negotiate, plus two *fida'i* presumably acting as bodyguards.

They sat around the King during the interview in such a way that his life could easily be taken by them and then presented their demands in the form of an implicit threat: they wished Louis to pay tribute to their order just as, they claimed, such other western kings as the German Emperor and the King of Hungary. These kings realized that their lives could be terminated at any moment by the Old Man, and willingly paid a tribute to guarantee their own safety from Assassin attack. Louis promised to consider their demands, but when they met again ensured that he was well protected by the Masters of the Temple and the Hospital. These men, well versed in Assassin ways, addressed the embassy in Arabic and ordered them to present themselves for a private interview the next day.

At the third meeting, the two Grand Masters pointed out that the original message and implied threat had been a great offence to the honour of King Louis, and that only the envoy's diplomatic status prevented them from throwing him into the sea. Joinville relates that the envoy immediately left for the Old Man's castle, but soon returned bearing gifts. These included a crystal elephant, amber ornaments, an engraved ring offered as the first stage of an exchange of rings, and a shirt. This latter gift, to western eyes of little value, was in fact of particular significance, since it was the garment worn closest to the body and therefore implied a special intimacy and trust.

St Louis then sent his own messenger, a certain Brother Yves the Breton, with gifts for the Old Man. The most interesting result of this visit was the fact that Brother Yves learned something of the doctrines of the Assassins. The story gains authenticity when we hear that he found a book which appeared to be a Christian treatise, referring to some sayings by Jesus to St Peter. Yves discovered that the Old Man often read this book, but that he interpreted it in terms of the reincarnation of past religious leaders. The words of the Old Man quoted by Joinville were supposed to have appeared absurd and to ridicule the ideas of the sect, but in fact they accurately reflect the Isma'ili doctrines we have examined:

I hold St Peter in the highest esteem, because at the beginning of the world, when Abel was killed, his soul went to the body of Noah, and when Noah died it went to the body of Abraham, and from Abraham's body, when he died, it passed to the body of St Peter when God came to earth.[21]

Thus it seems likely that Brother Yves really did visit the Old Man in his castle, and that Joinville based his account on reliable information. Certainly Joinville was the only western chronicler who made some attempt to understand Isma'ili doctrine, even though, not surprisingly, he gave a very muddled account of it. There were no further attempts in the medieval period, and in fact there are few records of contact between Assassins and crusaders after the epoch of St Louis. [22]

Louis led the last great crusade, and shortly after his departure from the Holy Land the delicate balance of circumstances which had enabled the Assassins to survive and had caused the crusaders to be near their territory was irrevocably destroyed by Baybars. As the Assassins fell into an irreversible decline, so the crusading ideal of recapturing Jerusalem also declined. From that moment, the story and doctrines of the Assassins were to become the exclusive preserve of legend.

PART III:
MYTHS AND LEGENDS OF
THE ASSASSINS

THE CONTEMPORARY LEGEND

AS THE Assassins of Syria grew in power and importance throughout the twelfth century, so they came into contact with crusading knights and their reputation reached the ears of western chroniclers who recorded for us the wars and struggles of the Holy Land. But these early writers had little information on which to base their accounts. They knew nothing about Isma'ilism as a deviant form of Islam, little about the parent sect in Persia and its origins, and quite often muddled their accounts as the result of this paucity of real knowledge. Yet their accounts were rich and fascinating, and soon entered the legend and literature of the crusaders. With no attempt to verify accuracy, these accounts were passed on to writers in Europe who repeated them and elaborated them until often the tales they tell bear little resemblance to the history of the Assassins as we now understand it.

But the dramatic and heroic nature of the tasks of the Assassins, the bloodiness of the deed which came to bear their name, and the accounts of such quasi-fantastic features as the garden of paradise and the death leap of the faithful, fixed them indelibly in the minds of credulous western men and women so firmly that even today echoes of the legends remain. They form part of the rich texture of crusading history — impermeated with similar heroic, larger-than-life characters and events — to which future ages look back nostalgically. Regardless of the facts of their doctrine, of their religious role, their long and interesting history, the Assassins entered the European historical and literary imagination for one reason alone.

The word 'assassin'

The complexity of the legend is not simplified by the fact that the

Old Man of the Mountains first appeared in European literature in an anachronistic context, where he was supposed to have participated in an early twelfth century event. The French poet Graindor de Douay introduced this character into his revised version of the much older *Chanson de l'Antioche,* where, basing his story on an incident we have seen occurring to Louis IX of France, Baldwin (Godfrey of Bouillon's brother and later King of Jerusalem) marries the daughter of the Old Man ('Li Vius de Montaigne') and receives a shirt from him as a sign of fidelity. [1]

But the words 'assassin' and 'assassinate' entered western European languages with their modern meaning at the end of the thirteenth century. Guido delle Colonne is recorded as having used it in the slightly different form of 'assessino' as early as 1290. The story of the Old Man of the Mountains demonstrating his men's obedience by ordering them to jump to their deaths from a rock was already mentioned in the anonymous *Novellino,* with Frederick II of Sicily as the observer during his crusading venture. This famous early collection of prose stories was published in the last decade of the thirteenth century. Dino Compagni, a contemporary of Dante noted for having written a chronicle of Florence from 1270 to 1312 in the vulgar tongue, used the verb in the modern sense of killing 'for hatred, vendetta or kidnapping'. [2] But the word definitely entered the literary vocabulary when it was used by Dante.

It appears first in a sonnet attributed with some certainty to Dante's youth, in which he presents a striking image using the concept of Assassin fidelity. The 'Lover' is said to be devoted to love:

Più che Assassino al Veglio . . .

or, even more than the Assassin is devoted to the Old Man of the Mountains. [3] This illustrates an understanding of the blind obedience of the Assassins. Yet more pertinent and more celebrated than this fine use of the word is Dante's line in the Inferno (*The Divine Comedy: Hell,* Book XIX, verses 49–50), where he uses the word in a context that demands the most abominable of crimes. Dante describes himself as 'like a friar who is confessing the wicked assassin':

'Io stava come il frate che confessa
Lo perfido assassin, . . .

Here the strongest possible noun is required since the criminal being confessed is being buried alive head down, thus denoting a sin of particular horror. The connection of assassin with wickedness reinforces the clarity and precision with which Dante uses the word, and it was in this sense that 'assassin' then passed into other European languages.

Early accounts of the Assassins

Gerhard, or Burchard, of Strasburg travelled to Syria in 1175 on a diplomatic mission for the Emperor Frederick Barbarossa. He reported that there was a sect known as the 'Heyssessini' who lived between Damascus and Aleppo. The accusations that had already been laid at the door of the Assassins by Moslem writers were repeated, that they ate pork and abused their mothers and sisters. He stresses the fear which their leader, at that time Sinan, strikes into them and then goes on to provide the first account of a procedure that was repeated by nearly all later writers:

. . . this prince possesses in the mountains numerous and most beautiful palaces, surrounded by very high walls, so that none can enter except by a small and very well-guarded door. In these palaces he has many of the sons of the peasants brought up from early childhood. He has them taught various languages, as Latin, Greek, Roman, Saracen as well as many others. These young men are taught by their teachers from their earliest youth to their full manhood, that they must obey the lord of their land in all his words and commands; and that if they do so, he, who has power over all living gods, will give them the joys of paradise. They are also taught that they cannot be saved if they resist his will in anything. Note that, from the time when they are taken in as children, they see no other one but their teachers and masters and receive no other instruction until they are summoned to the presence of the Prince to kill someone. When they are in the presence of this Prince, he asks them if they are willing to obey his commands, so that he may bestow paradise upon them. Whereupon, as they have been instructed, and without any objection or doubt, they throw themselves at his feet and reply with fervour, that they will obey him in all things that he may command. Thereupon the Prince gives each one of them a golden dagger and sends them out to kill whichever prince he has marked down. [4]

The confusion of fact and fantasy is obvious in this report. The fear of the Assassin leader and the technique of murder with which he inculcates that fear derive from the truth. But the boys being taken from their families and learning so many languages already seems a slight exaggeration. Above all, the story of the golden dagger presented to neophyte Assassins shows the extent to which Burchard elaborates his tale.

Soon after this date, another account of the Assassins was provided by Archbishop William of Tyre, one of the greatest of early historians. William had been asked by Amalric to write the history of the Latin kings of Jerusalem. He had been born, around 1130, in the Holy Land and understood Arabic and Moslem ways; above all, he was usually an impartial historian whose experience and great knowledge of the East led to immediate recognition of his work as a reliable source for the history of Latin Syria. He wrote, probably around 1182–4, in his *History of Deeds Done Beyond the Sea:*

There is in the province of Tyre, otherwise called Phoenicia, and in the diocese of Tortosa, a people who possess ten strong castles, with their independent villages; their number, according to what we have often heard is about 60,000 or more. It is their custom to install their master and choose their chief, not by hereditary right, but solely by virtue of merit. Disdaining any other title of dignity, they called him the Elder. The bond of submission and obedience that binds this people to their Chief is so strong, that there is no task so arduous, difficult or dangerous that any one of them would not undertake to perform it without the greatest zeal, as soon as the Chief has commanded it. If for example there be a prince who is hated or mistrusted by this people, the Chief gives a dagger to one or more of his followers. At once whoever receives the command sets out on his mission, without considering the consequences of the deed nor the possibility of escape. Zealous to complete his task, he toils and labours as long as may be needful, until chance gives him the opportunity to carry out his chief's orders. Both our people and the Saracens call them Assissini; we do not know the origin of this name.[5]

The difference between these two accounts is obvious, and probably represents the difference between the experience of a man who visited the Holy Land and picked up second-hand information, and a man who had spent much of his life amidst the Arabs. The basis of future legends and elaborations is already present in Burchard's account, while William of Tyre is sober and severe. He gives precise topographical details, provides a relatively accurate idea of total Assassin strength, but above all emphasizes the obedience and zeal of the companions. This demonstrates his solid local knowledge, since we have seen that in fact the obedience noted by many observers derived from the certainty and fanaticism of their religious faith.

Marco Polo

Perhaps the most widely read account in modern times, however, has been that of Marco Polo, whose *Book of Marco Polo, Citizen of Venice, Called Million, Wherein is Recounted the Wonders of the World* is justly better known than the above specialized histories.

Marco Polo's uncle and father had already spent seven years travelling as far as the Great Khan's court at Khanbaliq, now Pekin but known to literature as Coleridge's Xanadu. On their second journey to the East, beginning in 1270, they took the young Marco, then seventeen, with them. From this celebrated journey, with various periods of residence in oriental cities, Marco Polo returned to Venice twenty-five years later. Then, imprisoned by the Genoese during a war with the Republic of Venice, he committed his memories of his travels to paper with the aid of a fellow prisoner, Rustichello of Pisa, who transcribed them in French.

Thus the account that Marco Polo 'wrote' of his visit to Alamut in the year 1273, on his way south from Trebizond on the Black Sea to Kerman in south-eastern Persia via Tabriz, was written nearly thirty years after the event — although he may have used notes made during the journey. Yet although his description of the castle and valley of Alamut is unique in being the only detailed description by a westerner who may actually have visited Alamut, it must be remembered that his visit was made nearly twenty years after the fortress was taken by Hulegu. The description is worth quoting in full, since it has been the basis for so many elaborations:

Milice [e.g. mulehet, which derives from the Arabic word for heretic] is a district where the Old Man of the Mountains used to live. Now I shall tell you the story, as Messer Marco heard it from several men.

The Old Man is called in their language Aloodin. He had caused to be made the biggest and most beautiful garden of the world in a valley between two mountains. In it could be found all the fruits and the most beautiful palaces in the world, all painted with gold or animal and bird designs; there were channels — from one came water, from another honey and from another wine; there were the most beautiful ladies of the world, who sang and played instruments and danced better than any. And the Old Man made them believe that this was paradise; for this reason he made it, since Mohammad said that whosoever goes to paradise would have as many lovely women as he could desire, and would find rivers of milk, wine and honey. This is why he made it similar to that described by Mohammad; and the Saracens of that district believed firmly that this place was really paradise.

No one save those who wished to be Assassins (assesin) could enter into this garden. At the entrance of the garden there was a castle that was so strong that it feared no man in the world. The Old Man kept at his court such boys of twelve years old as seemed to him destined to become courageous men. When the Old Man sent them into the garden in groups of four, ten or twenty, he gave them hashish to drink [sic]. They slept for three days, then they were carried sleeping into the garden where he had them awakened.

When these young men woke, and found themselves in the garden with all these marvellous things, they truly believed themselves to be in paradise. And these damsels were always with them in songs and great entertainments; they received everything they asked for, so that they would never have left that garden of their own will. And the Old Man maintained a good and rich court so that those men of the mountains believed that it was really paradise as they had been told.

And when he wished to send one of these young men on a mission, he would give them the drink to make them sleep and have them carried from the garden to his own palace. When they awoke and found themselves in that place they were astonished, and very sad that they were no longer in paradise. They were taken immediately to the Old Man, and kneeled before him in the belief that he was a great prophet. He would then ask them whence they came, and they would reply 'From paradise', and tell him of all the things they had found there and their wish to return. When the Old Man wished to have someone assassinated, he would choose the one he considered strongest and have him do the killing. They did it willingly in order to return into paradise: if they survived they would return to their lord; if they were captured they wished to die, believing that they would go to paradise.

And when the Old Man wished to kill someone, he would take him and say: 'Go and do this thing. I do this because I want to make you return to paradise'. And the assassins go and perform the deed willingly. In this way no man who the Old Man has decided to kill can escape, and it is said that more than one king pays tribute to him in fear of his life. [6]

The essential elements of the Assassin legend, the garden of paradise, use of hashish and blind obedience of the *fida'i* appear in Marco Polo's account, and it does conform to the Syrian versions. The narrator in fact tells us that Marco Polo himself had the story from 'several men'. In fact, in a country where oral history is notoriously unreliable and subject to change as new rulers appear, local sources are less likely to have been precise than the western sources concerning the Assassins in Syria. It is also likely that in a Genoese prison at the end of the thirteenth century there were prisoners who had heard of the Assassins in the Italian trading communities of the Latin East. However, this version is usually taken to be a melange of local knowledge and some generally accepted notions about the Assassins that Marco Polo may have heard before his journey, or even after it. It is the best known account, and contains those aspects of the Assassin legend which came to be most closely identified with them: the vision of paradise and the death leap.

The garden of paradise

The idea of paradise as a place of rest and refreshment in which the righteous live in the presence of God appears in Judaism and thence in both Christianity and Islam. It is interesting in the context of the Assassins that the word itself is said to derive from Old Persian *pairidaeze,* meaning an enclosed area, usually a royal park or pleasure garden, although some derive the word more simply from the Persian *firdaws* or garden. Whichever is the case, the origin is undoubtedly Persian.

Furthermore, it was in Islam that the idea of paradise received its most explicit descriptions of a garden in which man would be able to enjoy his spiritual and physical desires. In this case, the transference of an idea of a vision of paradise before going to one's death seems to be an extension of orthodox Islam rather than a new feature of Isma'ilism. Even the Christian topographical location of paradise as Eden placed the original 'garden' squarely within the realms of Islam — in the north of Mesopotamia near the confluence of the Tigris and the Euphrates rivers.

The Koran refers to paradise in terms that are reminiscent of the Judaic or Christian garden. The abode of the just is called the Garden, *al-janna,* often described as a Garden through which rivers flow but also as the 'Garden of Eden' or the 'Garden of delight'. Curiously, in view of Moslem prohibition of alcohol and the ambiguous accounts concerning the Assassins on this matter, these fortunate blessed recline on couches, eat fruit and have wine served to them 'by ever-youthful boys'. In addition, the milk, honey and springs of the Christian paradise are also present. But the most important aspect is that they 'experience forgiveness, peace and the satisfaction of the soul in God'.[7]

From the beginning of Moslem history, the locality of the garden in which God had placed Adam and Eve aroused discussion and controversy. The Mutazili heretics propounded, in accordance with biblical tradition, the view that Adam and Eve had been expelled by God from the highest mountain in the East. The description of this version of paradise was made popular through its inclusion in the *Rasa'il Ikhwan al-Safa* of the Brethren of Sincerity. We have seen that there were striking general similarities between their ideas and Assassin doctrine, and that both Hasan-i Sabbah and Sinan were influenced by their thought. It is especially interesting to note the precise parallels in the concept of paradise. In one of the epistles of the Brethren of Sincerity earthly paradise is described as follows:

Lying on the summit of the Mountain of the Hyacinth, which no human being may ascend, paradise was a garden of the East; a soft breeze blew day and night, winter and summer, over its perfumed ground. The garden was well watered by streams and shaded by lofty trees; it was full of luscious fruit, of sweet-smelling plants, of flowers of different kinds; harmless animals lived there and birds of song . . .[8]

The terms used here are evidently close to the western descriptions of the Assassin garden, whether it be on Alamut or in the Syrian castles, with the streams, luscious fruit, sweet-smelling flowers and birds.

Yet a more elaborate description of paradise was written by the Arab writer Shakir ibn Muslim of Orihuela, who lived about 1136. This extraordinary passage, originally written in rhymed verse, begins by describing the journey of the souls through hell and purgatory across the plain that leads them to paradise; as they approach, a perfume-laden breeze brings comfort to them. At this point the author's fantasy is given full reign:

At the gate of paradise stand two mighty trees, lovelier than any ever seen on earth. Their fragrance, the richness of their foliage, the beauty of their blossom, the perfume of their fruit, the lustre of their leaves — nothing could ever surpass. The birds on their branches sing in sweet harmony with the rustling of the leaves . . . at the foot of either tree there springs a fountain of the purest water, clearer than beryl, cooler and whiter than freshly melted snow . . .[9]

In his study of Islamic influences on Dante, Palacios demonstrated that this most complete and classical form of the description of paradise, of which a very brief passage is quoted here, is so close to Dante's description in his *Divine Comedy* that its derivation is obvious.[10] In addition, the spiritual interpretation which Dante gives to the garden, and Dante's meeting with Beatrice in it, also have Islamic traditions behind them. From the point of view of a study of the Assassins, it is worth noting that these influences on Dante were operating at a time when our major Christian sources for the story of the Assassins were writing. We know that great theologians such as Raymond Lull and Raymond Martin, writing in the same period, quoted and were influenced by Moslem concepts of paradise and divine bliss.[11] Thus, while it cannot be proved, it is not at all unlikely that the same literary influences were at work on authors such as Joinville, William of Tyre, Marco Polo and Odoric of Pordenone.

That Hasan-i Sabbah and other early Assassin Masters had gardens seems likely since the garden is such an important part of Persian noble life and of mysticism. The water channels and meticulous care to ensure regular water supplies at Assassin castles echo the care which Persian and Arab villages and country houses today give to the presence of running water. So the legend of the garden in which Assassins were taken probably has its origins in fact. But it seems certain that the elaborations in western descriptions derive from the introduction of a wider concept of the garden as paradise into the Assassin legend. The vivid fantasies of writers like Shakir ibn Muslim are extremely attractive, and it is easy to see how the inclusion of similar passages enriched the accounts of something which, it must be remembered, the western authors had never actually seen.

The death leap

One of the other aspects recurrent in the western chronicles is the

Assassin 'death leap' ordered by various Grand Masters in Syria in order to show off the discipline and absolute obedience of their *fida'i*. This fanatical loyalty was noted by most of the later chroniclers and travellers. Arnold of Lubeck reported that the Assassins were so enchanted by the magical arts of their Master that they revered him as God and threw themselves from high walls, at his command. [12] He admits that his account will seem ridiculous, but adds that many reliable witnesses have seen it happen. Yet the most celebrated account of this spectacular demonstration of obedience comes from the visit of Count Henry of Champagne to the successor of Sinan in 1194.

Immediately after the death of Saladin in 1193, the crusading kingdom was threatened by Armenian attacks in the Principality of Antioch. The following year Count Henry of Champagne, nephew of Richard I of England and titular King of Jerusalem, travelled northwards in order to assist the defence of Antioch. His route necessarily passed through the Assassin state, where he was met by ambassadors sent by Sinan's successors. The Old Man sent apologies for the recent murder of Conrad of Montferrat and invited Henry to visit him at the castle of al-Kahf in the Nosairi Mountains.

One day Henry was walking in the grounds of the castle with Sinan's successor. He remarked to Henry that he believed no Christians were as obedient to their prince as his *fida'i* were to him, and in order to demonstrate the truth of his statement made a sign to some youths sitting at the top of a high tower. Two of them instantly jumped to their deaths on the rocks below, and the Old Man offered to repeat this spectacle by ordering the others to follow suit. But Henry agreed that they were far more obedient than Christian soldiers, and said that it was not necessary to repeat the demonstration. [13]

To sacrifice their lives was perceived as performance of duty, and was therefore an honour. We must remember that the *fida'i* expected entry to paradise from these 'shows' just as much as from a suicide mission. It seems, too, that the families of the *fida'i* considered it an honour that a son should die in this way. On one occasion, a mother cut off her hair and blackened her face to show the shame she felt when her son actually returned from a dangerous mission in which his colleagues had died. [14]

This part of the legend was in many ways more powerful in establishing the Assassins' name than the act of murder. Such blind and total obedience was sinister, and could only be explained by means of some enchantment. It fired the imagination as few other ideas could, since it probably appeared to come from some fantastic tale of oriental princes that could never be equalled in Europe. Yet it might also tell us something about the western attitude to obedience, and the ease with which a man might change loyalties. It was the absoluteness of the death leap that appealed to the western imagination, where the Moslem concept of absoluteness was alien.

The story is well-attested, and repeated by many authors. We may therefore assume that it is based upon factual occurrences, although it would appear a waste of good manpower at a time when the Assassins were not particularly strong. It is, however, one of the most revealing and durable aspects of the Assassin legend. We have seen that one use of the word 'assassin' by Dante was in this context of obedience. It was also in this sense that the word appears in contemporary poems by the troubadours. One states that his love 'has him more fully in her power than the Old Man has his Assassins', while another assures his lady that 'I am your Assassin, who hopes to win paradise through doing your commands'.[15] Thus the death leap, and its rich and impressive testimony to *fida'i* loyalty and obedience, is one of the most important aspects of the contemporary legend of the Assassins.

The Assassins were literally fantastic, oriental and incomprehensible in their faith and loyalty. It is not surprising that these dramatic aspects of their sect should be emphasized and become the basis of western ideas about them. The image of the Assassins was indelibly fixed in the collective imagination by these early accounts to such an extent that even serious historians were swayed by them until recently.

THE HISTORIOGRAPHY
OF THE ASSASSINS

THE earliest accounts of Assassin history were disseminated in manuscript until the sixteenth century. Then published accounts slowly became available as the most celebrated chronicles were published. But the first modern work, and first ever entire book, dedicated to the history of the Assassins was the *Traicte de L'Origine des Anciens Assasins porte-couteaux,* by Denis Lebey de Batilly. That book also carried the subtitle: 'With examples of their attempts and homicides against certain kings, princes and lords of Christianity'. It was a small volume of sixty-four pages, published at Lyon in 1604.

Beginnings of a modern historical tradition

Lebey de Batilly was a high royal official, Master of Petitions at the Royal Palace and for the Kingdom of Navarre, and President of the Court at Metz delegated by Henry IV of France (reigned 1594–1610). It is very much from this point of view that his short book is written, with obvious interest in and concern for the idea of political assassination.

France was at that time recovering from a period of anarchy which followed the assassination of Henry III, who had been stabbed to death by a fanatical Jacobin friar in 1589. Before his coronation as King of France, Henry IV had become the Protestant leader of the French Wars of Religion, but abjured the Protestant faith and became King in 1594. The following year he forced the Spanish out of Paris and declared war on Philip I of Spain. It was not until 1598 that Henry IV eventually brought the Wars of Religion to an end. But in that period of violence and religious fanaticism, it was only to be expected that several murder attempts were made against Henry IV. On one of these attempts, in 1594, he had been badly wounded with a dagger. It was presumably this concern with current events and the very urgent problem of contemporary political assassination that led Lebey de Batilly to his interest in the word 'assassin' and its origins.

The book consists of a direct and fairly straightforward survey of the major European medieval authors, especially William of Tyre, Jacques de Vitry and Joinville. Following the line of argument in Chapter 10, it is interesting to see his insistence on and repetition of the concept of an earthly paradise: he stresses the abundance of 'pleasant fruits', perfumed flowers, beautiful damsels and the streams of wine, milk and honey[1]. The only unusual note is his history of the origins of the Assassins, in which he describes them as deriving from a pre-Mohammadan sect and to be already in existence at the time of Alexander the Great. The same lack of historical perspective influences his comments about the founder of the sect, from whom the magical powers that its leaders possess derive. He names him as Aloadin, the name that Marco Polo uses referring to the penultimate Master of Alamut Ala-ad-Din Muhammad, but describes him as the 'first abbot of Islam' and companion of Mohammad.[2] Throughout the book he refers to the Old Man as 'Le Sarrazin'.

But even with these mistakes and some confusion, this little book announces itself as distinctly 'modern' in comparison with the earlier chronicles in the extent to which Lebey de Batilly allows himself speculative observations and considerations which reveal original insights into the Assassins. One section in which this new attitude is apparent is that in which he discusses the 'qualities and affections' of the Assassins with regard to murder. Whenever this 'Prince of the Beduins' rode in the countryside he always had a man in front of him carrying a bag with his weapons. This man has his sleeves full of knives, and shouted to everyone to flee before the man who brought the death of kings in his hands. In the same paragraph he makes a curious reference to the borders between the Assassin state and its Christian neighbours: the milestones marking this frontier are said to be shaped like knives.[3]

The most interesting part of his book comes, however, after he has traced the history of the Assassins and named some of the main victims of the sect in Syria. Here the real purpose of his research and writing becomes apparent. It will be left to the reader, he says, to compare the history of the Assassins with the events of his own time and the miserable effects which men have had to suffer for some time. For unfortunately there exist even in his day religions with 'assassins porte couteaux' quite as bad as those medieval fanatics who, encouraged by another 'Old Man of the Mountains', are prepared to kill kings and princes who do not happen to belong to the same sect.[4] That Lebey de Batilly had correctly identified a contemporary evil is shown by the ironical fact that his own royal patron Henry IV was himself assassinated seven years later. In 1610, a religious fanatic worthy in style and technique of the best *fida'i* stabbed him to death with a long knife while the King was driving through Paris in his coach.

The motivation behind Lebey de Batilly's work clearly belongs to the turn of the sixteenth and seventeenth centuries, and employs features that were only possible after an important change in historical writing, when speculation and author's insights became a valid part of the historian's task. For the rest, in order to understand Lebey de Batilly's contemporary point of view in the France of 1603, it will be sufficient for an English reader to consider the plot against Queen Elizabeth I in 1601, and the obsession with violent death, blood and murder in the contemporary theatre — revenge tragedies and the obvious public delight in the political murders at the heart of such Shakespearean plays as *Richard III*.

Scholarly reassessment of the Assassins

The placing of the Assassins in their correct historical perspective began with the publication of the *Bibliotèque Orientale* by Bartholomé d'Herbelot in 1697. This was a four volume encyclopedia of current western knowledge about the history, religion and literature of Islam, in which eastern sources were used in addition to the crusading chroniclers. The article on the Isma'ilis showed convincingly how they were a dissident sect of Islam, and explained how Isma'ili leaders claimed to be imams deriving through Isma'il ibn Ja'far from Ali, and ultimately from Muhammad himself. This 'encyclopedia' of the current state of knowledge about Islam set the way for future studies.[5]

It was followed by a century of relative inactivity on the part of European scholars and orientalists. In 1751, M. Falconnet wrote a *Dissertation sur les Assassins* which again ran through the main medieval western sources in exemplary manner but added nothing essentially new. He does make one ironic observation revealing his continuation of Lebey de Batilly's values, when he states, after a probably false letter in which Sinan referred to himself as 'Simplicitas' that the Assassins' simplicity consisted in the inhuman killing of their enemies. He also believed that the Assassins carried out murders for money on commission for any client.[6] The English historian Gibbon said in *Decline and Fall of the Roman Empire,* published 1776–88, that all that could be learned of the Assassins at that time was 'poured from the copious, and even profuse, erudition' of Falconnet. Gibbon himself refers to the Assassins as 'odious sectaries', and was both of his time and loyal to the tradition in stating that their extirpation by Hulegu 'may be considered as a service to mankind'.[7]

Interest in the Assassins, the history of assassination and the concept of political murder seem once again to have been aroused by relevant historical events. Just as in a period of political turmoil like the early seventeenth century an inquiring mind such as that of Lebey de Batilly looked into the history of the sect, so the consequences of the French Revolution in 1789 stimulated new interest at the beginning of the nineteenth century.

Yet up to that moment neither the etymology of the name of the sect nor the full extent of their activities had been explained satisfactorily. A curious instance of the possible disputes concerning the origin of the name, and consequent European use of the verb 'assassinate' by then in common usage, came with the article written by Simone Assemani, a professor of oriental languages at the University of Padova. In an article published in an obscure scholarly review in 1806 Assemani sought to show how the sect 'vulgarly known as the assassini' should in fact be called 'la setta Assissana' or Assissan sect.

Assemani once again covers the medieval sources, concentrating on Benjamin of Tudela, William of Tyre and Joinville. Then he presents a more original review of the eastern authors, who, he argues, 'knew that people much better than the Franks did'.[8] He then considers the versions of their name found in oriental sources, such as Isma'ili, Batini, Maleheda (from the Persian for 'heretic') and offers a better interpretation of the title and significance of the 'Old Man of the Mountains' as 'Lord of the mountainous part of Persia'.[9] After studying the series of Grand Masters of Alamut as reported by Arab historians, he correctly repeats that the European authors know nothing of the religious doctrines of the Assassins. [10]

Then Assemani comes to the most curious part of his argument with a hypothesis which was soon to be dismissed by another oriental scholar with even greater authority. He relates that whilst in Syria he had heard Isma'ilis who visited Tripoli from their mountain fastness use the phrase 'Assissani la moslem vala nasrani', which means that the 'Assissano is neither a Moslem nor a Christian'. He argues that the historians of the crusades accidentally transposed the two vowels 'i' and 'a' so that Assissani was written in the incorrect form Assassini. He argues that the word 'assissani' derives from Arabic assissath, meaning fortress or strong and secure place. Thus 'assissani' means men who live in mountainous and strong places. Assemani concludes sophistically that we can imagine how convenient it was for the Assassins that no one understood their real name as the result of these false etymologies. [11]

Within three years of the publication of Assemani's article, however, appeared the 'Mémoire sur la Dynastie des Assassins et sur l'origine de leur nom', which the French orientalist, Silvestre De Sacy, read to the Institut de France on 19 May 1809. This memoir, described by Lewis as a 'landmark in Assassin studies', [12] used Arabic manuscript sources from the Bibliotèque Nationale in Paris which had never been studied in this context. He states explicitly at the outset that his aim is to fill in the gaps left in the account by a non-orientalist, Falconnet. He then proceeds to give an accurate account of the origins of the Isma'ilis, discussing the Carmathians and other pre-Assassin sects. But De Sacy shows himself to be very much a man of his time in observing during his discussion of the use of hashish that even Napoleon found it necessary to ban the sale and use of the drug while he was in Egypt.

De Sacy's most important achievement was to provide a definitive answer to the etymological problem of the word 'assassin'. Having made a critical analysis of the sources for the history of the Assassins, he demonstrated that the name derived from the Arabic hashish and went on to explain how variant forms appearing in crusading texts (e.g. Assassini, Assissini, Heyssisini and Joinville's Hausaci) were in fact based upon the same word given in its alternative Arabic forms of 'hashishi' and 'hashshash'. He provided quotations from Arabic texts as evidence, although it has been shown that he was not entirely correct since the latter form has never been satisfactorily verified.[13] Nevertheless, excluding this erroneous hypothesis, De Sacy deserves credit for resolving the problem of etymology and opening the way for more precise studies. From that moment there could be no serious doubt that the word is based on the Arabic 'haschischi' and the plural form 'haschischin'.[14] Nevertheless, this etymology was not universally received: we find Colonel Monteith in the account of his visit to Alamut twenty-five years later explaining the word 'Assassin' as deriving from the 'corruption of Hassain, one of their most celebrated leaders'.[15]

The first major book on the Assassins

This renewed interest in turn stimulated the second entire book devoted to the Assassins, the *Geschichte der Assassinen* by Joseph von Hammer-Purgstall, which appeared in Stuttgart in 1818. It was published in Paris in 1833, and in London in 1835. This work, two-hundred-and-forty pages in the English translation, was far more complete than that of Lebey de Batilly. But, unfortunately, in view of its enormous influence — it was still being cited by Freya Stark as the most authoritative history of the Assassins in 1933 — it was also more biased.

Hammer-Purgstall has been called by a modern writer on the Assassins 'leisured, industrious, but scarcely profound',[16] although he was a distinguished orientalist with dozens of publications to his name. The fact is that, like his immediate predecessors, the historical period and political ideas of the author are vital in understanding his work. Hammer-Purgstall wrote his history from the perspective of a cyclical theory of history, as he himself states on the first page of his argument, with a precise polemical and political purpose. Towards the end of his book, he specifies what he describes as his twin objective: beyond 'exhuming' rare and often disdained historical information from oriental literature he wished to 'show the disastrous influence of secret societies on weak governments'.[17]

Once again the Assassins served as fuel for a historian's argument as he manipulated their story in terms of a polemic against the danger of secret societies. He stresses that his book should be read as a warning 'against the pernicious influence of secret societies . . . and . . . the dreadful prostitution of religion to the horrors of unbridled ambition'.[18] The Assassins, with little concern for the philosophical writings of such as Hasan-i Sabbah and their elaborate doctrines, were simply:

... a union of impostors and dupes which, under the mask of a more austere creed and severer morals, undermined all religion and morality; that order of murderers, beneath whose daggers the lords of nations fell; all powerful, because, for the space of three centuries, they were universally dreaded, until the den of ruffians fell with the khaliphate, to whom, as the centre of spiritual and temporal power, it had at the outset sworn destruction, and by whose ruins it was itself overwhelmed.[19]

This is a brilliant *melange* of accurate historical knowledge and heavily charged emotional language. In the course of his argument throughout the book he uses such prejudiced ridicule-inviting phrases as 'their hideous doctrine',[20] their 'impious and immoral doctrine'[21] and refers to the Assassins as 'the criminal propagators of atheism'.[22] Hasan-i Sabbah is dismissed as a 'terrible instrument of Providence, a scourage of weak sovereigns like the plague of war'.[23] These excesses are in strange disaccord with the author's own emphasis on the 'sacred duty' of the historian to be impartial.[24]

He argues that the Assassins had rules and structures which associate them with other powerful secret societies: initiation into a hierarchy consisting of master, companion and apprentice; a public doctrine with a second, secret doctrine: passive obedience. These aspects meant that even after their suppression these 'secret societies' could continue to exert influence, since only the public aspect was exterminated. But this polemic is rendered to the modern reader at the very least eccentric by his choice of European secret societies such as the Templars and the Jesuits,[25] especially since he had earlier compared these societies with brigands and pirates.[26]

The influence of Hammer-Purgstall's book was immense and long, and fuelled two fundamental misconceptions about the Assassins: first, it linked the Templars and Templar-derived beliefs indissolubly with the Assassins; second, in connection with the first, it suggested an occult or magical basis to Assassin doctrine and activity. This second aspect will be examined in the next chapter.

The essential fact in common between the Assassins and the Templars, according to Hammer-Purgstall, is that both constitute an order which carries out a political interpretation of their doctrines. Just as the Templars in their secret doctrines rejected the cross, so did the Assassins reject the fundamental tenets of Islam. Both 'orders' had as their basic rule for expansion the acquisition of fortresses in order to maintain the people around them in subjection.[27] This comparison appears as a leitmotiv throughout the book, and yet there is little evidence adduced by Hammer-Purgstall for such a comparison: the only concrete evidence he offers is that the Assassins were said to wear a white mantle and red headbands, while the Templars wore a white mantle with a red cross. The assertion made in the same passage that the two orders had the same secret rules is extremely evocative, but unprovable since there is no evidence at all of the Assassins having had a secret rule.[28]

Hammer-Purgstall's book was evidently, for all its scholarly pretensions and claims of impartiality, as much a tract for its time as its predecessors. It was not until a full century later that historians began to approach the history of the Assassins without bias and polemical preconceptions.

The twentieth century

The publication of original sources, Arabic manuscripts and other important materials from about the middle of the nineteenth century onwards has made research into the history of the Isma'ilis generally and the Assassins in particular a much more feasible task. The very secrecy of Isma'ilism and hiding away of crucial documents, together with frequent refusal to allow access to materials in possession of various branches of the sect, had always made the historian's task difficult. But during the course of the nineteenth century it was realized how many members of the sect existed throughout the world, especially in Syria and India. The discovery of a new leader in the person of the Aga Khan, which we shall review in the last chapter of this survey, served to galvanize attention and leave Isma'ilis, as it were, to 'come out'. Their doctrines have received scholarly analysis, and often publication, while in London today there is an 'Institute of Isma'ili Studies'.

Four historians in particular have forwarded the study of the Assassins in this century: one Frenchman, one Russian, one

Englishman and one American, upon whose work any work — whether scholarly analysis or general survey such as this — will necessarily be indebted for the forseeable future. They may be roughly divided into two groups: those who vehemently deny the use of the epithet 'Assassins' attributed to the Isma'ilis, and those who refer to the Assassins as Assassins, although the terminological dispute (Nizaris, Isma'ilis, Assassins, Khojas, Bohras and Imamites) is far deeper than such a simplified distinction.

The first of these scholars was a Russian, W. Ivanow, who published a series of at least thirty books and articles over a period of some forty years. These works have introduced much new light on Isma'ili doctrines and history, but Ivanow has often published or quoted texts which other scholars have not been able to see, and his translations have often been dubious in their precision. [29] Furthermore, he has often been unnecessarily scathing in his comments on western authors, such as Freya Stark, whose descriptions of Alamut and the Assassins in general he dismissed — although her account published in the same issue of the *Journal of the Royal Society of Geography* in 1931 is remarkably similar and in no way less accurate. Nevertheless, Ivanow's work and astonishing singlemindedness in hunting down texts stand at the centre of modern studies of the Isma'ilis.

Henry Corbin was a French scholar who spent long periods of his life in Turkey, Syria, Egypt and Iran. He was for twenty years a director of studies at the Ecole Pratique des Hautes Etudes in Paris and director of the collection of Persian and Arabic texts known as the Bibliotèque Iranienne in Tehran. His interest in Isma'ilism departed from a philosophical point of view and his pioneering work was in the ideas and doctrines of the Isma'ilis. His *Trilogie Ismaélienne* (1961) and *Cyclical Time and Isma'ili Gnosis* (1983) are of fundamental importance in understanding the doctrines of the Isma'ilis.

This concern with the philosophical ideas of the Isma'ilis led Henry Corbin to give short thrift to those who continued to refer to them as the 'Assassins'. An example of this insistence occurred during an international conference on 'Persia in the Middle Ages' at Rome in 1971. During the discussion following the reading of a paper by Bernard Lewis, Corbin asked — referring to himself as an 'ismaélologue' — how long they would be imprisoned by habits inherited from the time of the crusaders. He continued as follows:

For too long we have, whenever encountering the word "Isma'ili" in a text, followed the habit of translating it simply as "assassin". Perhaps one thereby achieves a sensational effect, but this effect is disastrous . . . I believe that even for the Syrian Isma'ilians, and not only for those in Persia, we must give up this terminology. [30]

Notwithstanding this plea, however, outside the world of specialist historians it is usual to refer to the Isma'ilis of both Syria and Persia as Assassins, and no amount of special pleading is likely to change this state of affairs.

Marshall G. S. Hodgson's book *The Order of the Assassins,* published at the Hague in 1955, represents the modern landmark in Assassins' studies that De Sacy's study represented in 1809. It is, to date, the most accurate and complete study of the sect known as the Assassins — although Hodgson refers to them more precisely as the Nizari Isma'ilis. Nearly three-hundred pages of closely reasoned argument based upon all the known western and eastern sources make a mark which no future author will be able to avoid. The basis of his argument, however, rests upon a solid discussion of Isma'ili doctrines that is often technical and requires a good background in Islamic history and philosophy. He also skims over, probably deliberately, some of the issues that are most likely to be of interest to a general reader and provides little topographical detail — although the maps and charts provided are exemplary.

Bernard Lewis has devoted an entire academic career to what he himself refers to as Assassin studies. He first prepared the way with an early study of Isma'ili origins in 1940, and has since provided a series of specialized articles on many aspects of the Assassins' history with a particular concentration on the Syrian Assassins. His short book aimed for a less specialist readership than his many articles. *The Assassins: A Radical Sect in Islam,* was originally published in 1967. On the basis of his scholarly work Professor Lewis wrote a fascinating account which, unlike Hodgson's work, did discuss the less 'academic' areas of interest concerning the Assassins. However, it does presuppose some knowledge of Islamic history and concentrates on the Syrian history. The bibliography contained in the notes to this work constitutes one of the most useful tools to any modern reader in Assassin history, and he himself has continued to publish further articles since that book.

With such excellent studies available for consultation, it should be easy to avoid the pitfalls and clichés of the history of the Assassins. Yet this is not the case: the legends persist and their popular acceptance seems not to have changed at all. We shall see in the following chapter how connections with the Templars and Freemasons have aroused speculation which has taken on a life of its own, irrespective of evidence to the contrary. The story of the Assassins has been adopted for particular purposes in the past, notably by Lebey de Batilly and Hammer-Purgstall, and continues to be used in this way today. It seems that the images and fantasies of medieval authors such as Marco Polo created a vision which modern historical research can do nothing to dispel.

THE ASSASSINS
AND THE OCCULT

A SENSE of the supernatural pervades many of the early accounts of
the Assassins, especially the anecdotes which Abu Firas reports in his
hagiographical version of Sinan's life. Works on sciences nowadays
considered occult, such as alchemy, formed an important part of the
Neoplatonic school which provided so many of the ideas germane
to the creation of Isma'ili doctrine. Studies in alchemy had been
translated from Greek to Coptic texts as early as the eighth century
under the Umayyads at Baghdad.[1] The Umayyad prince Khalid b.
Yazid studied alchemy with a monk named Marianus, and composed
three treatises on occult science.[2] Sufis such as al-Husayn b. Mansur,
the 'wool carder', admired by many Isma'ilis, and Sufi poets with
Isma'ili affiliations such as Attar, were spoken of as 'conjurors' and
'alchemists' and were thought to be in league with the Carmathians.[3]
The epistles of the 'Brethren of Purity' from whom many ideas of
Isma'ili doctrine derive, included among the 'mundane' studies of
the aspiring philosopher that he should have completed *before*
approaching the *Rasa'il* the science of omens and portents, and the
science of magic, amulets, alchemy and legerdemain.[4]

At least part of the veneration of Sinan was based on his well-attested
powers of telepathy and clairvoyance, such as the cases reported by
Abu Firas of him answering questions *thought* outside his window.[5]
Hasan-i Sabbah himself was renowned in his own day as an alchemist.
That the Assassins engaged in what would now be described as occult
practices seems therefore to be beyond doubt. The 'sciences' of alchemy
and astrology were then part of philosophical studies. But the problem
is that we have no concrete evidence, and no examples of their occult
activities. None of the historical records provides us with instances
of occult power, and even the supposed supernatural events in the

life of Sinan are quite likely to have been invented by his biographer.

The Hammer-Purgstall connection

As we have seen in the previous chapter, it was Hammer-Purgstall who made the decisive connection between the Assassins and the occult. The method was simple, and persuasive. From generic statements of the nature that 'it is likely' that through the influence of the crusades the spirit of the East is reflected in the West, which is obviously true to a certain extent but impossible to pin down, he moved to much wilder and unsubstantiated assertions which were then accepted by the reader without question. The very insistence on his impartiality and the historian's sacred duty to maintain it, inspire confidence in whatever he says.

He begins by presenting the history of the Isma'ilis in a light which reflects his notion of the Assassins as a 'secret society' in a very modern sense. The precise historical and oriental knowledge at his disposal increases this effect for readers unable to control the facts. He explains that Abdullah, the occultist from Basrah who developed the allegorical interpretation of the Koran in the ninth century, saw how dangerous it was to attack openly the dominant religion of his time and therefore resolved to 'undermine secretly that which he could not attack openly'. That is why — and here we move into the zone of emotional language — he enveloped the subversive doctrines he was evolving in 'the shadow of mystery'. The next step is to assert that Abdullah at that stage decided to subvert *all* religion and replace it with a doctrine based upon seven grades inspired by the example of Pythagoras and the Indians.[6]

But the key to the whole argument concerning the occult, and the passage to which all discussion of magical practices by later writers on Assassins can be traced, is a single extraordinary paragraph. Beginning his history of Hasan-i Sabbah after a lengthy introduction, he starts from the quite unexpected and tangential point of ancient Egypt. In a long digression he refers to the practices of the priests of ancient Egypt, whose doctrines were hidden in symbols and hieroglyphs. Then he makes the surprising assertion that these doctrines and secrets were passed on to the Isma'ilis in the Middle Ages. The entire corpus of occult practices and secrets of the ancient

Egyptian priests, such as alchemy, rhabdomancy, the search for the philosopher's stone and the use of talismans, were passed on from the ancient 'Academy of Heliopolis' to the Isma'ili 'House of Science' in Fatimid Cairo.[7]

Then, in the paragraph mentioned above, comes the series of assertions which underpin any modern theory of the occult concerning the Assassins. Hammer-Purgstall asserts that in 1004 Hakim founded the *Lodge* of Cairo under the Fatimids in order to preserve these 'secrets' — although he does not specify what they were. From that moment the Isma'ili Chief *Da'i* was always resident in Cairo, and sent out *da'is* to propagate these secret doctrines throughout the world. It was here that Hasan-i Sabbah studied during his brief residence in Cairo.[8] The use of such emotive phrases as 'the immoral mysteries of the Isma'ilites[9] serves to increase the aura of certainty that Hammer-Purgstall provides merely by suggestion. But above all this introduction of masonic terminology into a completely alien context paved the way for future speculative writers, who never bothered to verify Hammer-Purgstall's assertion and accepted it on his authority as an orientalist.

Now it remains to add this occult connection to the association with the Templars, but not so much with the historical Templars as with the various 'Templarist' orders which flourished in Germany in the late eighteenth century, and whose successors survive today in the masonic orders of 'The Knights Templar' and 'The Knights Templar Priests'.

Peter Partner has shown how the 'forces of unreason' caused many men at the end of the eighteenth century to take refuge in supposed hidden knowledge from the reduced limits which reason had imposed upon them.[10] This flight from reason led to the foundation of numerous secret societies in that period, especially in Germany. There, forms of 'Templarism' within the masonic movement were of great importance, and nearly took over the entire movement. Its members were often men who tended towards aristocratic exclusiveness and 'fanatical mystery-mongering' and were deeply affected by 'alchemical and occult practice'.[11] It was then that the search for material gains led these 'Templarists' to look for the hidden treasures that the Templars were supposed to have left behind after their dissolution. The 'Strict Templar Observance' for many years dominated German masonry, and new Templar orders were invented which drew on ideas from

Persia, Assyria and Egypt — including the controversial Baphomet figure. All these groups were to become part of a general conspiracy theory at the time of the French Revolution.

It was widely believed, and argued in books, that French masonic lodges had been behind the Revolution, and consequently action was taken against oath-taking and secret societies — including the 1799 'Unlawful Societies Act' in Britain. [12] A French political radical and freemason called Nicholas de Bonneville had claimed that the Jesuits were the secret inspirers and organizers of masonic Templarism. Another author, Louis Cadet de Gassicourt, propagated an even more fantastic theory in a book published in 1796 called *Le Tombeau de Jacques de Molay.* He argued that in a long chain of secret anarchist conspirators, which had culminated with the storming of the Bastille, the essential link had been the Templars, whose 'evil beginnings stretched back to the Old Man of the Mountains in medieval Syria'. [13]

Ironically, it was a Jesuit scholar who established a common parentage for these wildly disparate notions in a book written *against* the occultists. In his *Mémoires pour servir à l'histoire du Jacobinisme* published in three volumes from 1797 to 1798, Barruel derived all evils from Mani and the Manicheans and demonstrated the existence of a continuous historical conspiracy. In Peter Partner's words:

In the minds of Barruel and Cadet de Gassicourt there was an invincible belief in a continuous historical conspiracy, through which anarchist beliefs had passed from the medieval heretics in the west and the Assassins in the east to the Templars, and thence through the four Templar lodges which were set up after the death of Jacques de Molay in 1314. [14]

All revolutionaries and murderers since then had been part of a single 'Templar' society — including Cromwell, the murderer of Henry IV of France, conspirators in Portugal, Brazil and Sweden, and of course Robespierre and Danton.

Now we can understand Hammer-Purgstall's twin obsession with the Templars and the Jesuits. Could it be that the works of Cadet de Gassicourt and Augustin de Barruel directly inspired the orientalist to look into the history of Assassins? Whether that is the case or not, Hammer-Purgstall's book had a long and perfectly comprehensible pedigree. His reduction of Isma'ili doctrine at the last grade of initiation to a contemptuous 'believe nothing, dare all' demonstrates the thesis that he set out to demonstrate with all his specialized learning.

Furthermore, we can understand his part in the series of writers about the Assassins who perceived the sect from a particular historical perspective. Since the murders of Henry III and IV of France belong to the same grand conspiracy, Hammer-Purgstall clearly fits into the historiographical tradition which began with Lebey de Batilly.

But the damage had been done. Thenceforth, the greatest and most authoritative study of the Assassins by common consent — and in the absence of any alternative until the publication of Marshall Hodgson's study in 1955 — had made the connection between the Assassins and the occult.

The Assassins and modern occultists

When the Assassins do appear in the context of modern studies of the occult or of magic, it is usually as the result of the supposed connection with the Templars.

In a book entitled *Masonry and Medieval Mysticism: Traces of a Hidden Tradition,* for example, assumptions are made beyond the simple connection that Hammer-Purgstall attempted to prove. It is argued that the Templars took over the possessions of the Old Man of the Mountains completely, because they had perceived the *'supernatural courage'* of the Assassins. The *fida'i* were admitted into the Order of the Temple, and then the Templars themselves accepted the rules and institutions of the people they had just taken over. Apart from the unusual nature of this enterprise, this argument is followed by the remarkable and unsubstantiated assertion that 'Gauthier von Montbar was acquainted with these teachings, and transplanted them into Europe'. [15] There is really no basis in the contemporary accounts for such a supposition.

Similarly, a classical text like Maurice Bouisson's *Magic, Its Rites and History* seems to include the Assassins rather as if they ought to be there than as if they actually play an important part in his story. Whereas he adduces evidence to support his claims in other chapters, that on the 'The Grand Master of the Assassins' appears as an unnecessary interlude.

After a chapter on the devil, he suggests that we turn to the 'magic of the Near East' in the eleventh century, where there was an astonishing sect and a magician 'whose life has no need to be romanticized'.[16] Bouisson then uncritically relates the lift of Hasan-i Sabbah, including the story of the three school-friends. He tells the well-founded story of Hasan's sickness and conversion, and then how the young man left for Cairo.

Here, however, emotionally charged language and the vocabulary of freemasonry combine to give a new edge to the unsuspecting reader. Bouisson reveals his acceptance of the Hammer-Purgstall connection and even adds to it. For Hasan was initiated 'into the highest grade of the Ismaili Grand Lodge'. The account continues with some elaboration beyond his source:

In Cairo he began to take hashish. Made from the leaves of Indian hemp, it was either drunk as a liqueur, eaten in the form of sugared pastilles, or smoked. Hashish charmed the nights of the *fellahin* and of the *dahabiyah* rowers as well as those of great lords. The virtues of hashish were celebrated at length in the secret archives of the Grand Lodge for it heightened desire and courage, it multiplied the visions of the mystics and rendered insensitive to suffering and contemptuous of death the warriors who rushed, madly laughing, into the fray.[17]

References to hashish, grand lodges, madly laughing warriors and secret archives are muddled together to pass over the gap in our knowledge. The picture of Hasan-i Sabbah is quite different from that given even by his enemies Juvayni and Rashid al-Din: Juvayni especially pours contempt upon Hasan, but never doubts the austerity and asceticism of the Assassin leader. As for hashish, as we have seen there is no mention of that drug in connection with the Persian Assassins — especially in the library of Alamut ('the secret archives').

In fact, there is no argument at all here, or any illustration of exactly what the 'magical' power of Hasan-i Sabbah derived from. Any power that the historical Grand Master had is simply attributed to the conventional picture of the prospective Assassin being given a glimpse of the garden of paradise before being sent on a mission. On a personal level, Hasan is said to have owed his power to 'a profound knowledge of intoxicants and to an extraordinary hypnotic power', which, if there is any truth in the idea of 'the magnetism of his look' bending wills, would be more plausible if applied to Sinan.

The chapter ends on an even more fanciful note. Just as Lebey de Batilly three-hundred years before him, Bouisson reflects on the more recent outbreaks of terrorism in the Moslem world; without, as a matter of fact, recognizing that modern terrorism in its essentially random nature is quite different from specific assassination. He concludes with the statement that our laws were not made to deal with such as the *fida'i*, in which there is some truth, but undermines his own conclusion by the irrelevant statement that 'hashish and its little pipes are still sold in the *medinas* and the secret of Hassan Sabbah has not been lost'.[18] This odd non-sequitur is typical of arguments used to create magical associations with the Assassins.

Since this chapter is followed by one on alchemists, the reader is left with the suggestion that the Assassins lie half way between the devil and the alchemists. Yet it is difficult to see what this little chapter is doing in the book. It would be interesting to read a more accurate account of alchemism in Syria in the twelfth century, since Sinan has been more plausibly connected with the practice of that ancient art. These few examples will suffice to show the way in which the Hammer-Purgstall connection is uncritically accepted.

The occult in literature

Given the immense fascination and terror which the Assassins generated in the western imagination, it is strange that they have appeared so little in European literature. One curious instance is the romance entitled *The Assassins* which Shelley began dictating to his sister Mary on 25 August 1814 while they were staying at Brunen, on Lake Lucerne in Switzerland.[19] The work was never completed, and remains in fragmentary form.

The romance contains an endearing confusion between the facts of the Assassins and Shelley's imagination, in which the Assassins become a Christian sect which had escaped after the fall of Jerusalem to Saladin in 1187 and established themselves in a remote valley in Lebanon. Neither do his assassins have any of the qualities usually associated with the Islamic sect: they live an idyllic existence in a kind of perpetual bliss: 'They were already disembodied spirits: they were already the inhabitants of paradise'.[20] Shelley has evidently transposed the vision of paradise given to the assassin before setting out on his suicidal mission into the normal everyday living circumstances of his sect. The fact that this sect was Christian may be derived from a confusion with the Druzes, who in their remote and secret valleys in Lebanon have often been thought to preserve some of the original teachings of Christ.

The most interesting fact about this fragment derives from a piece of detective work by one of Shelley's biographers, Jean Overton Fuller. She demonstrated how an alternative idea of the magical spirit Ariel, who most scholars believe Shelley knew only through Shakespeare's *Tempest*, was actually derived from a legend connected with the Assassins. Thus the magical association of the Assassins came to have an unexpected resonance in English literature. In Shakespeare's play it was Ariel who managed the storm which caused the shipwreck at the beginning of the play.

Mary Shelley had been reading a book entitled *Le Vieux de la Montaigne*, published in 1799 in four volumes, in which the anonymous author claims to be translating an Arabic manuscript known as the 'story of Ariel'. Jean Overton Fuller demonstrates convincingly that the basis of Shelley's story derives from this tale of Ariel, although his own version dwells on the classic conflict between good and evil which reappears elsewhere in his work in the similar symbolic form of a contest between a snake and a vulture.[21]

In Shelley's unfinished story, a stranger enters the idyllic world of the Assassins. Desperately wounded, he is discovered by a young man while a serpent and a vulture await his death. The stranger is taken to the young man's home, where he observes children playing with a pet snake. Here the fragment ends, but it is noteworthy that the benign spirit these people had worshipped is described by Shelley as 'the delight that is bred among the solitary rocks'. He also states that 'no Assassin would submissively temporize with vice . . . His path through the wilderness of civilized society would be marked with the blood of the oppressor and the ruiner'.[22] This strange reversal of the current beliefs discussed above is curiously English and romantic. Yet there would seem to be justice in Jean Overton Fuller's claim that 'the meaning of the name Ariel becomes enormously enriched, in the context of Shelley's studies, when one realizes that the Ariel of this little known, but strangely magical, work was also known to him'.[23]

While the physical source for the version of paradise was, as Norman White has shown in his biography of Shelley,[24] the valleys near Lake Lucerne, the poetical inspiration was the magical tale of the magician known as the Old Man of the Mountain.

This demonstrates that Shelley's affinity for the name Ariel, and the magical powers associated with that spirit, derive from an unexpected and non-Shakespearean source. In an unusual way, and with several unconventional aspects, the story of the Old Man of the Mountains entered into English romantic literature as a trope for the occult. Although there was very little concern with the history of the Assassins, who were transformed into something far from the truth, the connection with Ariel in Shelley's poetical imagination remains fascinating. It adds a further element to the curious process of European assimilation and transformation of the story of the Assassins.

Were the Assassins occultists?

We have seen that at least the most celebrated leaders of the Assassin sect practised sciences which are considered occult. It is also evident that the Assassins constituted an occult society whose structures was at least to some degree initiatic. But the extent to which a highly secret, heretical doctrine can be described as approximating to magic is dubious.

As so often in this area, 'proof' is by association, parallels or even juxtaposition. Hammer-Purgstall was right to point out a certain similarity between Assassin and Templar hierarchy. It is indeed extremely likely that an Order so intimately involved in eastern life as the Templars in the Holy Land in the twelfth century should be influenced to some degree by what went on around them. Relations between the Assassins and the Templars are proven by documentary evidence. But to attribute occult practices to the Assassins by way of their relationship to the Templars is a double imaginative leap, since there is as yet no evidence of the Templars *as an Order* being involved in such practices. An uncritical person, who accepts on vague grounds that the Templars were guilty of some magical practice, may as well accept the same of the Assassins.

Yet there is a more interesting argument against such ideas, which relates not to Hammer-Purgstall but to medieval writers about the Assassins. The absolute power of the Old Man over his *fida'i*, their blind obedience, and their spirit of sacrifice, which were the real conditions behind the power of the sect, were incomprehensible both to their enemies and to the chroniclers[25]. In the total absence of information, then, these powers were attributed to occult powers and magical practices employed by the Old Man to hold sway over his followers. In this classic instance of the logical fallacy of *argumentum ad ignorantium,* magic was called in to substitute for western ignorance.

It is interesting that this phenomenal power was mysterious even to some Moslem sources, so that the stories of the western chroniclers seem to gain added weight from the anecdotes of Abu Firas. But even here, it is essential to recall that these stories were only ever told of Sinan. That he dabbled in magic and was an expert on astrology is extremely likely, and by no means unusual in the world in which he lived; but he is atypical even within the story of the Assassins. It would be harder to make the same imaginative connection with the austere and ascetic Hasan-i Sabbah, and it was his pure and spiritual mind which remained the fundamental impulse throughout Assassin history.

It was more than likely the search for some non-occult explanation of *fida'i* loyalty that led to hashish. The use of hashish has never been uncommon in that part of the world, and was used by mystics in order to intensify religious experiences. Yet the long-term effects of hashish use are debilitating, and create the opposite of the cold-blooded determination required to spend months in disguise, acquire new languages and techniques for special purposes, or assassinate a well-guarded man in public. The modern usage, cited above, of *hashasheen* in Egypt to mean noisy or riotous in a pejorative sense could equally well be the real reason for the use of the word. Again, as modern scholars have shown, the term Assassin and implicit accusation of use of hashish were used exclusively of the Syrian Assassins. Those at Alamut and elsewhere in Persia never had this name, or the practice it suggests, attributed to them. We might therefore assume that this too was part of the attempt to describe an incomprehensible phenomenon.

It would seem likely that the Assassins were occult only in the literal sense of that word, that doctrines — and often, as we have seen, imams — were *hidden* from the view of the uninitiated. Like so many other legends about the Assassins, that of their magical practices has stuck in spite of later evidence and information.

MODERN TRAVELLERS
TO ALAMUT

THE symbolic and imaginative centre of the Assassins has always remained Alamut. It was there that the sect began, and whence the Syrian leaders departed; after its fall the sect declined inexorably throughout the East, and even today the name 'Alamut' suggests the Old Man of the Mountains with all its connotations — although that is historically inaccurate. The magical coincidence of the numerological value of the name being the date of its foundation as an Assassin base, and its very remoteness and mysteriousness, made Alamut the spiritual centre of the medieval Assassins. It was not surprising, therefore, that early travellers in search of the Assassins and their sites should choose Alamut beyond all other castles.

This period of revived 'physical' interest in the Assassins opened with the importance given to the British presence in Persia as the result of its position on the threshold of India. Until the end of the eighteenth century little had been known about the huge expanse of Persia. Early British interest through the East India Company, who established settlements in Persia as early as the seventeenth century, was exclusively commercial in operation and concentrated in the south close to the sea route from England to India. The first diplomatic mission was sent under Captain (later Sir) John Malcolm in 1800 as a result of fears about a possible invasion of India through Persia by Napoleon.[1] From 1808 there was a permanent British mission in Tehran, and it is interesting to see specified among the tasks of Sir Gore Ousley on his appointment in 1810 as the first permanent envoy that he should obtain information about the history, customs and geography of the country and also buy Arabic and Persian manuscripts for the British Museum.[2] This new government interest in Persia stimulated the many important discoveries that were to take place during the next century, culminating with the discovery of the Persian oil fields.

One of the first problems, specified in the 1814 Anglo–Persian Treaty, concerned the establishment of permanent and well-defined frontiers. After the loss of the Caucasian provinces to the north of Persia during war with Russia, it was urgently necessary to draw that new frontier. One of the British officers involved, who spent nineteen years in that region and assisted in delimiting the new frontier, was Colonel William Monteith of the Madras Engineers.[3] He was also employed by the Government of India to map and collect information about north-western Persia. His 'Journal of a tour through Azerbaijan and the shores of the Caspian', published in 1833, was the first of many publications on Persia in the *Journal of the Royal Geographical Society* in the nineteenth century. In it, he described the first attempt to identify Alamut.

The other pioneer in identifying Alamut was Lieutenant Colonel Justin Shiel. He had been seconded by the Bombay Light Infantry to train Persian soldiers in 1833, but three years later became secretary to the British Legation at Tehran and in 1844 became Minister Plenipotentiary. He remained in Tehran until 1853, travelled widely through the entire country, and was a good Persian and Arabic scholar.[4] In May of 1837, Shiel became the first person to visit Alamut in modern times, publishing his account once again in the *Journal of the Royal Geographical Society.* Thus, as we shall see in the next chapter, ironically the British allies with whom the first Aga Khan was in contact from his Indian exile were setting the first steps in a new period of understanding about the sect he led.

The visits of Monteith and Shiel to Alamut

Monteith does not appear to have known exactly what he was looking at or for. Furthermore, he never visited the rock of Alamut itself. He appears to have visited a site where the Alamut River joins the main Shah Rud Valley and another Assassin fortress guards the easiest route into the Alamut district from the south.[5] Referring to the leader of the sect, he argues mysteriously that 'the power of this chief, whom I cannot help considering as the head of some religious sect of the

Ismailites, is said to have extended over both the districts of Taroom and Rood Bar'.[6] He then goes on to provide an interesting idea of the state of knowledge about the Assassins in the early nineteenth century when he refers to them as 'schismatics in the very commencement of Mahommedamism' who adopted the practice of assassination as the result of persecution by the early caliphs.

The castle he visited was a walled enclosure on a steep mountainside, with part of a tower surviving and the remains of a 'considerable residence' which suggested to Monteith that this was the fortress home of Hasan-i Sabbah. Although this identification was mistaken, he makes a comment that is just as valid of Alamut: 'The lower part of the mountain has been formed into terraces, but the whole is far from answering the description of the terrestrial Paradise described by some authors; the climate is decidedly cold, and for at least half the year it must have been a disagreeable habitation'.[7] The description of this castle, called Duruyon by Ivanow, confirms the hypothesis that most of these mountain sites were in fact fortified villages — perhaps only to be used in time of emergency.

The next journey to Alamut of which we have record was that of Shiel, who marched through the Alamut district in three days in May 1837. His topographical description is more precise, with all distances and compass readings given so that it is easy to follow his itinerary. But the account is disappointing since Shiel mentions that he had read Hammer-Purgstall's book but does not allow himself to indulge in historical speculation or seek evidence for the historical importance of the Assassins in the area. It would have been fascinating to have an account of the state of the Assassin castles at that time by such a precise observer.

His description of the district of Alamut is as good as any since: it is 'enclosed by a high range to the north, which separates it from Gilan and Mazanderan; on the south is the Pishakuh range; on the east are El-burz and Siyalan; and on the west is Rud-bar, and may be about 30 miles in length and 20 in breadth'.[8] At that time there were no buildings nearer to the rock than the village of Ghuzur Khan, nor were there any visible ruins although he refers to a burying ground not far from the rock that seems to have disappeared. Most interestingly, but without details, he mentions 'several remains of walls belonging to apartments at the top of the rock'[9]. Unlike Monteith, however, he does refer to the rock and district as Alamut and shows more awareness of the site he was visiting. But after noting the desolation of the site, with no living things except lizards and eagles, and the superb views from the top of the rock, he continues his journey through the Alborz Mountains.

Neither of these early travellers visited Alamut for historical or archeological reasons. Monteith only visited the valley and never discovered the site of the real fortress of Hasan-i Sabbah. Shiel correctly identified the rock and localized it with enough precision to guide later visitors, but only gave a brief description during an essentially military and explorative mission. These two pioneer accounts remain interesting and important for the information they provide, although their authors did not provide decisive evidence that the valley known as Alamut or the rock above Gazar Khan were the same as the Alamut of the Assassins. This confirmation came with a visit in 1927 by the archeologist Ernst Herzfeld, who did not leave a written report of his impressions although he passed them on verbally to Lawrence Lockhart. Three visits made in quick succession shortly after Herzfeld's own journey by Lockhart, Ivanow and Freya Stark provided the first detailed historical evidence of the 'Eagle's Nest'.

Twentieth century visits: Ivanow and Lockhart

Ivanow begins his account published in the *Geographical Journal* by noting that there had been no full description of Alamut, and that this was strange given the familiarity of the western public with the fortress. The most interesting part of his article is that in which he explains the administrative importance of Alamut, and its meaning amongst the people of the valley. Similarly, his insistence on the misuse of the word 'castle' in discussing the Assassins is salutary:

In a poor district like that of Alamut, where nowadays thirty villages cannot subsist by themselves alone, it would be impossible to expect fifty castles in addition, with strong garrisons. The term 'castle' is a very unhappy rendering of the original term *ga'la*, which means simply, and first of all, a fortified village or town, as well as a specially fortified refuge, used in the time of danger, and left unoccupied in ordinary times.[10]

Thus 'Alamut' means an entire district whose importance was due to its position on the shortest route between the Caspian Sea and the Persian highlands — a strange comment, since he presumably means the plateau which begins south of Qazvin. He himself took the easy route up from Qazvin, described in the introduction to this book. He states that the district contained sixty-six villages, although he himself seems to doubt the figure[11] and later in the article refers to thirty.

His strangest paragraph is that in which he makes totally unsubstantiated comments about the 'traces of degeneration' probably due to poverty and hardships in the Alamuti peasant. He considers this peasant to be 'much inferior from the point of racial type to Persians from other provinces', which is most likely due to the admixture of Turkish blood 'which everywhere in Persia has had a very disastrous influence on the Iranian race'.[12] These comments do not of course tell us much about the Assassins, or of their potential descendants in the area. He gives fairly detailed information about the dialects spoken locally. All the local inhabitants are said to be Shiites, which is not surprising since ancient Daylam was always a refuge for Shiites and now the Shi'a is the official religion of the state. He attributes legends that he heard concerning Hasan-i Sabbah to book learning, but does not state what these legends were. Then, working in no apparent order, he goes on to describe the road up from Qazvin to Alamut.

The article concludes very weakly, mentioning the work of Monteith and Shiel and noting that they actually refer to two different sites but not making any conclusion about this fact. He notes some strange rectangular holes in the rock, and found some fragments of apparently Ming pottery; which confirmed, he stated, Chardin's observation that the fortress had been used as a prison in Safavid times. On the whole, for someone who has the reputation of being a founder of modern Isma'ili studies, this article is muddled and inconclusive.

It was perhaps in tacit recognition of this fact that the article was followed by 'Some notes on Alamut' by the British scholar Lawrence Lockhart, who begins on a polemical note by criticizing Ivanow's eccentric transliterations of local names and some topographical details. He seems to be surprised that Ivanow doubted the position of the castle of Alamut, and also Ivanow's assertion that nothing could be decided about the fortress without special excavations. In fact, Ivanow does not seem to have bothered either to measure the surviving ruins or attempted to understand the buildings from the disposition of walls and entrances.

Lockhart published his own version in 1930 as an appendix to an article on Hasan-i Sabbah in the *Bulletin of the School of Oriental and African Studies*. His aims are more modest, to give a straightforward description of the journey and site. Interestingly, especially in view of the proliferation of such diggings in Templar castles, the headman of Shotorkhan was convinced that Lockhart and his two friends were treasure hunters: 'But surely,' he said, 'you must have come all this way to dig for the treasure which, they say, is still buried somewhere amid the ruins of the castle! Others have been here before, and they have *all* tried to find this treasure'. [13] Although the headman knew the history of Hasan-i Sabbah and answered the historical questions which Lockhart asked, he remained convinced to the end that they were treasure hunters.

The headman repeated a legend about the taking of Alamut by Hasan-i Sabbah concerning the three-thousand dinars which he is said to have paid. In this version, Hasan offered the governor of the castle, Mahdi, this sum for the space of ground covered by an ox-hide. The governor was overwhelmed by this apparently generous offer and accepted, but Hasan was too shrewd for him: as soon as the governor had accepted, he found an ox-hide and cut into thin strips so that it could surround the entire rock on which the castle stands. He then demanded that the castle be handed over. Yet another version, current in the village of Shotorkhan at the foot of the Alamut valley, stated that Hasan recognized that the man was ignorant because while they were talking he had been too stupid to put down a heavy load that he had been carrying. That is what made him think of the ruse concerning the ox-hide.

His analysis of the site, measurements and building materials to be found is far more precise and interesting than that of Ivanow. He observes that, although most of the walls were made of stone, good burnt brick was also used and the quality of the mortar was excellent. [14] Even though his account is precise, however, he allows himself a romantic flourish when returning to their camp after an afternoon exploring the rock. With an impressionist touch he describes the scene by soft moonlight, concluding that 'what with the wonderfully clear mountain air, the beautiful moonlight, and — above all — the romantic surroundings, it needed but little further stretching of our imaginations to picture Hasan-i Sabbah and his faithful Fida'is as being once again in possession of Alamut'.[15] It is hardly surprising that medieval travellers were so influenced by the Old Man, when the ruins themselves can have such an effect six-hundred years later.

In her article published in the same issue of the *Geographical Journal* as Ivanow's, Freya Stark does not give a detailed description of Alamut, but does pass on the interesting information that there were said to be fifteen-thousand inhabitants of Alamut and Rudbar. This figure appears to contradict Ivanow's statements about the difficulty of maintaining a large population.

The main body of her contribution is devoted to her journey through the mountains *beyond* Alamut. But in the course of her account she does put forward the interesting theory that the castle described by Marco Polo was not Alamut at all but Nevisar Shah, which controlled the eastern 'gate' into the Alamut valley system. Marco Polo spoke of a 'delicious valley' where Aloadin built a castle to defend the valley with only one secret opening into it. Miss Stark argues that this description is still perfectly recognizable:

The reason why it has escaped other travellers is that they have never followed the old way from one end of the valley to the other. It is only by so doing that one would notice the 'two' mountains, the castle or castles at the entrances, and — according to native reports — the remains of water conduits above Shirkuh. The delicious fragrance of the shrubs is still noticeable as one comes down into the valley from the west, and the whole passage bears the stamp of an authentic report without only those parts exaggerated which the reporter could not see for himself.[16]

The care of her descriptions, and the maps and transliterations of place names, would not appear to warrant the vituperation that Ivanow elsewhere uses against Freya Stark — unless it is for her dependence on the biased work of Hammer-Purgstall that he attacked her.

Freya Stark and The Valleys of the Assassins

Freya Stark's fullest account of the Assassins appeared in a well-known book published a few years later, *The Valleys of the Assassins,* in which thirty-seven pages are given to her journey to Alamut, and a further eighteen pages to the castle of Lammassar. Notwithstanding the title given to this collection of five travelogues, the greater part of the book has little to do with the Assassins.

The first striking thing is again the difficulty of establishing topographical names, not merely Alamut itself but the names of hills and valleys in the area. She relates that 'Six people would each give me a different name for the selfsame hill: when in doubt they invented or borrowed one from somewhere else to please me'.[17] Above all, in the villages and valleys further from Alamut, no one had ever heard of Hasan-i Sabbah or the Assassins. Folk myths were embroidered around the epic heroes of ancient Persian history. It was only nearer to the rock that the inhabitants knew anything, as is the case today, and Freya Stark may be correct to assume that their stories have been learned from modern western travellers — although there had only been ten or so foreign visitors as far as we know in the previous century. For commercial or military reasons there would have been little reason for others to visit Alamut, while there is little of artistic or archeological interest to compare with such cities and sites as Esfahan or Persepolis in southern Persia.

Later the village headman mentioned visitors who frequently came to see the castle, and that he would call the man who 'always' acted as guide. This, Freya Stark remarks, made the whole place sound a bit like a tourist resort, but on pressing them she discovered that the adjective 'frequent' bore a typical Persian exaggeration: there had been two parties within the previous two years and an 'English Ambassador' and his wife from Tehran a few years earlier.[18] It would appear likely that these two parties were the groups led by Professor Herzfeld and Ivanow; it is interesting to speculate whether the 'English Ambassador' who had visited a few years before was not Harold Nicholson and his wife Vita Sackville-West. Certainly, the headman's explanation makes Alamut sound far from a tourist resort at that time.

That such a dauntless lady, still admired and respected in her nineties in the north Italian village where she lives, should have travelled from Baghdad to make this journey and forgotten her climbing shoes is almost comical. She walked inside the castle walls, so it would seem, and noted the wild tulips among the stones and mortar, but was unable to see the rooms and water tanks in the lower part of the castle for want of these climbing shoes. Thus in the end Miss Stark says almost nothing about the rock itself, although her stories about the headman and other characters have an interest beyond their charm.

The local people, as so often happens, appear to have been influenced by the foreigners' romantic vision of their austere valley:

Down there [e.g. beneath the rock], so they say at Shutur Khan, seven black dogs guard the treasure and breathe fire, but fly — rather inadequately — as one approaches. The vine of Hasan spreads over the face of the Rock — perhaps of that second Hasan who released the valley from teetotalism; and the rose of Hasan grow on a narrow ledge whence my host had brought slips for his garden and gave me an Assassins' bouquet before I left. [19]

This sounds very much like the men mentioned above changing names to suit the guest. Travellers were, and have been more recently, a rare source of income, with mules to be hired and guides to be provided. Why not, the local inhabitants certainly reason, give these visitors the sort of stories they want to hear? Then we shall earn more money from them. As a matter of fact an ancient, gnarled and sprawling vine is still visible today on the south face of Alamut Rock.

But for all the picturesqueness of her descriptions, and the rather romantic nature of her journey — inspired by Fitzgerald's translations of the *Rubaiyyat* of Omar Khayyam — Freya Stark does manage to convey more of the feeling of Alamut. The care with which she collated topographical information means that her maps are the most accurate of all early travellers.

The current political situation has made it almost impossible to visit the Alborz Mountains in safety. It is difficult to imagine when more precise measurements or even excavations might be possible. To have an accurate picture of life in an Assassin castle would add much to the rather vague picture we can draw of them. Alamut and the other great castles of the Rudbar like Lammassar and Maymun Diaz would be the obvious candidates. For the moment we possess the descriptions and photographs published in the book which Peter Willey wrote after his expedition's visit to the castles in 1967. Now that these traveller's impressions have been strengthened by scholarly studies of texts and manuscripts, it is easier to form a picture of Assassin life.

Yet without these descriptions — even those as fanciful as that of Marco Polo — the scholarly studies would be dry. For it is indisputable, as Lockhart and Freya Stark emphasize, that the inebriation of high mountain valleys aid the imagination and help us to understand the incredible power of the Grand Masters of the Assassins over the *fida'i*.

RE-EMERGENCE :
THE AGA KHANS

AFTER the destruction of Alamut by Hulegu in 1256, many members of the Nizari Isma'ili sect are thought to have fled to Afghanistan, the Himalayas and above all Sind. Once again, as so often in their history, a sect of the Isma'ilis went underground at a time of great danger.

Tradition has it that, shortly before the fall of Alamut in 1256, the last Grand Master of the Assassins Khwurshah sent his seven-year-old son Shams al-Din Muhammad into hiding with his uncle. Like his hidden predecessors, Shams took a profession which gave him a 'cover' to hide his real importance. The Persian poet Nizari Quhistan states that he worked as an embroiderer (*zardoz*) and thus became known as Muhammad Zardoz in the north-western province of Azerbaijan where he chose to live. In the same area another important refugee from Alamut was Shams-i Tabriz, who became the spiritual master of the great Persian poet Jalal al-Din Rumi. Later, Rumi wrote a volume of poems in honour of his Isma'ili master, the *Diwan* of Shams-i Tabriz.[1]

Bohras and Khojas in India

Yet it seems that many of these refugees did not travel without direction or hope, since Isma'ili missionaries had already been established in the East for some time. Several of them had travelled to India as early as the eleventh century, but the founder of the branch of the sect known as the Bohras was probably a certain Abdullah who travelled from the Yemen and arrived in Cambay in about 1067. He travelled and preached extensively in the province of Gujerat, where still today the Bohras are a powerful and secretive presence.[2]

The other major branch of the Isma'ilis in the East today are known as the Khojas, who are particularly strong in what was once the Punjab but is now part of Pakistan. Their tradition relates that a missionary known as Nur Satagur, which means literally 'teacher of true light', was the first to arrive in India. He is thought to have travelled to north-western India some time between 1166 and 1242.[3] It was the Khoja sect which descended directly from the Nizari Isma'ilis or Assassins, and on whose support the Aga Khan's leadership of the Isma'ilis today is based. An early Nizari missionary called Sadr al Din created a form of Isma'ilism acceptable to Hindus and, giving himself a Hindu form of his name as Sahadev, developed the Khoja religious customs. The result was a curious amalgam of Hindu and Islamic ideas which reminds us of Sinan's adaptations of Isma'ili doctrine, and of the upper initiated grades where a universal religion beyond specific doctrines was the aim.

The north-western province of Azerbaijan was the first step on a journey which took the sect and its leaders through most of Persia and neighbouring countries in the following centuries. In a certain sense, as we shall see, this long migration has not finished yet. Information about the precise details of this long, forced migration is necessarily vague since the various periods of fixed residence were carried out in the greatest secrecy. But the general pattern can be formed.

The hidden imams

The residence of the hidden imams seems to have continued in Azerbaijan until about 1400. After that date there is evidence that they moved south east towards the city of Esfahan — which under Hasan-i Sabbah's teacher ibn-Attash had been one of their first bases in Persia. During the fifteenth century they appear to have been established in the area between Qom and Sultanabad, north west of Esfahan, where the Isma'ili leader Shah Mustansir bi-Llah III died in 1480 at a place called Anjudan between Qom and Sultanabad, south of Qazvin.[4] This may be the modern village of Anjilavand just outside Saveh, which was a well-known Assassin stronghold. It would appear that these isolated sites maintained the traditions almost intact through long periods of time.

From 1480, in fact, all traces of the hidden imams disappear for about three centuries until they appear again slightly further to the south with the death of Shah Nizar at Kahak, south of Qom, in 1722. Then from Kahak they seem to have moved much further south east to Kerman. A plausible hypothesis in this case would be that an Isma'ili imam of the time gave his support to the tribal leader Karim Khan Zand — whose name the present Aga Khan bears — when he rose against the decaying Safavid dynasty in mid-century. It was in fact towards the end of the eighteenth century that the history of the line again becomes clearly discernible, when the Nizari Isma'ili imams appear already established as important members of the Persian nobility. The presumed forty-fourth imam, Abu al-Hasan Ali Shah, in fact became Governor of the city of Kerman under Karim Khan Zand and died in that city in 1780.[5]

But the real emergence of the Isma'ilis who trace their origins to the Assassins occurred in the early nineteenth century under the new Qajar dynasty of Persia. And it was in the fluid situation after the death of the first great Qajar Shah, Fath-Ali Shah, in 1834, that the first man to bear the title Aga Khan managed by force of personality and clever deployment of his limited resources and spiritual hold over the Isma'ilis to create for himself and his successors a new and unexpected role in the modern world.

Aga Khan I

Abu al-Hasan's governorship was under the ruler Karim Khan Zand (1750–79). Karim Khan was a tribal leader from Luristan who managed to establish his authority over southern and central Persia in the vacuum which followed the decay of the great Safavid dynasty (1501–1736). He never styled himself Shah and preferred the title 'Regent of the People'. His first capital was Shiraz, but he was gradually forced to retreat to Kerman as the bloodthirsty Turkoman leader Agha Muhammad Qajar (1743–97) imposed the new dynasty. Qajar rule lasted in Persia until 1921, when the Pahlavis in turn usurped the Persian throne.[6]

Karim Khan Zand was succeeded by the dynastically complex but short and relatively unimportant reigns of two brothers and three nephews. We have no evidence of the whereabouts of Abu al-Hasan's son Khalilu'llah (1790–1817) during the violent sacking of Kerman by Agha Mohammad Qajar in 1796. But we may assume that he returned to Kahak after his father's death. The founder of the Qajar dynasty took out the eyes of prisoners and granted twenty-thousand women and children to his soldiers as slaves.[7] He then managed to bring the entire country under his power and was crowned at his new capital of Tehran in 1796. But his reign was short, and within one year he was succeeded by his son Fath-Ali, who reigned until 1834. This prolific Shah became famous for his immensely long beard and enormous number of wives and children: he was survived by fifty-seven sons and forty-six daughters.

Fath-Ali Shah played a vital role in the modern history of the Assassins, since it was he who formally recognized Khalilu'llah as head of the Isma'ilis in Persia. The new spiritual leader of the Isma'ilis was visited at Kahak by the French Consul-General at Aleppo, M. Rousseau, who travelled through the area in 1811. Rousseau described him as living in great wealth and honour, and discovered that Isma'ilis came to pay homage to him, and literal tribute, from as far away as India.[8] This veneration and the attendant obedience were probably behind Fath-Ali's move, since to have the support of such a man could be important. But the recognition had unforeseen repercussions. It seems that Khalilu'llah later lived in Yazd, where he was a supporter of the tyrannic Governor Muhammad Zeman Khan.[9] In 1817, he was murdered in his own home by a mob in that city, some writers believe as a result of his support for the despot. But it seems more likely, given the high-running religious fervour of the time, that it was the official recognition by the Shah which inspired envy amongst the Shiite mullahs, who in turn instigated the mob that took his life.[10] As if in confirmation of the medieval loyalty to the 'Old Man', the leader's followers immediately killed the assassins.

The following year Khalilu'llah's son was made Governor of Mahallat and Qom by Fath-Ali Shah, and given the title of Aga Khan, which his descendants have used down to the present day. For the next sixteen years we must imagine that he fulfilled his duties as Governor, and received homage as the head of the Isma'ilis. But after Fath-Ali Shah's death in 1834, he seems to have become involved in the violent struggle of succession which was eventually won by Fath-Ali's grandson Muhammad. Persia had been seriously weakened by Fath-Ali's inattention to such important matters as the national economy and defence. He had been content to increase his personal wealth by hoarding jewels and gold. Territory had been lost to the encroaching power of Russia, to which country Fath-Ali had signed away much of the old Persian Empire in 1813.

Muhammad Shah set out to create a stronger Persia, and in 1836 attempted to restore Persian sovereignty over the Afghan province of Herat. This city, and all of Afghanistan, was perceived as a bulwark against Russian advance by the British in India, who resisted Muhammad Shah's claim and went to war against Persia that year. Meanwhile, for reasons which are not completely clear, the Aga Khan found himself in conflict with Muhammad Shah, either attempting to usurp power for himself or leading a genuine popular revolt. He took castles and towns, openly opposed the Shah and at one time was thought to be behind many of the rebellions spontaneously breaking out throughout southern Persia. This situation lasted until the spring of 1841, when Muhammad Shah prepared to send an army against the Isma'ili leader. At that point, the Aga Khan took what turned out to be a historic decision both for his family and for the sect. Escorted by a hundred soldiers he left Persia in the summer of 1841 and rode to Kandahar, in southern Afghanistan on the main road from Herat to Kabul.

Announcing himself as Aga Khan Mehalatee, the leader of the Isma'ilis presented himself to the British political agent Henry Rawlinson as an important ally of the British against the Shah. From this moment began a remarkable series of promises, requests, British payments, strange episodes in which the Aga Khan actually led troops in an important battle for the British, and engaged in long and polite correspondence with military and political leaders regarding his privileges, and his eventual transfer to Sind. This enigmatic leader offered to take Persia for the British without fighting and impressed all who saw him by his unusual habits and the loyalty of his devotees. He cleverly made himself almost indispensable as the only Moslem ally of the British, and then used his British contacts to reach an unassailable position of prestige and wealth in India. Whatever the real value of his presence and rhetoric, he himself always seemed to derive benefit from any situation in which he artfully positioned himself. At one time, he even seems to have imagined himself becoming Shah of Persia with British support.[11]

But he had managed by 1844 to become the owner of estates in Hyderabad and receive pensions from the British Government. As a recent biographer puts it, up to that moment the first Aga Khan had been a rebel; now, for the next seven years, he was to be an intriguer.[12] He intrigued and procrastinated with great success, insisting on his being a member of a family with nine-hundred years standing. It is a curious irony that in his dealings with the British in Persia at this time, he negotiated with Lieutenant-Colonel Justin Shiel, who had been appointed Minister Plenipotentiary at Tehran in 1844,[13] and who a decade earlier had been one of the first travellers to seek the castle of Alamut. Now he continued his nomadic exile, first moving to Bombay and then to Calcutta — in constant diplomatic and personal conflict with the British, but always seeming to get the better of them and receive the money he claimed to be owed as a result of losses in Persia, and his combat in Afghanistan. At this time his family was in Kerbala, the holy city in Iraq, where, he claimed, they were in great distress.[14]

The story of these years is a remarkable one, recounted in all its fascinating detail by Mihir Bose. From nothing, with little more than extraordinary powers of persuasion and the backing of small scattered communities of followers, Aga Khan Mehalatee had created for himself a solid power base in India. When Muhammad Shah died in 1848, he began the last stage of an almost unbelievable series of cases of outwitting his 'Masters'. He was sent off from Calcutta on his way back to Persia, but never arrived further than Bombay, where he found himself surrounded by admirers and supporters. Now, the Government of Bombay, the Indian Government in Calcutta, the British Minister in Tehran, and the Foreign Office in London all became engaged in solving the 'problem' of the Aga Khan. Threatened with loss of all pensions unless he took ship to the Middle East, he still remained in Bombay.[15]

It was in Bombay that the Aga Khan secured with British assistance the greatest coup of his life, and guaranteed the future power and wealth of his family. This culminating series of events began with a dispute over the tribute which the Aga Khan claimed from the Bombay Khojas. A dissident group called the *Barbhai,* or twelve, who had been excommunicated nearly twenty years earlier, won a court case against the Aga Khan over a huge inheritance. These *Barbhai* began to hold their own meetings in a separate hall, and on 13 November 1850 — in the best tradition of his family — the Aga Khan's followers murdered four of them in revenge. An interesting fact supporting the Aga's hand in the matter and linking him with medieval tradition is that the *Times of India* reported him as comforting the widows of his murderers after their judicial execution with the argument that they would go straight to heaven.[16] But for the moment, the episode was quickly forgotten.

In the 1860s this simmering dispute again came to the surface, this time more spectacularly with resonances in the newspapers. Dissidents publicly charged the Aga Khan with avoiding progress by preventing the community from being educated and otherwise abusing his position. Some Moslems claimed to be Sunni, and that the Aga Khan had no right to demand tribute or give them orders of any kind. One of the most important charges was that he used the immense income derived from his followers for horse racing, instead of using it to the general benefit of the Isma'ili community. For ten years the argument went on, in the Indian press and even the London newspapers; the entire history of the Isma'ilis was recounted, the dissidents were threatened, and at last the whole affair came to court.

The case was heard by Sir Joseph Arnould, Chief Justice of Bombay, in April and June 1866. Complex legal arguments, with lengthy historical and genealogical discussions, and the examination of witnesses lasted for twenty-five days. In his final judgement, Sir Joseph Arnould legally established the Khojas as a community of the Isma'ili sect and the Isma'ilis as the heirs of the Assassins. Thus, with the backing of historical argument and British legal sanction the Aga Khan became the official heir of the imams of Alamut with every right to expect allegiance and tribute from the Indian Khojas.[17]

That the ancient Assassin traditions and faith had been maintained is obvious in two references to the first Aga Khan. Sir Charles Napier, Commander of the British forces in Sind, writing in 1844 describes the 'old Persian Prince' as a 'great crony' of his, a man recognized by his followers as a god and with an immense income. But then, in confirmation of the medieval tales of obedience, he comments that '. . . his followers do not refuse him anything he asks . . . He could kill me if he pleased. He has only to say the word and one of his people can do the job in a twinkling and go straight to heaven for the same'.[18]

Earlier, in a letter repeating many of these observations, Napier makes an even more interesting allusion: 'However, I put an end peremptorily to his rights whenever any of his people chose to resist him which is awkward for the divinity of the "Old Man of the Mountain" '.[19]

Whether this alternative title had survived with the Isma'ilis or had been gleaned from literary and historical sources, it is now impossible to know. But it does demonstrate a remarkable continuity. So it was that this extraordinary character, supported by the British, achieved a success worthy of the 'magic' of such predecessors as Sinan in having his lineage officially legitimized by a British court.

Aga Khans II and III

When the Aga Khan I died in 1881 at Bombay, his son and heir Ali Shah was a man of fifty, most of whose life had been spent in Kerbala and Baghdad. He would appear to have been a most unsuitable candidate for the succession, but in any case his passion for hunting led him to an early death. In 1885, the Aga Khan II died of pneumonia after getting soaked during a shooting expedition.[20]

His son, Sultan Muhammad, at that time only eight years old, was to reign as Aga Khan III from 1881 to 1957. This Aga Khan, in many ways as remarkable as his grandfather, managed to fulfil a double role that only a man of extreme diplomatic accomplishment, subtlety and personal charm could have pulled off: presenting himself as the leader of Moslems loyal to the Raj he created an important international political career that culminated with his presidency of the League of Nations; in complete contrast, captivated on an 1898 visit by society life on the French Riviera, he established the European jet-setting style that has since characterized his family in the popular imagination.

In 1906 Aga Khan III presented himself at the head of a delegation representing the sixty-million Moslems — about one-fifth of the population — of India to the British Viceroy Lord Minto at his summer residence in Simla. This presentation in fact emphasized the fundamental division of India into British power, the nascent nationalist Congress movement, and the Moslem elite. The Aga Khan was known to be close to the British rulers. On his first visit to England, he had been received by Queen Victoria, and when the future Edward VII visited India as Prince of Wales in 1906 he had taken tea at the Aga's Calcutta home.[21] He was shrewd enough to perceive that he could use this friendship to place himself at the head of all Indian Moslems. The idea of a separate Moslem state for Indian Moslems was born. Thus he had cleverly made himself the spokesman for a movement that was to create the All India Muslim League in Dacca, taking the first steps in the process that was to create Pakistan and later Bangladesh — of which Dacca is the capital. It must be remembered that the Punjab, and Sind, where the first Aga had developed important support, were in that part of north-western India which is now part of Pakistan.

In Europe Aga Khan III presented himself in a completely different light. Associated in the public mind with such luxury hotels at the Ritz in London and the Hotel de Paris in Monaco, he took as his second wife an Italian dancer who he first saw in the casino ballet corps in Monte Carlo.[22] She was to be the mother of his heir Aly Khan, thus beginning a process in which there was always less and less of 'Indian' or 'Persian' in the Aga Khans. He threw a party in 1912 at the London Ritz with Nijinsky dancing, became a friend of Lord Beaverbrook and Lord Astor, and a fixture in the world that included such celebrated socialites as Lady Diana Cooper and Lady Emerald Cunard. He enjoyed huge meals and extravagant dinner parties, and was renowned for his gifts of food to favourite friends whenever he arrived in London. He was known to the general public as one of the greatest owners of racehorses, who in a long career won all the major English races. He married two beautiful French women as the last two of his four wives, and had numerous mistresses during his long sojourns in the South of France.

Politically, he identified his cause with Moslems throughout the world, with the Turks suffering as the result of the Balkan war in 1912 or with the Palestinian cause in 1939 and after the Second World War. Although his public-relations work and constant letter-writing were in fact generally rewarded by failure, his importance seemed to grow. While publicly in favour of reforms in India, in 1933 he attempted to obtain the grant of a territory with ruling powers in order to guarantee himself and his descendants 'the permanent and influential status in India consistent with the prestige and dignity' of his ancient lineage.[23] Iraq and Syria had been suggested in the past, and now areas in Kalat and on the Persian Gulf were also considered for the formation of an Aga-state; but nothing was ever to come of these plans. His most important offices were achieved in 1934 and

1937 when he became, respectively, Vice-President and President of the League of Nations.[24] Aga Khan III died in 1957 after a public life on two continents that had lasted more than half a century.

His son and heir Aly Khan brought the family to the fore in European gossip columns and developed for himself the reputation of one of the world's greatest playboys. He lived between a villa at Deauville, a house in Paris, a stud farm in Ireland and a castle near Cannes. His celebrated love affair and marriage with Rita Hayworth in 1949, and later affair with Gene Tierney, were carefully exploited by the international gossip press and virtually inaugurated the concept of a jet-set. The idea of a playboy religious leader was obviously irresistible to the press, but not to Aga Khan III. Aly was passed over in the battle for the succession to the title, and died tragically in 1960 in a car accident on his way to a dinner party in Paris. His son Karim, then twenty-one, from his first marriage with Loel Guinness, inherited both the title and his father's notoriety as he suddenly became one of the world's richest men and most eligible bachelors while still a student at Harvard.

Aga Khan IV

The present Aga Khan, correctly known as Prince Karim El Husseni, Aga Khan IV, is recognized as the forty-ninth hereditary imam of the Isma'ilis and claims direct descent from the Prophet Muhammad. He is recognized as head of the world-wide Isma'ili sect, today estimated at between four and twenty million in number. His income from voluntary contributions was estimated by Mihir Bose in 1985 to be seventy-five million pounds a year.[25]

But beyond his highly publicized racing and business activities he has gained wide respect for his role as a moderate Moslem leader, and has contrived to increase loyalty amongst the Isma'ilis by providing loans to set up business and financial advice through his 'Industrial Promotion Services'[26]. In managing to walk the delicate tightrope between a wealthy and extravagant existence and the spiritual leadership of a large religious sect, he exhibits some of the diplomatic and political skill of his grandfather Aga Khan III.

★   ★   ★

The story of the medieval Assassins is an extraordinary one, moving as it does within the ambiguous area between fact and fiction, or between reality and legend.

But the story of their successors is no less extraordinary. As a matter of fact, the right to use the title 'Royal Highness' is extremely recent, having been granted in 1959 by the then Shah of Persia. It might therefore be reasonably argued that the title fell into disuse with the end of Pahlavi rule in 1979. Similarly, we have seen that the direct line back from the Aga Khans reaches to Buzurg'umid, the second Grand Master of the Assassins of Alamut: from Buzurg'umid to Hasan-i Sabbah there is no blood link, and neither does there appear to be a direct link back from Hasan to Ali, and thence to the Prophet. But to such a family the arguments which might interest the readers of *Burke's Peerage* are largely irrelevant.

Above all, we have seen that both Hasan-i Sabbah and Sinan, the two greatest medieval leaders of the sect, gained authority and obedience through *force of personality*. In this respect we may safely assert that at least two of their modern descendants — Aga Khans I and III — have been equal to their exploits in a very different world.

The story of the Aga Khans serves to illustrate that it is the spiritual and doctrinal beliefs of the Nizari Isma'ilis which are ultimately the most interesting aspects of their history. In fact, Isma'ilism can be said to have exerted an important influence on Persian mystical thought[27]. It has been argued that there was a certain 'warrior-enthusiast' impulse amongst the various mystical-religious components behind the historical resurrection of Persia under the Safavids[28]. The word *fida'i* reappeared in modern times when a group of Ottoman conspirators used the word in their secret oaths in the nineteenth century[29]. It is also clear that similar impulses underlie the promise of external life by Khomeini to his *fida'i* as they go to the front in Iraq, or the same faith which fires the suicidal missions of Arab terrorists from Lebanon, where such ideas are deep-rooted.

In a history of Persian spirituality, Filippani-Ronconi has argued that from time to time enigmatic personalities emerge in the spiritual history of Persia to whom the qualities of an Isma'ili can be attributed[30]. He mentions Shams-i Tabriz, the teacher and initiator of Rumi, as an example. Similarly the gnostic aspect of Persian Islam often bears an Isma'ili stamp. The theology and politics of the revolutionary of genius Hasan-i Sabbah can in fact be seen as the first original creation — both religious and political — of a specifically Persian ethos after the conquest of the country by the Arabs and consequent conversion to Islam. In this wider sense the thought and doctrines of the inventor of the 'Assassins' may be said to have an enduring influence in the religious and political life of the Middle East. This legacy is shared both by the Aga Khans and by contemporary revolutionary groups in Lebanon and Persia.

SELECT BIBLIOGRAPHY

Abu-Izzedin, Nejla M., *The Druzes: A New Study of their History, Faith and Society*. Leiden: E. J. Brill (1984).

Ambraseys, N. N., 'Historical Seismicity of North-Central Iran', in *Materials for the Study of the Seismotectonics of Iran: North-Central Iran*. Tehran: Geological Survey of Iran (1974).

Arberry, A. J., *Sufism: An Account of the Mystics of Islam*. London: George Allen and Unwin (1950).

Assemani, Simone, 'Ragguaglio storico-critico sopra la setta Assissana detta volgarmente degli Assassini', *Giornale dell'Italiana Letteratura*. Padova, XIII (1806), pp.241–62.

Aubin, Jean, 'Elements pour l'Etude des Agglomerations Urbaines dans l'Iran Medieval', in *The Islamic City: A Colloquium* (Hourani, A. H., & Stern, S. M., eds), pp.65–75. Oxford: Bruno Cassirer (1970).

Bausani, A., *Persia Religiosa*. Milan: Il Saggiatore (1959).

Benvenisti, Meron, *The Crusaders in the Holy Land*. Jerusalem: Israel Universities Press (1970).

Bose, Mihir, *The Agha Khans*. Kingswood: World's Work (1984).

Bouisson, Maurice, *Magic: Its Rites and History* (trs. G. Almayrac). London: Rider (1960).

Bouthoul, Madame B., *Le Grand Maitre des Assassins*. Paris: Librairie Armand Colins (1936).

Boyle, J. A., *The History of the World Conqueror* (2 vols). Manchester University Press (1958).

Broadhurst, R. J. C. (trs.), *The Travels of Ibn Jubayr*. London: Jonathan Cape (1952).

Brown, John P., *The Darvishes, or Oriental Spiritualism*. London: Frank Cass (1968; 1st edn 1868).

Browne, Edward Granville, 'A Chapter From the History of *Cannabis Indica*', *St Bart's Hospital Journal*. (March 1897), pp.1–15.

—— *A Literary History of Persia, Vol I: From the Earlier Times to Firdawsi.* Vol II: *From Firdawsi to Sa'di.* Cambridge University Press (1902; 1906).

Chambers, F. M., 'The Troubadours and the Assassins', *Modern Language Notes.* lxiv (1949), pp.245–51.

Cooper-Oakley, Isabel, *Masonry and Medieval Symbolism: Traces of a Hidden Tradition.* London: Theosophical Publishing House (1977).

Corbin, Henry, *Trilogie Ismaelienne.* Paris: Adrien-Maisonneuve (1961).

—— *Cyclical Time and Ismaili Gnosis.* London: Routledge (1983).

De Boer, T. J., *The History of Philosophy in Islam* (trs. Edward R. Jones). London: Luzac (1970; 1st edn 1903).

De Goeje, M. J., *Mémoire sur les Carmathes du Bahrain et les Fatimides.* Leiden: E. J. Brill (1886).

De Sacy, Silvestre, 'Mémoire sur la Dynastie des Assassins', Paris: *Mémoires de l'Institut Royal,* iv (1818), pp.1–85.

—— *Exposé de la Religion des Bruzes.* Paris: Imprimerie Royale (1888).

Defrémery, M., *Histoire des Seldjoukides et Des Ismaeliens ou Assassins de l'Iran: Extraite du Tarikh Gazideh ou Histoire Choisie d'Hamd-Allah Mustaufi.* Paris: Imprimerie Nationale (1849).

Falconnet, M., 'Dissertation sur les Assassins, peuple d'Aise', *Mémoires de l'Académie Royale des Inscriptions et belles-lettres,* XVII (1751), pp.127–70.

Filippani-Ronconi, Pio, *Ismaeliti e Assassini,* Basle: Troth (1973).

Gabrieli, Francesco (ed.), *Storici Arabi delle Crociate.* Turin: Einaudi (1963).

Gibb, H. A. R., *The Damascus Chronicle of the Crusades.* London: University of London Historical Series, Vol V (1932).

——, *The Life of Saladin, from the works of 'Imad ad-Din and Baha' ad-Din.* Oxford: Clarendon (1973).

Grunebaum, Gustave E. von, *Medieval Islam: A Study of Cultural Orientation.* University of Chicago Press (1946).

Guyard, M. Stanislaus, *Fragments Reliatifs à la Doctrine des Ismaelis.* Paris: Imprimerie Nationale (1874).

——, *Un Grand Maître des Assassins au temps du Saladin.* Paris: Imprimerie Nationale (1877).

Hammer-Purgstall, J. von, *The History of the Assassins, derived from Oriental Sources* (trs. O. C. Wood), New York: Burt Franklin (1968; reprint of 1835 edn).

Hamill, John, *The Craft: a History of English Freemasonry.* Wellingborough: Crucible (1986).

Harris, Walter B., *A Journey Through the Yemen.* Edinburgh and London: William Blackwood (1893).

Hitti, Philip K., *The Origins of the Druse People and Religion, with extracts from their Sacred Writings.* New York: Columbia University Press (1928).

——, *Lebanon in History.* London: Macmillan (1957).

——, 'Salah-al-Din: Hero of the Anti-Crusades', in *Makers of Arab History,* pp.116–42. London: Macmillan (1969).

——, *History of the Arabs, from the Earliest Times to the Present,* 10th edn. London: Macmillan (1970).

Hodgson, Marshall G. C., *The Order of the Assassins: The Struggle of the Early Nizari Isma'ilis against the Islamic World.* The Hague: Mouton (1955).

Hollister, John Norman, *The Shi'a of India.* London: Luzac (1953).

Hourani, A. H., & Stern, S. M. (eds), *The Islamic City: A Colloquium.* Oxford: Bruno Cassirer and University of Pennsylvania Press (1970).

Ibn Alatyr, *Extrait de la Chronique intitulée Kamel-Altevarykh,* Paris: Recueil des Historiens des Croisades, Historiens Orientaux, 5 Vols. 1872-1906, Vol 1, pp.187-744.

Ibn Khaldun, *The Muqaddimah* (trs. F. Rosenthal). London: Routledge and Kegan Paul (1978).

Irwin, Robert, *The Middle East in the Middle Ages: The Early Mamluk Sultanate 1250-1382.* London: Croom Helm (1986).

Ivanow, W., *A Creed of the Fatimids.* Bombay: Qayyimah Press (1936).

——, 'Alamut', *Geographical Journal,* lxxvii (1931), pp.38–45.

——, *Guide to Ismaili Literature.* London: Royal Asiatic Society (1933).

——, *Ismaili Tradition concerning the Rise of the Fatimids.* Oxford: Humphrey Milford, for the Islamic Research Association (1942).

——, *The Alleged Founder of Ismailism.* Bombay: Thacker, for the Ismaili Society (1946).

Lane, Edward William, *An Account of the Manners and Customs of the Modern Egyptians.* London: John Murray (1860).

Laoust, Henri, *Les Schismes dans l'Islam: Introduction à une étude de la religion musalmane.* Paris: Payot (1977).

Lebey de Batilly, Denis, *Traicte de l'origine des Anciens Assasins.* Lyon: V. Vaspase (1603).

Le Strange, Guy, *Palestine Under the Moslems: A Description of Syria and the Holy Land from AD 650-1500.* London: Alexander P. Watt, for the Palestine Exploration Fund (1890).

——, *The Lands of the Eastern Caliphate.* Cambridge University Press (1905).

Lewis, Bernard, *The Origins of Isma'ilism.* Cambridge: Heffer (1940).

——, 'The Sources for the History of the Syrian Assassins', *Speculum,* xxvii (1952), pp.475-89.

——, 'Saladin and the Assassins', *Bulletin of the School of Oriental and African Studies,* xv (1953), pp.239–45.

——, 'Kamal al-Din's Biography of Rasid al-Din Sinan', *Arabica,* xiii (1966), pp.225–60.

——, *The Assassins: A Radical Sect in Islam.* London: Weidenfeld and Nicholson (1967).

——, 'The Ismaelites and the Assassins', in *A History of the Crusades* (Setton, ed.), Vol. 1, pp.99–132. Madison, Milwaukee and London: University of Wisconsin Press (1969).

——, 'Assassins of Syria and Isma'ilis of Persia', in *La Persia nel Medioevo*, pp.573–80. Rome: Accademia Nazionale dei Lincei (1977).

Lings, Martin, *What is Sufism?* London: George Allen and Unwin (1975).

Lockhart, Lawrence, 'Hasan-i-Sabbah and the Assassins', *Bulletin of the School of Oriental and African Studies,* v (1928–30), pp.689–96.

Lyons, M. C. & Jackson, D. E. P., *Saladin: The Politics of the Holy War.* Cambridge University Press (1982).

Maalouf, Amin, *The Crusades Through Arab Eyes.* London: Al Saqi (1984).

Madelung, Wilfred, 'Aspects of Isma'ili Theology: The Prophetic Chain and the God Beyond Being', in *Isma'ili Contributions to Islamic Culture* (Seyyed Hossein Nasr, ed.). Tehran: Imperial Academy of Philosophy (1977).

Marco Polo, *Il Milione* (Antonio Lanza, ed.). Rome: Editori Riuniti (1971).

Matheson, Sylvia A., *Persia: An Archeological Guide.* London: Faber and Faber (1972).

Meck, Bruno, *Die Assassinen: Die Moderskete der Haschischesser.* Dusseldorf: Econ Verlag (1981).

Meshkati, Nosratollah, *A List of the Historical Sites and Ancient Monuments of Iran* (trs. H. A. S. Pessyan). Tehran: National Organization for the Protection of the Historical Monuments of Iran (nd, but Persian original 1966).

Minasian, Caro Owen, *Shah Diz of Isma'ili Fame: Its Siege and Destruction.* London: Luzac (1971).

Monteith, W., 'Journal of a Journey through Azerbijan and the Shores of the Caspian', *Journal of the Royal Geographical Society,* iii (1833), pp.15–16.

Morgan, M. R. (ed.), *La Continuation de Guillaume de Tyr.* Paris: Paul Guethner (1982).

Nowell, C. E., 'The Old Man of the Mountains', *Speculum,* xxii (1947), pp.497–519.

Nicholson, Reynold A., *A Literary History of the Arabs.* London: T. Fisher Unwin (1907).

O'Leary, De Lacy, *A Short History of the Fatimid Caliphate.* London: Kegan Paul, Trench, Trubner (1923).

Overton Fuller, Jean, *The Magical Dilemma of Victor Neuburg.* London: W. H. Allen (1965).

——, *Shelley: A Biography*. London: Jonathan Cape (1968).

Olschki, Leonardo, *Storia Letteraria delle Scoperte Geografiche*. Florence: Leo S. Olschki (1937).

Palacios, Miguel Asin, *Islam and The Divine Comedy*, London: Frank Cass (1968).

Partner, Peter, *The Murdered Magicians: The Templars and Their Myth*. Oxford University Press (1982).

Petrushevsky, I. P., *Islam in Iran* (trs. Hubert Evans). London: Athlone (1985).

Poonawala, Ismail K., *Biobibliography of Isma'ili Literature*. Malibu: Undena Publications (1977).

Prawer, Joshua, *The Latin Kingdom of Jerusalem: European Colonisation in the Middle Ages*. London: Weidenfeld and Nicholson (1972).

Rockhill, W. W. (ed.), *The Journey of William of Rubruck to the Eastern Parts of the World, 1253-55*. London: The Hakluyt Society (1900).

Rosenthal, Erwin I. J., *Political Thought in Medieval Islam*. Cambridge University Press (1968).

Runciman, Steven, *A History of the Crusades* (3 vols). Harmondsworth: Peregrine (1978).

Sachedina, Abdulaziz A., *Islamic Messianism: the Idea of Mahdi in Twelver Shiism. Albany: State University of New York* (1981).

Saunders, J. J., *Aspects of the Crusades*. Christchurch, NZ: University of Canterbury Publications, No. 3 (1962).

——, *The History of the Mongol Conquests*. London: Routledge (1971).

Setton, Kenneth M. (ed.), *A History of the Crusades, Vol I, The First Hundred Years. Vol II, The Later Crusades 1189-1311*. University of Wisconsin Press (1969).

Shiel, J., 'Itinerary from Tehran to Alamut and Khurramabad in May 1837', *Journal of the Royal Geographical Society*, viii (1838), pp.430–4.

Sivan, Emmanuel, *Radical Islam: Medieval Theology and Modern Politics*. New Haven & London: Yale University Press (1985).

Smail, R. C., 'Crusaders' Castles of the Twelfth Century', *The Cambridge Historical Journal*, Vol X, No 2 (1951), pp.133–49.

——, *Crusading Warfare: (1097-1193)*. Cambridge University Press (1956).

Stark, Freya, 'The Assassins' Valley and the Salambar Pass', *Geographical Journal*, lxxvi (1931), pp.48–60.

——, *The Valleys of the Assassins, and Other Persian Travels*. London: John Murray (1936).

Stern, Samuel M., 'Isma'ilis and Qarmatians', from *L'Elaboration de l'Islam: Colloque de Strasbourg 12-14 Juin 1959*. Paris: Presses Universitaires de France (1961), pp.99–108.

——, 'Cairo as the Centre of the Isma'ili Movement', in *Colloque International*

Sur l'Histoire de Caire, pp.437–50.

——, 'The Constitution of the Islamic City', in *The Islamic City: A Colloquium* (Hourani, A. H., & Stern, S. M., eds), pp.25–50. Oxford: Bruno Cassirer (1970).

Sykes, Sir Percy, *A History of Persia* (2 vols). London: Macmillan (1915).

Watt, W. Montgomery, *Bell's Introduction to the Qur'an.* Edinburgh University Press (1970).

White, Norman Ivey, *Shelley* (2 vols). London: Secker & Warburg (1947).

Willey, Peter, *The Castles of the Assassins.* London: George G. Harrap (1963).

William of Tyre, *A History of Deeds done beyond the Sea* (2 vols), (trs. Emily Atwater Babcock & A. C. Krey). New York: Octagon Books (1976).

Wright, Denis, *The English Amongst the Persians: During the Qajar Period 1787-1921.* London: Heinemann (1977).

REFERENCES

CHAPTER 1

1. Hitti, *History of the Arabs*, pp. 140–6.
2. *Ibid.*, p. 175.
3. Browne, *History of Persian Literature*, I., p. 217.
4. Hitti, *op. cit.*, p. 180.
5. *Ibid.*, p. 182.
6. *Ibid.*, p. 190.
7. *Ibid.*, p. 191.
8. Lewis, *The Assassins*, p. 23; Abu-Izzedin, *The Druzes*, p. 21.
9. Abu-Izzedin *Ibid.*
10. Hitti, *op. cit.*, pp. 282–7.
11. Abu-Izzedin, *op. cit.*, p. 19.
12. Hitti, *op. cit.*, p. 290.
13. Abu-Izzedin, *op. cit.*, p. 19.
14. Lewis, *op. cit.*, pp. 28–9.
15. Hitti, *op. cit.*, pp. 443–4.
16. Abu-Izzedin, *op. cit.*, p. 22.
17. *Ibid.*, p. 24.
18. Hitti, *op. cit.*, p. 617.
19. *Ibid.*, p. 620.
20. Lewis, 'Ismaelites and Assassins', p. 104.
21. Abu-Izzedin, *op. cit.*, p. 56.
22. *Ibid.*, p. 62.
23. Lewis, *op. cit.*, p. 105.
24. Abu-Izzedin, *op. cit.*, p. 85.
25. Lewis, *op. cit.*, p. 105.
26. cf. Abu-Izzedin, *op. cit.*, pp. 133-41.
27. Lewis, *op. cit.*, p. 106.
28. *Ibid.*, pp. 106-7; cf. Hodgson, *Assassins*, pp. 1–2.

CHAPTER 2

1. Boyle, *World Conqueror*, II, p. 667; Hodgson, *Assassins*, p. 43.
2. Boyle, *op. cit.*, II, p. 666.
3. cf. Lewis, *The Assassins*, p. 146.
4. Boyle, *op. cit.*, II, p. 667.
5. Quoted from Hodgson, *op. cit.*, p. 44.
6. *Ibid.*, p. 45.
7. Boyle, *op. cit.*, II, p. 668.
8. Minasian, *Shah Diz*, pp. 11–16.
9. Boyle, *op. cit.*, II, p. 668.
10. Browne, *Literary History*, II, p. 191.
11. Lockhart, 'Hasan-i Sabbah', p. 676.
12. Hitti, *History of the Arabs*, p. 477.
13. *Ibid.*, p. 478.
14. Boyle, *op. cit.*, II, p. 669.
15. *Ibid.*, p. 677.
16. Hodgson, *op. cit.*, pp. 46–7; Lewis, *op. cit.*, p. 41.
17. Boyle, *op. cit.*, II, pp. 668–9.
18. *Ibid.*, p. 669.
19. *Ibid.*
20. Boyle, *op. cit.*, II, p. 670.
21. *Ibid.*
22. *Ibid.*, p. 675.
23. *Ibid.*, p. 680.
24. *Ibid.*, pp. 679–80.
25. Hodgson, *op. cit.*, p. 82.
26. Petrushevsky, *Islam in Iran*, pp. 255–6.
27. Hodgson, *op. cit.*, p. 111.
28. Boyle, *op. cit.*, II, pp. 676–7.

CHAPTER 3

1. Avery, P., *Modern Iran*, London: Ernest Benn (1965), p. 6.
2. Ambraseys, 'Historical Seismicity', p. 56.
3. Matheson, *Persia*, p. 57; Lockhart, 'Hasan-i Sabbah', p. 688.
4. Defrémery, *Histoire des Seldjoukides*, p. 137.
5. Lockhart, *art. cit.*, p. 693.
6. Willey, *Castles of the Assassins*, p. 220.
7. Aubin, 'Elements pour l'étude', pp. 68–9.
8. Ivanow, 'Alamut', p. 38.
9. Matheson, *op. cit.*, p. 59.

10. Quoted in Willey, *op. cit.*, p. 84.
11. Le Strange, *Lands of the Eastern Caliphate*, p. 226.
12. *Ibid.*
13. Boyle, *World Conqueror*, p. 679.
14. Willey, *op. cit.*, p. 274.
15. Stark, *Valleys of the Assassins*, p. 247.
16. Quoted in Le Strange, *op. cit.*, p. 221.
17. Boyle, *op. cit.*, p. 682.
18. Willey, *op. cit.*, p. 173.
19. Minasian, *Shah Diz*, pp. 17–20.
20. *Ibid.*, p. 27.
21. *Ibid.*, p. 52.
22. *Ibid.*, pp. 58–9.
23. Le Strange, *op. cit.*, p. 365.
24. Boyle, *op. cit.*, p. 679.
25. Matheson, *op. cit.*, pp. 194–5.
26. Le Strange, *op. cit.*, p. 362.
27. *Ibid.*, p. 355.
28. *Ibid.*, p. 360.
29. *Ibid.*, p. 227.
30. *Ibid.*, p. 269.

CHAPTER 4

1. Hitti, *History of the Arabs*, p. 372; Nicholson, *Literary History of the Arabs*, pp. 370–1.
2. Abu-Izzedin, *The Druzes*, p. 89.
3. *Ibid.*, p. 90.
4. Hitti, 'Salah-al-Din', p. 164.
5. Hitti, *op. cit.*, p. 373.
6. Abu-Izzedin, *op. cit.*, p. 90.
7. Browne, *Literary History*, II, pp. 378–81; De Boer, *History of Philosophy*, pp. 81-96.
8. De Boer, *op. cit.*, p. 93.
9. *Ibid.*, pp. 82–3.
10. Petrushevsky, *Islam in Iran*, p. 253; Browne, *op. cit.*, II, p. 206.
11. Browne, *op. cit.*, I, p. 412.
12. *Ibid.*, I., pp. 413–5.
13. Madelung, 'Aspects', pp. 54–5.
14. *Ibid.*
15. Hodgson, *Assassins*, p. 325.
16. *Ibid.*, p. 326.

17. *Ibid.*
18. *Ibid.*, p. 56.
19. Quoted in Hodgson, *op. cit.*, p. 327.
20. *Ibid.*, p. 59.
21. Russell, *History of Western Philosophy*, p. 326. London: Allen and Unwin (1946).
22. cf. Corbin, *Cyclical Time*, pp. 151–93; Christie-Murray, D., *A History of Heresy*, pp. 21–32. London: New English Library (1976); Cox, M., *Mysticism*, pp. 56–7. Wellingborough: The Aquarian Press (1983).
23. Madelung, *op. cit.*, p. 56.
24. Abu-Izzedin, *op. cit.*, p. 117.
25. De Boer, *op. cit.*, pp. 100–6.
26. *Ibid.*, p. 103.
27. Madelung, *op. cit.*, p. 59.
28. *Ibid.*, p. 56.
29. Hodgson, *op. cit.*, p. 58.
30. Browne, *op. cit.*, I, p. 345.
31. De Boer, *op. cit.*, pp. 87–8.
32. Browne, op. cit., II, 203–4.
33. Brown, *The Darvishes*, p. 340; Lane, *Manners and Customs*, p. 330.
34. Lane, *op. cit.*, p. 412.
35. Brown, *op. cit.*, p. 341.
36. Browne, 'A Chapter', pp. 2–3.
37. Attar, Farid ud-Din, *The Conference of the Birds*, London: Routledge and Kegan Paul (1954). p. 16.
38. Hodgson, *op. cit.*, pp. 276–7.
39. cf. Guyard, *Fragments*, p. 8; Browne, *op. cit.*, II., pp. 204–5.
40. Lane, *op. cit.*, p. 334.
41. *Brihadaranyaka Upanishad*, IV, iii, 36, in Swami Nikhilananda, *The Upanishads: A Third Selection*, p. 285. London: Phoenix House (1957).
42. Sachedina, *Islamic Messianism*, p. 13.
43. Brown, *op. cit.*, p. 325.
44. Abu-Izzedin, op. cit., p. 116.
45. Guyard, *Grand Maître*, p. 117.
46. *Ibid.*, pp. 116–17.
47. Ivanow, *Creed*, p. 2.

CHAPTER 5

1. Boyle, *World Conqueror*, p. 682.
2. Lewis, *The Assassins*, p. 64.
3. Hodgson, *Assassins*, p. 99.

4. *Ibid.*, p. 115.
5. Hitti, *History of the Arabs*, pp. 473–80.
6. Hodgson, *op. cit.*, pp. 100–1; Lewis, *op. cit.*, p. 64.
7. Hodgson, *op. cit.*, pp. 101-3; Lewis, *op. cit.*, pp. 64–5.
8. Hodgson, *op. cit.*, p. 104; Lewis, *op. cit.*, p. 66.
9. Lewis, *op. cit.*, p. 67.
10. Boyle, *op. cit.*, p. 683.
11. *Ibid.*, p. 685.
12. Hodgson, *op. cit.*, pp. 143–4; Lewis, *op. cit.*, p. 68.
13. Hodgson, *op. cit.*, p. 145; Lewis, *op. cit.*, p. 70.
14. Hodgson, *op. cit.*, p. 147.
15. Boyle, *op. cit.*, p. 686.
16. *Ibid.*, p. 687.
17. Hodgson, *op. cit.*, p. 147.
18. Boyle, *op. cit.*, p. 687.
19. *Ibid.*
20. Ibn Khaldun, *Muqaddimah*, p. 105.
21. Hodgson, *op. cit.*, p. 149.
22. *Ibid.*, p. 157.
23. *Ibid.*, p. 158.
24. cf. Hodgson, *op. cit.*, p. 154.
25. *Ibid.*, p. 157.
26. *Ibid.*, p. 158.
27. cf. *Hodgson*, pp. 161–2.
28. *Ibid.*, p. 216.
29. *Ibid.*, p. 217.
30. *Ibid.*, p. 218.
31. *Ibid.*, p. 220.
32. *Ibid.*, p. 226.
33. *Ibid.*, p. 227.
34. *Ibid.*, p. 239.
35. *Ibid.*, p. 256.
36. *Ibid.*, p. 259.
37. Saunders, *Mongol Conquests*, p. 107.
38. *Ibid.*, p. 108.
39. Boyle, quoted from Willey, *Castles of the Assassins*, p. 167.
40. Lewis, *op. cit.*, p. 94.
41. Hodgson, *op. cit.*, p. 269.
42. Saunders, *op. cit.*, p. 111.
43. Rockhill, *Journey*, p. 222.
44. Saunders, *op. cit.*, p. 109.

CHAPTER 6

1. Hitti, *History of the Arabs*, pp. 633–4.
2. Lewis, 'Ismaelites and Assassins', p. 110.
3. Hodgson, *Assassins*, pp. 89–90; Lewis, *op. cit.*, pp. 110–11.
4. Hodgson, *op. cit.*, p. 90.
5. Lewis, *op. cit.*, p. 111; Hodgson, *op. cit.*, p. 95.
6. Hitti, *op. cit.*, pp. 637–8.
7. Hodgson, *op. cit.*, pp. 94–5.
8. *Ibid.*, pp. 92-3.
9. *Ibid.*, pp. 94-5.
10. Lewis, *The Assassins*, p. 103; Lewis, 'Ismaelites and Assassins', p. 114.
11. Lewis, 'Ismaelites and Assassins', p. 112.
12. *Ibid.*, p. 115.
13. Lewis, *The Assassins*, p. 105.
14. Runciman, *History of the Crusades*, II, p. 173.
15. Hodgson, *op. cit.*, p. 105.
16. Quoted in Benvenisti, *Crusaders in the Holy Land*, p. 148.
17. Hodgson, *op. cit.*, p. 105.
18. Runciman, *op. cit.*, II, p. 200.
19. Hodgson, *op. cit.*, p. 107.
20. Runciman, *op. cit.*, II, p. 130.
21. Runciman, *op. cit.*, III, p. 65.
22. Saunders, *Aspects of the Crusades*, p. 27.

CHAPTER 7

1. Smail, *Crusading Warfare*, p. 218.
2. Le Strange, *Palestine Under the Moslems*, p. 78.
3. *Ibid.*, p. 352.
4. *Ibid.*, p. 353.
5. *Ibid.*, p. 507.
6. *Ibid.*
7. *Ibid.*, p. 81.
8. Nicholson, *Literary History of the Arabs*, p. 357.
9. Le Strange, op. cit., p. 485.
10. Hitti, *Lebanon in History*, p. 295.
11. Benvenisti, *Crusaders in the Holy Land*, p. 148.
12. *Ibid.*, pp. 152–4.
13. Hourani & Stern, *The Islamic City*, pp. 21–2.
14. cf. Lea, H., *The Inquisition in the Middle Ages*, Vol. III, p. 252. New York: Macmillan (1908); Burman, *The Templars*, p. 45. Wellingborough: Crucible (1986).

CHAPTER 8

1. Lewis, 'Kamal al-Din's Biography', p. 229.
2. *Ibid.,* pp. 230–1.
3. *Ibid.,* p. 231.
4. *Ibid.*
5. *Ibid.,* pp. 231–2.
6. Hodgson, *Assassins,* p. 186, n2.
7. Lewis, 'Assassins of Syria and Ismailis of Persia', p. 575.
8. *Ibid.*
9. Hodgson, *op. cit.,* p. 186.
10. *Ibid.,* pp. 190–2.
11. Guyard, *Grand Maître,* p. 77.
12. Hodgson, *op. cit.,* p. 195.
13. *Ibid.,* p. 197.
14. Lewis, 'Kamal al-Din's Biography', p. 230.
15. Guyard, *Fragments,* p. 100.
16. Hodgson, *op. cit.,* p. 203.
17. *Ibid.*
18. Hitti, *'Salah-al-Din',* pp. 117–23; Gibb, *Life of Saladin,* pp. 563–89.
19. Gibb, *op. cit.,* p. 534.
20. Lewis, 'Saladin and the Assassins', p. 239.
21. Lewis, 'Ismaelites and Assassins', p. 123; Lewis, 'Saladin and the Assassins', pp. 239–40.
22. Lewis, *The Assassins,* p. 115.
23. Lewis, 'Kamal al-Din's Biography', pp. 236–7.
24. Lewis, 'Saladin and the Assassins', p. 244.
25. Lewis, 'Ismaelites and Assassins', p. 127.
26. Lewis, 'Assassins of Syria and Ismailis of Persia', p. 579.
27. Runciman, *History of the Crusades,* III, pp. 135–8.
28. *Ibid.;* Lewis, 'Ismaelites and Assassins', p. 126.
29. Nicholson, *Literary History of the Arabs,* pp. 447–8.
30. Mustafa Ziada, 'The Mamluk Sultans to 1293', in Setton, *History of the Crusades,* II, p. 746.
31. Lewis, 'Ismaelites and Assassins', pp. 130–1.
32. Hitti, *History of the Arabs,* p. 675.
33. Lewis, 'Ismaelites and Assassins', p. 131.

CHAPTER 9

1. Nowell, 'The Old Man of the Mountains', p. 507.
2. Lewis, *The Assassins,* p. 105.

3. Ibn Athir, *Extrait de la Chronique intitulée Kamel-Altevarykh*, p. 679.
4. e.g. Nowell, *op. cit.*, p. 504.
5. Burman, *The Templars*, Wellingborough: Crucible (1986). pp. 26–30.
6. Nowell, *op. cit.*, p. 504; Hammer-Purgstall, *History of the Assassins*, pp. 56–9.
7. Daniel-Rops, *Cathedral and Crusade*, pp. 77–86. London: Dent (1957).
8. cf. Burman, *op. cit.*, p. 49.
9. Nowell, *op. cit.*, p. 505.
10. Smail, 'Crusaders' Castles', pp. 148–9.
11. cf. Nowell, *op. cit.*, p. 505.
12. William of Tyre, *History*, II, pp. 390–4.
13. Nowell, *op. cit.*, p. 506.
14. Quoted in Nowell, *op. cit.*, p. 508.
15. Nowell, *op. cit.*, p. 508–9.
16. *Ibid.*, pp. 509–10
17. *Ibid.*, p. 512.
18. Burman, *op. cit.*, pp. 130–1.
19. Nowell, *op. cit.*, p. 512.
20. Runciman, *op. cit.*, III, pp. 261–71.
21. Quoted in Nowell, *op. cit.*, p. 514.
22. *Ibid.*, pp. 512–4.

CHAPTER 10

1. Nowell, 'The Old Man of the Mountains', p. 503; Olschki, *Storia Letteraria*, p. 216.
2. Cortellazzi & Zolli, *Dizionario etimologico della lingua italiana*, Vol. I, A-C. Bologna: Zanichelli (1979).
3. Olschki, *op. cit.*, p. 215.
4. Quoted in Lewis, *The Assassins*, p. 3.
5. William of Tyre, *History*, II, p. 391.
6. Trs. from Marco Polo, *Il Milione*, pp. 87–90.
7. Watt, *Bell's Introduction*, p. 161.
8. Quoted in Palacios, *Islam and the Divine Comedy*, p. 123.
9. *Ibid.*, p. 126.
10. *Ibid.*, pp. 127–71.
11. cf. *Ibid.*, p. 139.
12. Filippani-Ronconi, *Ismaeliti e Assassini*, pp. 4–5.
13. Lockhart, 'Hasan-i Sabbah', p. 683; Runciman, *History of the Crusades*, III, p. 89.
14. Lockhart, *art. cit.*, p. 683.
15. Chambers, 'Troubadours and Assassins', pp.245–51.

CHAPTER 11

1. Lebey de Batilly, *Traicte de l'origine*, pp. 8–9.
2. *Ibid.*, p. 7.
3. *Ibid.*, pp. 48–9.
4. *Ibid.*, pp. 61–2.
5. Lewis, *The Assassins*, p. 10.
6. Falconnet, 'Dissertation', p. 168.
7. Gibbon, *The Decline and Fall of the Roman Empire*, Chapter LXIV.
8. Assemani, 'Ragguaglio storico-critico', p. 254.
9. *Ibid.*, p. 255.
10. *Ibid.*, p. 260.
11. *Ibid.*, pp. 260–2.
12. Lewis, *op. cit.*, p. 11.
13. *Ibid.*, pp. 11–2.
14. De Sacy, 'Mémoire', p. 62.
15. Monteith, 'Journal', p. 16.
16. Hodgson, *Assassins*, p. 27.
17. Hammer-Purgstall, *History of the Assassins*, p. 341.
18. *Ibid.*, p. 1.
19. *Ibid.*, p. 1–2.
20. *Ibid.*, p. 168.
21. *Ibid.*, p. 136.
22. *Ibid.*, p. 46.
23. *Ibid.*, p. 117.
24. *Ibid.*, p. 208.
25. *Ibid.*, p. 340.
26. *Ibid.*, p. 3.
27. *Ibid.*, p. 90–1.
28. *Ibid.*, p. 339.
29. cf. Hodgson, *Assassins*, Appendix III.
30. Lewis, 'Assassins in Syria and Isma'ilis of Persia', p. 582.

CHAPTER 12

1. Nicholson, *Literary History of the Arabs*, p. 358.
2. Browne, *Literary History of Persia*, I, p. 274.
3. *Ibid.*, p. 362.
4. *Ibid.*, p. 379.
5. Hodgson, *Assassins*, pp. 196–7.
6. Hammer-Purgstall, *History of the Assassins*, p. 45.
7. *Ibid.*, pp. 61–5.
8. *Ibid.*, pp. 64–5.

9. *Ibid.*, p. 77.
10. Partner, *The Murdered Magicians*, pp. 115–6.
11. *Ibid.*, p. 116.
12. Hamill, *The Craft*, p. 49.
13. Partner, *op. cit.*, p. 130.
14. *Ibid.*, p. 131.
15. Cooper-Oakley, *Masonry and Medieval Symbolism*, p. 96.
16. Bouisson, *Magic*, p. 196.
17. *Ibid.*, p. 197.
18. *Ibid.*, p. 199.
19. White, *Shelley*, I p. 682.
20. Fuller, *Shelley*, p. 156.
21. cf. *Laon and Cynthia*, I, pp. 280–306.
22. Quoted in White, *op. cit.*, I, p. 682.
23. Fuller, *op. cit.*, p. 161.
24. White, op. cit., I, p. 682.
25. cf. Olschki, *Storia Letteraria*, p. 218.

CHAPTER 13

1. Wright, *English Amongst the Persians*, p. 4.
2. *Ibid.*, p. 13.
3. *Ibid.*, pp. 54, 139–40.
4. *Ibid.*, p. 22.
5. Ivanow, 'Alamut', p. 44.
6. Monteith, 'Journal', pp. 15–16.
7. *Ibid.*, p. 15.
8. Shiel, 'Itinerary', p. 431.
9. *Ibid.*
10. Ivanow, *art. cit.*, p. 43.
11. *Ibid.*, p. 39.
12. *Ibid.*, p. 41.
13. Lockhart, 'Hasan-i Sabbah', p. 691.
14. *Ibid.*, p. 693.
15. *Ibid.*, p. 694.
16. Stark, 'The Assassins' Valley', p. 54.
17. Stark, *The Valleys of the Assassins*, p. 212.
18. *Ibid.*, p. 219.
19. *Ibid.*, p. 221.

CHAPTER 14

1. Hollister, *The Shi'a of India*, pp. 331–3.

2. *Ibid.*, pp. 267–92.
3. *Ibid.*, p. 351.
4. *Ibid.*, p. 336.
5. *Ibid.*, pp. 332-8.
6. Pakravan, E., *Agha Mohammad Ghadjar*, Paris: debresse (1963), pp. 161–74.
7. Avery, P., *Modern Iran*, p. 24. London: Ernest Benn (1965).
8. Lewis, *The Assassins*, pp. 14–15.
9. Bose, *The Aga Khans*, p. 45.
10. Hollister, *op. cit.*, pp. 332-8.
11. Bose, *op. cit.*, pp. 17–42.
12. *Ibid.*, p. 55.
13. Wright, *English Amongst the Persians*, p. 22.
14. Bose, *op. cit.*, p. 60.
15. *Ibid.*, pp. 64–7.
16. *Ibid.*, pp. 70–1.
17. Lewis, *op. cit.*, pp. 15–17; Bose, *op. cit.*, pp. 76–80.
18. Bose, *op. cit.*, p. 44.
19. Bose, *op. cit.*, p. 41.
20. *Ibid.*, pp. 82–3.
21. *Ibid.*, pp. 92–121.
22. *Ibid.*, pp. 127–31.
23. *Ibid.*, p. 245.
24. *Ibid.*, pp. 251, 270.
25. *Ibid.*, p. 13.
26. *Ibid.*, p. 377.
27. Filippani-Ronconi, *Ismaeliti e Assassini*, p. 291.
28. *Ibid.*, p. 280.
29. Lewis, 'Assassins of Syria and Isma'ilis of Persia', p. 576.
30. Filippani-Ronconi, *op. cit.*, p. 269.

INDEX